George Washington Moon

The monograph Gospel:

Being the four Gospels arranged in one continuous narrative in the words of Scripture, without omission of fact or repetition of statement

George Washington Moon

The monograph Gospel:
Being the four Gospels arranged in one continuous narrative in the words of Scripture, without omission of fact or repetition of statement

ISBN/EAN: 9783337714215

Printed in Europe, USA, Canada, Australia, Japan

Cover: Foto ©ninafisch / pixelio.de

More available books at **www.hansebooks.com**

THE
MONOGRAPH

BEING

THE FOUR GOSPELS

ARRANGED IN ONE CONTINUOUS NARRATIVE IN THE
WORDS OF SCRIPTURE,

𝔚𝔦𝔱𝔥𝔬𝔲𝔱 𝔒𝔪𝔦𝔰𝔰𝔦𝔬𝔫 𝔬𝔣 𝔉𝔞𝔠𝔱 𝔬𝔯 𝔑𝔢𝔭𝔢𝔱𝔦𝔱𝔦𝔬𝔫 𝔬𝔣 𝔖𝔱𝔞𝔱𝔢𝔪𝔢𝔫𝔱.

BY

G. WASHINGTON MOON, F.R.S.L.

Member of the Council of the Royal Society of Literature,
AUTHOR OF
' THE SOUL'S INQUIRIES ANSWERED IN THE WORDS OF SCRIPTURE,' ETC.

Second Thousand.—Improved Edition.

NEW YORK:
ANSON D. F. RANDOLPH & CO.
38 WEST TWENTY-THIRD STREET.

PREFACE.

This little work is not intended for the analytical student of New Testament history desirous of comparing with each other the four evangelists' accounts of the life and teaching of Christ: that end may be better attained by a study of the Gospels arranged in tabular parallels.

The work is intended rather for the devotional student, to whom its chief value will be that it presents to him, for private and family reading, in the words of the evangelists, the scattered records of the life and teaching of Christ, arranged in one continuous narrative, without omission of fact or repetition of statement.

The compiler's object has been the focussing of the rays of "the light of the glorious gospel of Christ," so that they might by their combined intensity kindle in the heart a flame of more fervent devotion to HIM who "so loved the world that He gave His only begotten Son, that whosoever believeth in Him should not perish, but have everlasting life."

The carrying out of this object has necessitated the transposition of certain passages from the order in which they stand in one or other of the Gospels; but the general sequence of events has, as far as was consistent with the object of this work, been carefully made in accordance with the best authorities: though the compiler has, throughout, been obliged to exercise his own judgment in this matter, in consequence of no two writers of any eminence being agreed respecting the chronology of all the recorded events in the life of Christ; as may be seen by a comparison of the works of Lightfoot 1655, Doddridge 1739, Macknight 1756, Newcome 1778, Townsend 1821, Greswell 1830, Jarvis 1844, Robinson 1845, and Tischendorf 1851.

London, Nov. 1877.

PREFACE TO THE SECOND EDITION.

For the purpose of promoting and facilitating a systematic reading of the life of Christ, the sections in this edition have been rearranged under dates, so that if the book be begun on January 1st, and one section be read daily, the whole history will be read through exactly four times by the last day of the year.

Another important alteration that has been made in this little work is the addition of marginal references, showing where may be found every passage in the authorized version of the New Testament, as well as the quotations from the Old Testament. At the end there is an index, showing where the subject of every verse in each of the four Gospels may be found in this work.

The abbreviations in the marginal references are as follows:—M, Matthew; K, Mark; L, Luke; J, John; A, Acts; and C, Corinthians.

London, July, 1878.

INTRODUCTION.

Forasmuch as many have taken in hand to set forth in order a declaration of those things which are most surely believed among us, even as they delivered them unto us, which from the beginning were eyewitnesses, and ministers of the word; it seemed good to me also, having had perfect understanding of all things from the very first, to write unto thee in order, most excellent Theophilus, that thou mightest know the certainty of those things, wherein thou hast been instructed.—Luke i, 1-4.

THE GOSPEL

OF

JESUS CHRIST THE SON OF GOD.

I.

Jan. 1.   Apl. 2.   July 2.   Oct. 1.

The angel Gabriel appears to Zacharias and foretells the birth of John the Baptist; and to Mary and foretells the birth of Christ.

THERE was in the days of Herod, the king of Judæa, a certain priest named Zacharias, of the course of Abijah: and his wife was of the daughters of Aaron, and her name was Elisabeth. And they were both righteous before God, walking in all the commandments and ordinances of the Lord blameless; and they had no child, because that Elisabeth was barren, and they both were now well stricken in years.

And it came to pass, that while he executed the priest's office before God in the order of

L	1, 5
—	6
—	7
—	8

| Jan. 1. | | July 2. |
| Apl. 2. | The Four Gospels arranged | Oct. 1. |

L 1, 9 — his course,* according to the custom of the priest's office, his lot was to burn incense when
— 10 — he went into the temple of the Lord. And the whole multitude of the people were praying
— 11 — without at the time of incense; and there appeared unto him an angel of the Lord standing on the right side of the altar of
— 12 — incense. And when Zacharias saw him, he
— 13 — was troubled, and fear fell upon him; but the angel said unto him, Fear not, Zacharias: for thy prayer is heard; and thy wife Elisabeth shall bear thee a son, and thou shalt call his
— 14 — name John. And thou shalt have joy and gladness; and many shall rejoice at his birth;
— 15 — for he shall be great in the sight of the Lord, and shall drink neither wine nor strong drink; and he shall be filled with the Holy Ghost,
— 16 — even from his mother's womb; and many of the children of Israel shall he turn to the Lord
— 17 — their God. And he shall go before him in the spirit and power of Elijah, to turn the hearts of the fathers to the children, and the disobedient to the wisdom of the just; to make ready a people prepared for the Lord.
— 18 — And Zacharias said unto the angel, Whereby shall I know this? for I am an old man, and
— 19 — my wife well stricken in years. And the angel

* 1 Ch. xxiii, 6.

| Jan. 1. Apl. 2. | in one Continuous Narrative. | July 2. Oct. 1. |

answering said unto him, I am Gabriel, that stand in the presence of God; and am sent to speak unto thee, and to shew thee these glad tidings; and, behold, thou shalt be dumb, and not able to speak, until the day that these things shall be performed, because thou believest not my words, which shall be fulfilled in their season. L 1, 19
— 20

And the people waited for Zacharias, and marvelled that he tarried so long in the temple; and when he came out, he could not speak unto them; and they perceived that he had seen a vision in the temple, for he beckoned unto them, and remained speechless. — 21
— 22

And it came to pass, that, as soon as the days of his ministration were accomplished,* he departed to his own house;† and after those days his wife Elisabeth conceived, and hid herself five months, saying, thus hath the Lord dealt with me in the days wherein he looked on me, to take away my reproach among men. — 23
— 24
— 25

And in the sixth month the angel Gabriel was sent from God unto a city of Galilee, named Nazareth, to a virgin espoused to a man whose name was Joseph, of the house of David; and the virgin's name was Mary. — 26
— 27

* 1 Ch. ix, 25.   † Luke i, 39, 40.

| Jan. 1. Apl. 2. | The Four Gospels arranged | July 2. Oct. 1. |

L 1, 28   And the angel came in unto her, and said, Hail, thou that art highly favoured, the Lord is with thee: blessed art thou among women.
— 29   And when she saw him, she was troubled at his saying, and cast in her mind what manner of salutation this should be.
— 30   And the angel said unto her, Fear not, Mary: for thou hast found favour with God;
— 31   and, behold, thou shalt conceive in thy womb, and bring forth a son, and shalt call his name
— 32   JESUS. He shall be great, and shall be called the Son of the Highest: and the Lord God shall give unto him the throne of his
— 33   father David; and he shall reign over the house of Jacob for ever; and of his kingdom there shall be no end.
— 34   Then said Mary unto the angel, How shall
— 35   this be, seeing I know not a man? And the angel answered and said unto her, The Holy Ghost shall come upon thee, and the power of the Highest shall overshadow thee; therefore also that holy thing which shall be born of thee
— 36   shall be called the Son of God. And, behold, thy cousin Elisabeth, she also hath conceived a son in her old age; and this is the sixth month
— 37   with her, who was called barren; for with God nothing shall be impossible.
— 38   And Mary said, Behold the handmaid of the

Lord; be it unto me according to thy word. And the angel departed from her. | L 1, 38

II.

Jan. 2.   Apl. 3.   July 3.   Oct. 2.

Mary visits her cousin Elisabeth. The birth of John the Baptist.

AND Mary arose in those days, and went into the hill country with haste, into a city of Judæa; and entered into the house of Zacharias, and saluted Elisabeth.

And it came to pass, that, when Elisabeth heard the salutation of Mary, the babe leaped in her womb; and Elisabeth was filled with the Holy Ghost; and she spake out with a loud voice, and said, Blessed art thou among women, and blessed is the fruit of thy womb. And whence is this to me, that the mother of my Lord should come to me? For, lo, as soon as the voice of thy salutation sounded in mine ears, the babe leaped in my womb for joy. And blessed is she that believed; for there shall be a performance of those things which were told her from the Lord.

And Mary said, My soul doth magnify the Lord, and my spirit hath rejoiced in God my Saviour, for he hath regarded the low estate of

L 1, 39
— 40
— 41
— 42
— 43
— 44
— 45
— 46
— 47
— 48

| Jan. 2. | The Four Gospels arranged | July 3. |
| Apl. 3. | | Oct. 2. |

L 1, 48 — his handmaiden; for, behold, from henceforth
— 49 — all generations shall call me blessed; for he that is mighty hath done to me great things;
— 50 — and holy is his name; and his mercy is on them that fear him from generation to genera-
— 51 — tion. He hath shewed strength with his arm; he hath scattered the proud in the imagination
— 52 — of their hearts; he hath put down the mighty from their seats, and exalted them of low
— 53 — degree; he hath filled the hungry with good things; and the rich he hath sent empty away;
— 54 — he hath holpen his servant Israel, in remem-
— 55 — brance of his mercy; as he spake to our fathers, to Abraham, and to his seed for ever.*

— 56 — And Mary abode with her about three months, and returned to her own house.†

— 57 — Now Elisabeth's full time came that she should be delivered; and she brought forth
— 58 — a son; and her neighbours and her cousins heard how the Lord had shewed great mercy upon her; and they rejoiced with her.

— 59 — And it came to pass, that on the eighth day they came to circumcise the child;‡ and they called him Zacharias, after the name of his
— 60 — father. And his mother answered and said,
— 61 — Not so; but he shall be called John. And they said unto her, There is none of thy

* Gen. xii, 1-3.   † Luke ii, 39.   ‡ Gen. xvii, 12.

| Jan. 2.
Apl. 3. | in one Continuous Narrative. | July 3.
Oct. 2. |

kindred that is called by this name; and they made signs to his father how he would have him called. And he asked for a writing table, and wrote, saying, His name is John. And they marvelled all; and his mouth was opened immediately, and his tongue loosed, and he spake, and praised God. And fear came on all that dwelt round about them; and all these sayings were noised abroad throughout all the hill country of Judæa; and all they that heard them laid them up in their hearts, saying, What manner of child shall this be! And the hand of the Lord was with him.

And his father Zacharias was filled with the Holy Ghost, and prophesied, saying, Blessed be the Lord God of Israel; for he hath visited and redeemed his people, and hath raised up a horn of salvation for us in the house of his servant David; as he spake by the mouth of his holy prophets,* which have been since the world began; that we should be saved from our enemies, and from the hand of all that hate us; to perform the mercy promised to our fathers, and to remember his holy covenant; the oath which he sware to our father Abraham,† that he would grant unto us, that we being

L 1, 62
— 63
— 64
— 65
— 66
— 67
— 68
— 69
— 70
— 71
— 72
— 73
— 74

* 1 Sam. ii, 10. Psa. cxxxii, 17. Jer. xxiii, 5. Ezek. xxix, 21.
† Gen. xxii, 16-18.

| Jan. 3. Apl. 4. | The Four Gospels arranged | July 4. Oct. 3. |

L 1, 74 delivered out of the hand of our enemies might
— 75 serve him without fear, in holiness and righteousness before him, all the days of our life.
— 76 And thou, child, shalt be called the prophet of the Highest: for thou shalt go before the
— 77 face of the Lord to prepare his ways; to give knowledge of salvation unto his people by the
— 78 remission of their sins, through the tender mercy of our God; whereby the dayspring from on high
— 79 hath visited us, to give light to them that sit in darkness and in the shadow of death, to guide our feet into the way of peace.
— 80 And the child grew, and waxed strong in spirit, and was in the deserts till the day of his shewing unto Israel.

M 3, 4 And the same John had his raiment of camels' hair, and a leathern girdle about his loins; and his meat was locusts and wild honey.

III.

JAN. 3. APL. 4. JULY 4. OCT. 3.

The conception, divinity, and birth of Christ.

M 1, 18 NOW the birth of Jesus Christ was on this wise: when as his mother Mary was espoused to Joseph, before they came together, she was found with child of the Holy Ghost.

| Jan. 3. ApL 4. | in one Continuous Narrative. | July 4. Oct. 3. |

Then Joseph her husband, being a just man, and not willing to make her a public example, was minded to put her away privily; but while he thought on these things, behold, the angel of the Lord appeared unto him in a dream, saying, Joseph, thou son of David, fear not to take unto thee Mary thy wife: for that which is conceived in her is of the Holy Ghost; and she shall bring forth a son, and thou shalt call his name JESUS; for he shall save his people from their sins.

Then Joseph being raised from sleep did as the angel of the Lord had bidden him, and took unto him his wife; and knew her not till she had brought forth her firstborn son.

Now all this was done, that it might be fulfilled which was spoken of the Lord by the prophet* saying, Behold, a virgin shall be with child, and shall bring forth a son, and they shall call his name Emmanuel, which being interpreted is, God with us.

In the beginning was the Word, and the Word was with God, and the Word was God. The same was in the beginning with God: all things were made by him; and without him was not any thing made that was made. In him was life; and the life was the light of men;

M 1, 19
— 20
— 21
— 24
— 25
— 22
— 23
J 1, 1
— 2
— 3
— 4

* Isa. vii, 14.

Jan. 3.		July 4.
Apl. 4.	The Four Gospels arranged	Oct. 3.

J 1, 5	and the light shone in darkness; and the darkness comprehended it not.
— 6	There was a man sent from God, whose name was John. The same came for a witness,
— 7	to bear witness of the Light,* that all men
— 8	through him might believe. He was not that Light, but was sent to bear witness of that
— 9	Light. That was the true Light, which lighteth every man that cometh into the world.
— 10	He was in the world, and the world was made
— 11	by him,† and the world knew him not. He came unto his own, and his own received him
— 12	not; but as many as received him, to them gave he power to become the sons of God, even
— 13	to them that believe on his name; which were born, not of blood, nor of the will of the flesh,
— 14	nor of the will of man, but of God. And the Word was made flesh, and dwelt among us,
— 16	full of grace and truth; and of his fulness have
— 17	all we received, and grace for grace. For the law was given by Moses,‡ but grace and truth
— 14	came by Jesus Christ. And we beheld his glory, the glory as of the only begotten of the Father.
L 2, 1	And it came to pass in those days, that there went out a decree from Cæsar Augustus, that
— 2	all the world should be taxed. And this taxing

* Isa. xlix, 6.   † Eph. iii, 9.   ‡ Ex. xx, 1.

| Jan. 4. Apl. 5. | in one Continuous Narrative. | July 5. Oct. 4. |

was first made when Cyrenius was governor of Syria. And all went to be taxed, every one into his own city. And Joseph also went up from Galilee, out of the city of Nazareth, into Judæa, unto the city of David, which is called Bethlehem; (because he was of the house and lineage of David;) to be taxed with Mary his espoused wife, being great with child. And so it was, that, while they were there, the days were accomplished that she should be delivered; and she brought forth her firstborn son, and wrapped him in swaddling clothes, and laid him in a manger; because there was no room for them in the inn.

L 2, 2
— 3
— 4

— 5
— 6

— 7

IV.

Jan. 4. Apl. 5. July 5. Oct. 4.

The birth of Christ announced by angels; his circumcision.

AND there were, in the same country, shepherds abiding in the field, keeping watch over their flock by night. And, lo, the angel of the Lord came upon them, and the glory of the Lord shone round about them; and they were sore afraid. And the angel said unto them, Fear not; for, behold, I bring you

L 2, 8
— 9
— 10

| Jan. 4. | | July 5. |
| Apl. 5. | The Four Gospels arranged | Oct. 4. |

L 2, 10 — good tidings of great joy, which shall be to all
— 11 people; for unto you is born this day, in the city of David, a Saviour, which is Christ the
— 12 Lord. And this shall be a sign unto you; Ye shall find the babe wrapped in swaddling
— 13 clothes, lying in a manger. And suddenly there was with the angel a multitude of the
— 14 heavenly host praising God, and saying, Glory to God in the highest, and on earth peace, good will toward men.
— 15 And it came to pass, as the angels were gone away from them into heaven, the shepherds said one to another, Let us now go even unto Bethlehem, and see this thing which is come to pass, which the Lord hath made known unto
— 16 us. And they came with haste, and found Mary, and Joseph, and the babe lying in a
— 17 manger. And when they had seen it, they made known abroad the saying which was
— 18 told them concerning this child. And all they that heard it wondered at those things which
— 19 were told them by the shepherds; but Mary kept all these things, and pondered them in
— 20 her heart. And the shepherds returned, glorifying and praising God for all the things that they had heard and seen, as it was told unto them.
— 21 And when eight days were accomplished for

| Jan. 4. Apl. 5. | in one Continuous Narrative. | July 5. Oct. 4. |

the circumcising of the child, his name was called JESUS, which was so named of the angel before he was conceived in the womb. And when the days of her purification according to the law of Moses* were accomplished, they brought him to Jerusalem, to present him to the Lord; (as it is written in the law of the Lord,† Every male that openeth the womb shall be called holy to the Lord;) and to offer a sacrifice according to that which is said in the law of the Lord,‡ A pair of turtledoves, or two young pigeons.

And, behold, there was a man in Jerusalem, whose name was Simeon; and the same man was just and devout, waiting for the consolation of Israel;§ and the Holy Ghost was upon him; and it was revealed unto him by the Holy Ghost, that he should not see death before he had seen the Lord's Christ. And he came by the Spirit into the temple; and when the parents brought in the child Jesus, to do for him after the custom of the law, then took he him up in his arms, and blessed God, and said, Lord, now lettest thou thy servant depart in peace, according to thy word; for mine eyes have seen thy salvation, which thou hast prepared before the face of all people; a light to

L 2, 21
— 22
— 23
— 24
— 25
— 26
— 27
— 28
— 29
— 30
— 31
— 32

* Lev. xii, 4. † Ex. xiii, 2. ‡ Lev. xii, 6, 8. § Isa. xxv, 8, 9.

L 2, 32	lighten the Gentiles, and the glory of thy people Israel.
— 33	And Joseph and his mother marvelled at
— 34	those things which were spoken of him. And Simeon blessed them, and said unto Mary his mother, Behold, this child is set for the fall and rising again of many in Israel; and for a
— 35	sign which shall be spoken against; (yea, a sword shall pierce through thy own soul also,) that the thoughts of many hearts may be revealed.
— 36	And there was one Anna, a prophetess, the daughter of Phanuel, of the tribe of Asher;* she was of a great age, and had lived with a
— 37	husband seven years from her virginity; and she was a widow of about fourscore and four years, who departed not from the temple, but served God with fastings and prayers night and
— 38	day; and she coming in that instant gave thanks likewise unto the Lord, and spake of him to all them that looked for redemption in
— 39	Jerusalem. And when they had performed all things according to the law of the Lord, they returned into Galilee, to their own city Nazareth.

* Gen. xxx, 13.

Jan. 5. Apl. 6.   *in one Continuous Narrative.*   July 6. Oct. 5.

V.

Jan. 5. Apl. 6. July 6. Oct. 5.
Wise men from the east come to Bethlehem.
The murder of the innocents.

NOW when Jesus was born in Bethlehem of Judæa in the days of Herod the king, behold, there came wise men from the east to Jerusalem, saying, Where is he that is born King of the Jews? for we have seen his star in the east, and are come to worship him.   *M 2, 1 — 2*

When Herod the king had heard these things, he was troubled, and all Jerusalem with him. And when he had gathered all the chief priests and scribes of the people together, he demanded of them where Christ should be born. And they said unto him, In Bethlehem of Judæa; for thus it is written by the prophet,* And thou Bethlehem, in the land of Judah, art not the least among the princes of Judah, for out of thee shall come a Governor, that shall rule my people Israel.   *— 3 — 4 — 5 — 6*

Then Herod, when he had privily called the wise men, enquired of them diligently what time the star appeared. And he sent them to Bethlehem, and said, Go and search diligently for the young child; and when ye have found him, bring me word again, that I also   *— 7 — 8*

* Micah v, 2.

Jan. 5. Apl. 6.	The Four Gospels arranged	July 6. Oct. 5.

M 2, 9   may come and worship him. When they had heard the king, they departed; and, lo, the star, which they saw in the east, went before them, till it came and stood over where the
— 10   young child was. When they saw the star,
— 11   they rejoiced with exceeding great joy; and when they were come into the house, they saw the young child with Mary his mother, and fell down, and worshipped him; and when they had opened their treasures, they presented unto him gifts; gold, and frankincense, and myrrh.
— 12   And being warned of God in a dream that they should not return to Herod, they departed into their own country another way.

— 13   And when they were departed, behold, the angel of the Lord appeared to Joseph in a dream, saying, Arise, and take the young child and his mother, and flee into Egypt, and be thou there until I bring thee word; for Herod will seek the young child to destroy him.
— 14   When he arose, he took the young child and his mother by night, and departed into Egypt;
— 15   and was there until the death of Herod; that it might be fulfilled which was spoken of the Lord by the prophet,* saying, Out of Egypt have I called my son.
— 16   Then Herod, when he saw that he was

* Hosea xi, 1.

| Jan. 5. | | July 6. |
| Apl. 6. | in one Continuous Narrative. | Oct. 5. |

mocked by the wise men, was exceedingly wrath, and sent forth, and slew all the children that were in Bethlehem, and in all the coasts thereof, from two years old and under, according to the time which he had diligently enquired of the wise men. Then was fulfilled that which was spoken by Jeremiah the prophet,* saying, In Ramah was there a voice heard, lamentation, and weeping, and great mourning, Rachel weeping for her children, and would not be comforted, because they are not. But when Herod was dead, behold, an angel of the Lord appeared in a dream to Joseph in Egypt, saying, Arise, and take the young child and his mother, and go into the land of Israel; for they are dead which sought the young child's life.	M 2, 16 — 17 — 18 — 19 — 20
And he arose, and took the young child and his mother and came into the land of Israel. But when he heard that Archelaus did reign in Judæa in the room of his father Herod, he was afraid to go thither; notwithstanding, being warned by God in a dream, he turned aside into the parts of Galilee; and he came and dwelt in a city called Nazareth; that it might be fulfilled which was spoken by the prophets, He shall be called a Nazarene.	— 21 — 22 — 23

* Jer. xxxi, 15.

VI.

Jan. 6. Apl. 7. July 7. Oct. 6.

Christ with the doctors in the temple. The preaching of John the Baptist.

L 2, 40 — AND the child Jesus grew, and waxed strong in spirit, filled with wisdom; and the grace of God was upon him.

— 41 Now his parents went to Jerusalem every
— 42 year at the feast of the passover; and when he was twelve years old, they went up to Jerusalem
— 43 after the custom of the feast.* And when they had fulfilled the days, as they returned, the child Jesus tarried behind in Jerusalem; and
— 44 Joseph and his mother knew not of it. But they, supposing him to be in the company, went a day's journey; and they sought him
— 45 among their kinsfolk and acquaintance; and when they found him not, they turned back to
— 46 Jerusalem, seeking him. And it came to pass, that after three days they found him in the temple, sitting in the midst of the doctors, both hearing them, and asking them questions;
— 47 and all that heard him were astonished at his
— 48 understanding and answers. And when they saw him, they were amazed; and his mother

* Deut. xvi, 1-8.

Jan. 6.
Apl. 7.

in one Continuous Narrative.

July 7.
Oct. 6.

said unto him, Son, why hast thou thus dealt with us? behold, thy father and I have sought thee sorrowing. And he said unto them, How is it that ye sought me? wist ye not that I must be about my Father's business? And they understood not the saying which he spake unto them.

And he went down with them, and came to Nazareth, and was subject unto them; but his mother kept all these sayings in her heart. And Jesus increased in wisdom and stature, and in favour with God and man.

Now in the fifteenth year of the reign of Tiberius Cæsar, Pontius Pilate being governor of Judæa, and Herod being tetrarch of Galilee, and his brother Philip tetrarch of Ituræa and of the region of Trachonitis, and Lysanias the tetrarch of Abilene, Annas and Caiaphas being the high priests, the word of God came unto John the Baptist, the son of Zacharias, in the wilderness of Judæa.

And he came into all the country about Jordan, preaching the baptism of repentance for the remission of sins; and saying, Repent ye; for the kingdom of heaven is at hand.

This is he that was spoken of by the prophet Isaiah,* saying, The voice of one crying in the

* Isa. xl, 3.

L 2, 48
— 49
— 50
— 51
— 52
L 3, 1
— 2
M 3, 1
L 3, 2
M 3, 1
L 3, 3
M 3, 2
— 3
L 3, 4

| | Jan. 6. Apl. 7. | The Four Gospels arranged | July 7. Oct. 6. |

L 3,	wilderness, Prepare ye the way of the Lord,
— 5	make his paths straight. Every valley shall be filled, and every mountain and hill shall be brought low; and the crooked shall be made straight, and the rough ways shall be made
— 6	smooth; and all flesh shall see the salvation of God.
	Then went out to him Jerusalem, and all
M 3, 5	Judæa, and all the region round about Jordan,
— 6	and were baptized by him in Jordan, confessing their sins.
— 7	But when he saw many of the Pharisees and Sadducees come to his baptism, he said unto them, O generation of vipers, who hath warned
L 3, 8	you to flee from the wrath to come? Bring forth therefore fruits worthy of repentance, and begin not to say within yourselves, We have Abraham for our father; for I say unto you, that God is able of these stones to raise up
— 9	children unto Abraham. And now also the axe is laid unto the root of the trees; every tree therefore which bringeth not forth good fruit is hewn down, and cast into the fire.
— 10	And the people asked him, saying, What
— 11	shall we do then? He answered and said unto them, He that hath two coats, let him impart to him that hath none; and he that hath meat,
— 12	let him do likewise. Then came also publicans

| Jan. 7. Apl. 8. | in one Continuous Narrative. | July 8. Oct. 7. |

to be baptized, and said unto him, Master, what shall we do? And he said unto them, Exact no more than that which is appointed you. And the soldiers likewise demanded of him, saying, And what shall we do? And he said unto them, Do violence to no man, neither accuse any falsely; and be content with your wages.

L 8,12
— 13

— 14

VII.

Jan. 7. Apl. 8. July 8. Oct. 7.

Christ's baptism and temptation. John the Baptist's first testimony to Christ.

THEN Jesus, being about thirty years of age, came from Nazareth of Galilee to Jordan unto John, to be baptized by him; but John forbad him, saying, I have need to be baptized by thee, and comest thou to me? And Jesus answering said unto him, Suffer it to be so now: for thus it becometh us to fulfil all righteousness. Then he suffered him.

I. 3,23
K 1, 9
M 3,13
— 14

— 15

Now when all the people were baptized, it came to pass, that Jesus also being baptized, and straightway coming up out of the water, praying, the heaven was opened, and the Holy Ghost descended in a bodily shape like a dove

L 3,21

K 1,10
L 3,21
— 22

| | Jan 7.
Apl. 8. | 𝕿𝖍𝖊 𝖋𝖔𝖚𝖗 𝕲𝖔𝖘𝖕𝖊𝖑𝖘 𝖆𝖗𝖗𝖆𝖓𝖌𝖊𝖉 | July 8.
Oct. 7. |

L 8, 22 — upon him, and a voice came from heaven, which said, Thou art my beloved Son; in thee I am well pleased.

L 4, 1 — And Jesus being full of the Holy Ghost returned from Jordan, and was led by the Spirit

— 2 — into the wilderness, being forty days tempted by the devil. And in those days he did eat

M 4, 2 — nothing: and when they were ended, and he had fasted forty days and forty nights, he after-

L 4, 3 — ward hungered; and the devil said unto him, If thou art the Son of God, command this

— 4 — stone that it be made bread. And Jesus answered him, saying, It is written,* Man shall not live by bread alone, but by every word of God.

— 9
M 4, 5
L 4, 9 — And he brought him to Jerusalem, the holy city, and set him on a pinnacle of the temple, and said unto him, If thou art the Son of God,

— 10 — cast thyself down hence; for it is written,† He shall give his angels charge over thee, to keep

— 11 — thee; and in their hands they shall bear thee up, lest at any time thou dash thy foot against

— 12 — a stone. And Jesus answering said unto him,

M 4, 7 — It is written again,‡ Thou shalt not tempt the Lord thy God.

L 4, 5
M 4, 8
L 4, 6 — And the devil, taking him up into an exceeding high mountain, shewed unto him all

* Deut. viii, 3.   † Psa. xci, 11, 12.   ‡ Deut. v, 16.

	in one Continuous Narrative.	
Jan. 7. Apl. 8		July 8. Oct. 7.

the kingdom of the world and the glory of them in a moment of time; and the devil said unto him, All this power will I give thee, and the glory of them; for that is delivered unto me; and to whomsoever I will I give it; if thou therefore wilt fall down and worship me, all shall be thine. And Jesus answered and said unto him, Get thee behind me, Satan; for it is written,* Thou shalt worship the Lord thy God, and him only shalt thou serve.

And when the devil had ended all the temptation, he departed from him for a season. And Jesus was there in the wilderness with the wild beasts; and the angels came and ministered unto him.

And the people were in expectation, and all men mused in their hearts of John, whether he were the Christ, or not.

And this is the record of John, when the Jews sent priests and Levites from Jerusalem to ask him, Who art thou? And he confessed, and denied not; but confessed, I am not the Christ.† And they asked him, What then? Art thou Elijah? And he said, I am not. Art thou that prophet?‡ And he answered, No. Then said they unto him, Who art thou?

Side references:
M 4, 8
L 4, 5
— 6
— 7
M 4, 9
L 4, 7
— 8
— 13
K 1, 13
M 4, 11
L 3, 15
J 1, 19
— 20
— 21
— 22

* Ex. xxxiv, 14.   † Dan. ix, 25.   ‡ Deut. xviii, 15.

| | Jan. 7. Apl. 8. | The Four Gospels arranged | July 8. Oct. 7. |

J 1, 22	that we may give an answer to them that sent
— 23	us. What sayest thou of thyself? He said, I am the voice of one crying in the wilderness, Make straight the way of the Lord, as said the
— 24	prophet Isaiah.* And they which were sent
— 25	were of the Pharisees; and they asked him, and said unto him, Why baptizest thou then, if thou art not that Christ, nor Elijah, neither
L 3, 16	that prophet? John answered, saying unto
M 3, 11	them all, I indeed baptize you with water unto
J 1, 26	repentance; but there standeth one among you
K 1, 7	whom ye know not; one mightier than I; he
J 1, 27	it is, who coming after me is preferred before
— 15	me, for he was before me; the latchet of whose
L 3, 16 M 3, 11 K 1, 7 L 3, 16	shoes I am not worthy to bear, or to stoop down to unloose; he shall baptize you with the
— 17	Holy Ghost and with fire; whose fan is in his hand, and he will throughly purge his floor, and will gather the wheat into his garner; but the chaff he will burn with fire unquenchable.
— 18	And many other things in his exhortation preached he unto the people.
J 1, 28	These things were done in Bethabara beyond Jordan, where John was baptizing.

* Isa. xl, 3.

Jan. 8.　Apl. 9.　　*in one* 𝕮𝖔𝖓𝖙𝖎𝖓𝖚𝖔𝖚𝖘 𝕹𝖆𝖗𝖗𝖆𝖙𝖎𝖛𝖊.　　July 9.　Oct. 8.

VIII.

Jan. 8.　Apl. 9.　July 9.　Oct. 8.

John the Baptist's second testimony to Christ. Christ's first disciples.

THE next day John saw Jesus coming unto him, and said, Behold the Lamb of God, which taketh away the sin of the world. This is he of whom I said, After me cometh a man which is preferred before me; for he was before me. And I knew him not; but that he should be made manifest to Israel, therefore am I come baptizing with water. | J 1, 29
— 30
— 31

And John bare record, saying, I saw the Spirit descending from heaven like a dove, and it abode upon him; and I knew him not; but he that sent me to baptize with water, the same said unto me, Upon whom thou shalt see the Spirit descending, and remaining on him, the same is he which baptizeth with the Holy Ghost. And I saw, and bare record that this is the Son of God. | — 32
— 33
— 34

Again, the next day after, John stood, and two of his disciples; and looking upon Jesus as he walked, he said, Behold the Lamb of God! And the two disciples heard him speak, and they followed Jesus. | — 35
— 36
— 37

Then Jesus turned, and saw them following, | — 38

| Jan. 8. | | July 9. |
| Apl. 9. | The Four Gospels arranged | Oct. 8. |

J 1, 38 and said unto them, What seek ye? They said unto him, Rabbi, which is to say, being
— 39 interpreted, Master, where dwellest thou? He said unto them, Come and see. They came and saw where he dwelt, and abode with him that day; for it was about the tenth hour.
— 40 One of the two which heard John speak, and followed him, was Andrew, Simon Peter's
— 41 brother. He first found his own brother Simon, and said unto him, We have found the Messiah, which is, being interpreted, the
— 42 Christ; and he brought him to Jesus.

And when Jesus beheld him he said, Thou art Simon the son of Jonas, thou shalt be called Cephas, which is by interpretation, A stone.

— 43 The day following Jesus would go forth into Galilee, and found Philip, and said unto him,
— 44 Follow me. Now Philip was of Bethsaida,
— 45 the city of Andrew and Peter. Philip found Nathanael, and said unto him, We have found him, of whom Moses in the law,* and the prophets,† did write, Jesus of Nazareth, the
— 46 son of Joseph. And Nathanael said unto him, Can there any good thing come out of Nazareth? Philip said unto him, Come and
— 47 see. Jesus saw Nathanael coming to him, and

* Deut. xviii. 18.
† Isa. vii, 14; ix, 6; Micah v, 2; Zech. vi, 12.

| Jan. 9. Apl. 10. | in one Continuous Narrative. | July 10. Oct. 9. |

said of him, Behold an Israelite indeed, in whom is no guile! Nathanael said unto him, Whence knowest thou me? Jesus answered and said unto him, Before that Philip called thee, when thou wast under the fig tree, I saw thee. Nathanael answered and said unto him, Rabbi, thou art the Son of God; thou art the King of Israel. Jesus answered and said unto him, Because I said unto thee, I saw thee under the fig tree, believest thou? thou shalt see greater things than these. And he said unto him, Verily, verily, I say unto you, hereafter ye shall see heaven open, and the angels of God ascending and descending upon the Son of man.

J 1, 47
— 48
— 49
— 50
— 51

IX.
Jan. 9. Apl. 10. July 10. Oct. 9.

The marriage in Cana of Galilee. Christ's first expulsion of the money-changers from the temple.

AND the third day there was a marriage in Cana of Galilee; and the mother of Jesus was there; and both Jesus and his disciples were called to the marriage. And when they wanted wine, the mother of Jesus said unto him, They have no wine. Jesus said unto her, Woman, what have I to do with thee? mine hour is not yet come. His mother said unto the servants, Whatsoever he saith

J 2, 1
— 2
— 3
— 4
— 5

| Jan. 9. | The Four Gospels arranged | July 10. |
| Apl. 10. | | Oct. 9. |

J 2, 6 — unto you, do it. And there were set there six waterpots of stone, after the manner of the purifying of the Jews, containing two or three

— 7 — firkins apiece. Jesus said unto the servants, Fill the waterpots with water. And they filled

— 8 — them up to the brim. And he said unto them, Draw out now, and bear unto the governor of

— 9 — the feast. And they bare it. When the ruler of the feast had tasted the water that was made wine, and knew not whence it was; (but the servants which drew the water knew;) the governor of the feast called the bridegroom,

— 10 — and said unto him, Every man at the beginning doth set forth good wine; and when men have well drunk, then that which is worse: but

— 11 — thou hast kept the good wine until now. This beginning of miracles did Jesus in Cana of Galilee, and manifested forth his glory; and his disciples believed on him.

— 12 — After this he went down to Capernaum, he, and his mother, and his brethren, and his disciples; and they continued there not many days.

— 13 — And the Jews' passover* was at hand, and

— 14 — Jesus went up to Jerusalem, and found in the temple those that sold oxen and sheep and

— 15 — doves, and the changers of money sitting; and when he had made a scourge of small cords,

* Ex. xii, 12-49.

| Jan. 9. Apl. 10. | in one Continuous Narrative. | July 10. Oct. 9. |

he drove them, and the sheep, and the oxen, all out of the temple; and poured out the changers' money, and overthrew the tables; and said unto them that sold doves, Take these things hence; make not my Father's house a house of merchandise. And his disciples remembered that it was written,* The zeal of thy house hath eaten me up.

Then answered the Jews and said unto him, What sign shewest thou unto us, seeing that thou doest these things? Jesus answered and said unto them, Destroy this temple, and in three days I will raise it up. Then said the Jews, Forty and six years was this temple in building, and wilt thou rear it up in three days? But he spake of the temple of his body. When therefore he was risen from the dead, his disciples remembered that he had said this unto them; and they believed the scripture, and the word which Jesus had said.

Now when he was in Jerusalem at the passover, in the feast day, many believed in his name, when they saw the miracles which he did. But Jesus did not commit himself unto them, because he knew all men, and needed not that any should testify of man; for he knew what was in man.

* Psa. lxix, 9.

J 2, 15
— 16
— 17
— 18
— 19
— 20
— 21
— 22
— 23
— 24
— 25

X.

Jan. 10.   Apl. 11.   July 11.   Oct. 10.

Nicodemus comes to Christ by night.

J 3, 1 — THERE was a man of the Pharisees, named Nicodemus, a ruler of the Jews;
— 2 the same came to Jesus by night, and said unto him, Rabbi, we know that thou art a teacher come from God; for no man can do these miracles that thou doest, except
— 3 God be with him. Jesus answered and said unto him, Verily, verily, I say unto thee, except a man be born again, he cannot see
— 4 the kingdom of God. Nicodemus said unto him, How can a man be born when he is old? can he enter the second time into his
— 5 mother's womb, and be born? Jesus answered, Verily, verily, I say unto thee, except a man be born of water and of the Spirit, he
— 6 cannot enter into the kingdom of God. That which is born of the flesh is flesh; and that
— 7 which is born of the Spirit is spirit. Marvel not that I said unto thee, Ye must be born
— 8 again. The wind bloweth where it listeth, and thou hearest the sound thereof, but canst not tell whence it cometh, and whither it goeth; so
— 9 is every one that is born of the Spirit. Nico-

Jan. 10.
Apl. 11.

in one Continuous Narrative.

July 11.
Oct. 10.

demus answered and said unto him, How can these things be? Jesus answered and said unto him, Art thou a master of Israel, and knowest not these things? Verily, verily, I say unto thee, we speak that we do know, and testify that we have seen; and ye receive not our witness. If I have told you of earthly things, and ye believe not, how shall ye believe, if I tell you of heavenly things? No man hath seen God at any time; the only begotten Son, which is in the bosom of the Father, he hath declared him. And no man hath ascended up to heaven, but he that came down from heaven, even the Son of man which is in heaven. And as Moses lifted up the serpent in the wilderness,* even so must the Son of man be lifted up; that whosoever believeth in him should not perish, but have eternal life. For God so loved the world, that he gave his only begotten Son, that whosoever believeth in him should not perish, but have everlasting life; for God sent not his Son into the world to condemn the world; but that the world through him might be saved. He that believeth on him is not condemned; but he that believeth not is condemned already, because he hath not believed in the name of the only begotten Son of God. And this is the

* Num. xxi, 8, 9.

J 3, 9
— 10
— 11
— 12
J 1, 18
J 3, 13
— 14
— 15
— 16
— 17
— 18
— 19

J 3, 19	condemnation, that light is come into the world, and men loved darkness rather than
— 20	light, because their deeds were evil. For every one that doeth evil hateth the light, neither cometh to the light, lest his deeds should be
— 21	reproved; but he that doeth truth cometh to the light, that his deeds may be made manifest, that they are wrought in God.

XI.

JAN. 11. APL. 12. JULY 12. OCT. 11.

John the Baptist's third testimony to Christ. Imprisonment of John the Baptist.

J 3, 22	AFTER these things came Jesus and his disciples into the land of Judæa; and there he tarried with them, and baptized.
— 23	And John also was baptizing in Ænon, near to Salim, because there was much water there;
— 24	and they came, and were baptized; for John was not yet cast into prison.
— 25	Then there arose a question between some of John's disciples and the Jews about puri-
— 26	fying. And they came unto John, and said unto him, Rabbi, he that was with thee beyond Jordan, to whom thou barest witness, behold, the same baptizeth, and all men come to him.
— 27	John answered and said, A man can receive

| Jan. 11. Apl. 12. | in one Continuous Narrative. | July 12. Oct. 11. |

nothing, except it be given him from heaven. Ye yourselves bear me witness, that I said, I am not the Christ,* but that I am sent before him. He that hath the bride is the bridegroom; but the friend of the bridegroom, which standeth and heareth him, rejoiceth greatly because of the bridegroom's voice; this my joy therefore is fulfilled. He must increase, but I must decrease. He that cometh from above is above all: he that is of the earth is earthly, and speaketh of the earth. He that cometh from heaven is above all; and what he hath seen and heard, that he testifieth; and no man receiveth his testimony. He that hath received his testimony hath set to his seal that God is true. For he whom God hath sent speaketh the words of God; for God giveth not the Spirit by measure unto him. The Father loveth the Son, and hath given all things into his hand. He that believeth on the Son hath everlasting life: and he that believeth not the Son shall not see life; but the wrath of God abideth on him.

J 3, 27
— 28
— 29
— 30
— 31
— 32
— 33
— 34
— 35
— 36

Herod the tetrarch, being reproved by John for Herodias his brother Philip's wife, and for all the evils which Herod had done, added this yet above all, that he shut up John in prison.

L 3, 19
— 20

* Dan. ix. 25.

| | Jan. 11. Apl. 12. | The Four Gospels arranged | July 12. Oct. 11. |

K 6, 17	For Herod himself had sent forth and laid hold upon John, and bound him in prison for Herodias' sake, his brother Philip's wife: for
— 18	he had married her. For John had said unto Herod, It is not lawful for thee to have thy
— 19	brother's wife. Therefore Herodias had a quarrel against him, and would have killed
M 14, 5	him; but she could not; for Herod, when he would have put him to death, feared the multitude, because they counted John as a prophet.
K 6, 20	And he feared John, knowing that he was a just man and a holy, and observed him; and when he heard him, he did many things, and heard him gladly.
K 1, 14	Now after that John was put in prison, Jesus
L 4, 14	returned in the power of the Spirit into Galilee,
K 1, 14	preaching the Gospel of the kingdom of God,
— 15	and saying, The time is fulfilled, and the kingdom of God is at hand: repent ye, and believe
L 4, 14	the gospel. And there went out a fame of him
— 15	through all the region round about, and he taught in their synagogues, being glorified of all.
J 4, 1	When therefore the Lord knew how the Pharisees had heard that Jesus made and bap-
— 2	tized more disciples than John, (though Jesus
— 3	himself baptized not, but his disciples,) he left
— 4	Judæa, and departed again into Galilee; and he must needs go through Samaria.

| Jan. 12. | | July 13. |
| Apl. 13. | *in one Continuous Narrative.* | Oct. 12. |

XII.

Jan. 12. Apl. 13. July 13. Oct. 12.

Christ's conversation with the Samaritan woman at Jacob's well.

THEN came Jesus to a city of Samaria, which is called Sychar, near to the parcel of ground that Jacob gave to his son Joseph.* Now Jacob's well was there. Jesus therefore, being wearied with his journey, sat thus on the well; and it was about the sixth hour. There came a woman of Samaria to draw water: Jesus said unto her, Give me to drink; (for his disciples were gone away unto the city to buy meat.)

Then said the woman of Samaria unto him, How is it that thou, being a Jew, askest drink of me, who am a woman of Samaria? for the Jews have no dealings with the Samaritans. Jesus answered and said unto her, If thou knewest the gift of God, and who it is that saith to thee, Give me to drink; thou wouldest have asked of him, and he would have given thee living water. The woman said unto him, Sir, thou hast nothing to draw with, and the well is deep; whence then hast thou that living

* Josh. xxiv, 32.

J	,
—	6
—	7
—	
—	
—	10
—	11

| | Jan. 12. Apl. 19. | The Four Gospels arranged | July 13. Oct. 12. |

J 4, 12	water? Art thou greater than our father Jacob, which gave us the well, and drank thereof him-
— 13	self, and his children, and his cattle? Jesus answered and said unto her, Whosoever drink-
— 14	eth of this water shall thirst again; but whoso- ever drinketh of the water that I shall give him shall never thirst; but the water that I shall give him shall be in him a well of water springing
— 15	up into everlasting life. The woman said unto him, Sir, give me this water, that I thirst not,
— 16	neither come hither to draw. Jesus said unto her, Go, call thy husband, and come hither.
— 17	The woman answered and said, I have no hus- band. Jesus said unto her, Thou hast well
— 18	said, I have no husband; for thou hast had five husbands; and he whom thou now hast is not thy husband: in that saidst thou truly.
— 19	The woman said unto him, Sir, I perceive that
— 20	thou art a prophet. Our fathers worshipped in this mountain; and ye say, that in Jerusalem is
— 21	the place where men ought to worship. Jesus said unto her, Woman, believe me, the hour cometh, when ye shall neither in this moun- tain, nor yet at Jerusalem, worship the Father.
— 22	Ye worship ye know not what: we know what
— 23	we worship; for salvation is of the Jews.* But the hour cometh, and now is, when the true

* Gen. xxii, 18.

| Jan. 12. ApL 13. | in one Continuous Narrative. | July 13. Oct. 12. |

worshippers shall worship the Father in spirit and in truth; for the Father seeketh such to worship him. God is a Spirit; and they that worship him must worship him in spirit and in truth. The woman said unto him, I know that Messiah cometh, which is called Christ; when he is come, he will tell us all things. Jesus said unto her, I that speak unto thee am he.

And upon this came his disciples, and marvelled that he talked with the woman; yet no man said, What seekest thou? or, Why talkest thou with her? The woman then left her waterpot, and went her way into the city, and said to the men, Come, see a man, which told me all things that ever I did: is not this the Christ? Then they went out of the city, and came unto him.

In the mean while his disciples prayed him, saying, Master, eat. But he said unto them, I have meat to eat that ye know not of. Therefore said the disciples one to another, Hath any man brought him aught to eat? Jesus said unto them, My meat is to do the will of him that sent me, and to finish his work. Say not ye, There are yet four months, and then cometh harvest? Behold, I say unto you, lift up your eyes, and look on the fields; for they are white already to

J 4, 23
— 24
— 25
— 26
— 27
— 28
— 29
— 30
— 31
— 32
— 33
— 34
— 35

| Jan. 13. Apl. 14. | The Four Gospels arranged | July 14. Oct. 13. |

J 4, 36 harvest; and he that reapeth receiveth wages, and gathereth fruit unto life eternal; that both he that soweth and he that reapeth may rejoice
— 37 together. And herein is that saying true, One
— 38 soweth, and another reapeth. I sent you to reap that whereon ye bestowed no labour; other men laboured, and ye are entered into their labours.

— 39 And many of the Samaritans of that city believed on him for the saying of the woman, which testified, He told me all that ever I did.
— 40 So when the Samaritans were come unto him, they besought him that he would tarry with
— 41 them; and he abode there two days; and many more believed because of his own word,
— 42 and said unto the woman, Now we believe, not because of thy saying; for we have heard him ourselves, and know that this is indeed the Christ, the Saviour of the world.

XIII.

Jan. 13. Apl. 14. July 14. Oct. 13.

Christ heals the nobleman's son at Capernaum, and preaches in the synagogue at Nazareth.

J 4, 43 NOW after two days Jesus departed thence,
— 45 and went into Galilee; and the Galilæans received him, having seen all the things that he did at Jerusalem at the feast; for they

| Jan. 13. Apl. 14. | in one Continuous Narrative. | July 14. Oct. 13. |

also went unto the feast. So Jesus came again into Cana of Galilee, where he made the water wine: **J 4, 4;**

And there was a certain nobleman, whose son was sick at Capernaum. When he heard that Jesus was come out of Judæa into Galilee, he went unto him, and besought him that he would come down, and heal his son; for he was at the point of death. Then said Jesus unto him, Except ye see signs and wonders, ye will not believe. The nobleman said unto him, Sir, come down ere my child die. Jesus said unto him, Go thy way; thy son liveth. And the man believed the word that Jesus had spoken unto him, and he went his way. And as he was now going down his servants met him, and told him, saying, Thy son liveth. Then inquired he of them the hour when he began to amend. And they said unto him, Yesterday at the seventh hour the fever left him. So the father knew that it was at the same hour, in the which Jesus said unto him, Thy son liveth; and himself believed, and his whole house. This is the second miracle that Jesus did, when he was come out of Judæa into Galilee.

— 47
— 48
— 49
— 50
— 51
— 52
— 53
— 54

And he came to Nazareth, where he had been brought up; and, as his custom was, he **L 4, 16**

Jan. 13. Apl. 14.	The Four Gospels arranged	July 14. Oct. 13.

L 4, 16 — 17 went into the synagogue on the sabbath day, and stood up to read. And there was delivered unto him the book of the prophet Isaiah. And when he had opened the book, he found the
— 18 place where it was written,* The Spirit of the Lord is upon me, because he hath anointed me to preach the gospel to the poor; he hath sent me to heal the broken hearted, to preach deliverance to the captives, and recovering of sight to the blind, to set at liberty them that
— 19 are bruised, to preach the acceptable year of
— 20 the Lord. And he closed the book, and gave it again to the minister, and sat down.

— 21 And the eyes of all them that were in the synagogue were fastened on him. And he began to say unto them, This day is this
— 22 scripture fulfilled in your ears. And all bare him witness, and wondered at the gracious words which proceeded out of his mouth. And
— 23 they said, Is not this Joseph's son? And he said unto them, Ye will surely say unto me this proverb, Physician, heal thyself: whatsoever we have heard done in Capernaum, do also here in thy country.

— 24 And he said, Verily, I say unto you, no
J 4, 44 prophet is accepted, or hath honour, in his
L 4, 25 own country. But I tell you of a truth, many

* Isa. lxi, 1.

| Jan. 14. Apl. 15. | in one Continuous Narrative. | July 15. Oct. 14. |

widows were in Israel in the days of Elijah, when the heaven was shut up three years and six months, when great famine was throughout all the land;* but unto none of them was Elijah sent, save unto Sarepta, a city of Sidon, unto a woman that was a widow. And many lepers were in Israel in the time of Elisha the prophet;† and none of them was cleansed, saving Naaman the Syrian.

And all they in the synagogue, when they heard these things, were filled with wrath, and rose up, and thrust him out of the city, and led him unto the brow of the hill whereon their city was built, that they might cast him down headlong; but he, passing through the midst of them, went his way.

L 4, 25
— 26
— 27
— 28
— 29
— 30

XIV.
Jan. 14. Apl. 15. July 15. Oct. 14.

The miraculous draught of fishes; the exorcism of an unclean spirit; and the healing of Peter's wife's mother.

AND leaving Nazareth, Jesus came and dwelt in Capernaum, a city of Galilee, upon the sea coast, in the borders of Zabulon and Nephthalim; that it might be fulfilled which was spoken by Isaiah the prophet,‡

M 4, 13
L 4, 31
M 4, 13
— 14

* 1 Kings xvii, 1-16.   † 2 Kings v, 1-14.   ‡ Isa. ix, 1, 2.

	Jan. 14.		July 15.
	Apl. 15.	The Four Gospels arranged	Oct. 14.

M 4, 15 — saying, The land of Zabulon, and the land of Nephthalim, by the way of the sea, beyond
— 16 — Jordan, Galilee of the Gentiles; the people which sat in darkness saw great light; and to them which sat in the region and shadow of death, light is sprung up.

L 5, 1 — And it came to pass, that, as the people pressed upon him to hear the word of God, he
— 2 — stood by the lake of Gennesaret, and saw two ships standing by the lake; but the fishermen were gone out of them, and were washing
— 3 — their nets. And he entered into one of the ships, which was Simon's, and prayed him that he would thrust out a little from the land. And he sat down, and taught the people out of
— 4 — the ship. Now when he had left speaking, he said unto Simon, Launch out into the deep, and
— 5 — let down your nets for a draught. And Simon answering said unto him, Master, we have toiled all the night, and have taken nothing: nevertheless at thy word I will let down the net.

K 1, 16 — And when Simon and Andrew his brother
L 5, 6 — had this done, they enclosed a great multitude
— 7 — of fishes; and their net brake. And they beckoned unto their partners, which were in the other ship, that they should come and help them. And they came, and filled both the
— 8 — ships, so that they began to sink. When

Jan. 14.
Apl. 15. **in one Continuous Narrative.** July 15.
Oct. 14.

Simon Peter saw it, he fell down at Jesus' knees, saying, Depart from me; for I am a sinful man, O Lord. For he was astonished, and all that were with him, at the draught of the fishes which they had taken; and so were also James and John, the sons of Zebedee, which were partners with Simon, and were in the ship with their father mending their nets, for they were fishers. And he said unto them, Follow me, and I will make you fishers of men. And when they had brought their ships to land, they straightway left their nets and the ship and their father, with the hired servants, and forsook all and followed him.	L 5, 8 — 9 — 10 M 4, 21 — 18 — 19 L 5, 11 M 4, 20 — 22 K 1, 20 L 5, 11
And they went into Capernaum; and straightway on the sabbath day he entered into the synagogue, and taught. And the people were astonished at his doctrine; for his word was with power: he taught them as one that had authority, and not as the scribes.	K 1, 21 — 22 L 4, 32 K 1, 22
And in the synagogue there was a man, which had a spirit of an unclean devil, and cried out with a loud voice, saying, Let us alone: what have we to do with thee, thou Jesus of Nazareth? art thou come to destroy us? I know thee who thou art; the Holy One of God. And Jesus rebuked him, saying, Hold thy peace, and come out of him. And	L 4, 33 — 34 — 35

| Jan. 15. | | July 16. |
| Apl. 16. | **The Four Gospels arranged** | Oct. 15. |

L 4, 35
K 1, 26
L 4, 35
— 36

when the devil had thrown him in the midst, and had torn him, and cried with a loud voice, he came out of him, and hurt him not. And they were all amazed, and spake among themselves, saying, What a word is this! for with authority and power he commandeth even the

K 1, 27
— 28

unclean spirits, and they obey him and come out. And immediately his fame spread abroad throughout all the region round about Galilee.

— 29

— 30
L 4, 38
— 39

K 1, 31

And forthwith, when they were come out of the synagogue, they entered into the house of Simon and Andrew, with James and John. But Simon's wife's mother lay sick of a great fever; and they besought him for her. And he came and stood over her, and rebuked the fever; and took her by the hand, and lifted her up; and immediately the fever left her, and she arose and ministered unto them.

XV.

JAN. 15. APL. 16. JULY 16. OCT. 15.

Christ casts out the spirits by his word, heals the sick, and cleanses a leper.

L 4, 40
K 1, 32
L 4, 40

NOW when the sun was setting, all they that had any sick with divers diseases brought them unto Jesus, and they that were possessed with devils; and he laid his hands on

Jan. 15. Apl. 16.	in one Continuous Narrative.	July 16. Oct. 15.

every one of them, and healed them; that it might be fulfilled which was spoken by Isaiah the prophet,* saying, Himself took our infirmities, and bare our sicknesses. And all the city was gathered together at the door; and he cast out the spirits by his word, and they came out of many, crying out, and saying, Thou art Christ the Son of God. And he, rebuking them, suffered them not to speak; for they knew that he was Christ.

And in the morning, rising up a great while before day, he went out, and departed into a solitary place, and there prayed; and Simon and they that were with him followed after him; and when they had found him, they said unto him, All men seek for thee. And he said unto them, Let us go into the next towns, that I may preach there also. And the people came unto him, and stayed him, that he should not depart from them. And he said unto them, I must preach the kingdom of God to other cities also; for therefore am I sent.

And Jesus went about all Galilee, teaching in their synagogues, and preaching the gospel of the kingdom, and healing all manner of sickness and all manner of disease among the people, and casting out devils. And his fame went

M 8, 17

K 1, 33
M 8, 16
L 4, 41

K 1, 35
— 36
— 37
— 38

L 4, 42
— 43

M 4, 23

K 1, 39
M 4, 24

* Isa. liii, 4.

| | Jan. 15. Apl. 16. | The Four Gospels arranged | July 16. Oct. 15. |

M 4, 24	throughout all Syria : and they brought unto him all sick people that were taken with divers diseases and torments, and those which were possessed with devils, and those which were lunatic, and those that had the palsy ; and he
— 25	healed them. And there followed him great multitudes of people from Galilee, and from Decapolis, and from Jerusalem, and from Judæa, and from beyond Jordan.
L 5, 12	And it came to pass, when he was in a certain city, behold, there came a man full of leprosy; who seeing Jesus, fell on his face, and besought him, saying, Lord, if thou wilt, thou
K 1, 41	canst make me clean. And Jesus, moved with compassion, put forth his hand, and touched
— 42	him, saying, I will; be thou clean. And as soon as he had spoken, immediately the leprosy departed from him, and he was cleansed.
— 43	And he straitly charged him, and forthwith
— 44	sent him away, and said unto him, Tell no
L 5, 14	man; but go, and shew thyself to the priest, and offer for thy cleansing according as Moses
— 15	commanded, for a testimony unto them. But so much the more went there a fame abroad of him, for he went out and began to publish it much and to blaze abroad the matter; and great multitudes came together to hear, and to
K 1, 45	be healed by him of their infirmities; inso-

| Jan. 16. Apl. 17. | in one Continuous Narrative. | July 17. Oct. 16. |

much that Jesus could no more openly enter into the city. And he withdrew himself into the wilderness, and prayed; and they came to him from every quarter.

K 1, 45
L 5, 16
K 1, 45

XVI.

JAN. 16. APL. 17. JULY 17. OCT. 16.

Christ cures a man of the palsy. The call of Levi.

AND again Jesus entered into Capernaum after some days, and, as he was teaching, there were Pharisees and doctors of the law sitting by, which were come out of every town of Galilee, and Judæa, and Jerusalem; and it was noised that he was in the house, and straightway many were gathered together, insomuch that there was no room to receive them, no, not so much as about the door; and he preached the word unto them; and the power of the Lord was present to heal them. And, behold, four men brought in a bed a man which was taken with a palsy; and they sought means to bring him in, and to lay him before Jesus. And when they could not find by what way they might bring him in because of the multitude, they went upon the housetop, and uncovered the roof where he was, and when they had broken it up, they

K 2, 1
L 5, 17

K 2, 2

L 5, 17
K 2, 3

K 2, 3
L 5, 18

— 19

K 2, 4
L 5, 19

| | Jan. 16. Apl. 17. | The Four Gospels arranged | July 17. Oct. 16. |

L 5, 19	let him down through the tiling with his couch
— 20	into the midst before Jesus. And when he saw
M 9, 2	their faith, he said unto him, Man, be of good
— 3	cheer, thy sins are forgiven thee. And certain
L 5, 21 K 2, 6 L 5, 21	of the scribes and the Pharisees sitting there, began to reason within themselves, saying, Who is this which speaketh blasphemies?
— 22	Who can forgive sins, but God alone? But
K 2, 8 L 5, 22	when Jesus perceived in his spirit their thoughts, he answering said unto them,
M 9, 4	What reason ye, and wherefore think ye
L 5, 23	evil in your hearts? Whether is easier, to say, Thy sins are forgiven thee; or to say,
K 2, 9 L 5, 24	Arise, and take up thy bed and walk? But that ye may know that the Son of Man hath power upon earth to forgive sins, (he said unto the sick of the palsy,) I say unto thee, Arise, and take up thy couch, and go unto thy
— 25	house. And immediately he rose up before them all and took up that whereon he lay, and departed to his own house, glorifying
M 9, 8	God. And when the multitude saw it they
L 5, 26	were all amazed, and they glorified God, who
M 9, 8 L 5, 26	had given such power unto men, and were filled with fear, saying, We have seen strange things to-day.
K 2, 13	And he went forth again by the sea side; and all the multitude resorted unto him, and

he taught them. And as he passed by, he saw a publican, named Levi, surnamed Matthew, the son of Alphæus, sitting at the receipt of custom; and he said unto him, Follow me. And he left all, rose up, and followed him.

And Levi made him a great feast in his own house; and there was a great company of publicans and of others that sat down with Jesus and his disciples, for they were many, and they followed him. But the scribes and Pharisees murmured against his disciples, saying, Why do ye eat and drink with publicans and sinners? And Jesus answering said unto them, They that are whole need not a physician; but they that are sick. I came not to call the righteous, but sinners to repentance.

And the disciples of John and of the Pharisees used to fast. Then came to Jesus the disciples of John, saying, Why do we and the Pharisees fast oft, and make prayers, but thy disciples eat and drink and fast not? And he said unto them, Can ye make the children of the bridechamber mourn and fast while the bridegroom is with them? As long as they have the bridegroom with them they cannot fast. But the days will come, when the bridegroom shall be taken away from them, and then shall they fast in those days.

| Jan. 17. | | July 18. |
| Apl. 18. | **The Four Gospels arranged** | Oct. 17. |

L 5, 36
M 9, 16

L 5, 36
— 37

— 38
— 39

And he spake also a parable unto them; No man putteth a piece of new cloth into an old garment, for that which is put in to fill it up taketh from the garment, and the rent is made worse, and the piece that was taken out of the new agreeth not with the old. And no man putteth new wine into old leathern bottles; else the new wine will burst the bottles, and be spilled, and the bottles shall perish. But new wine must be put into new bottles; and both are preserved. No man also having drunk old wine straightway desireth new: for he saith, The old is better.

XVII.

Jan. 17. Apl. 18. July 18. Oct. 17.

The raising of Jairus's daughter, and the cure of a woman having an issue of blood.

M 9, 18
L 8, 41

K 5, 23
L 8, 41
K 5, 23

WHILE Jesus spake these things unto them, behold, there came a man named Jairus, and he was a ruler of the synagogue; and he fell down at Jesus' feet, and besought him greatly that he would come into his house; saying, My little daughter lieth at the point of death; I pray thee come and lay thy hands on her that she may be healed, and she shall live:

Jan. 17. Apl. 18.	in one Continuous Narrative.	July 18. Oct. 17.

for he had one only daughter, about twelve years of age, and she lay a dying. And Jesus arose and followed him, and so did his disciples. But as he went much people followed him and thronged him.

And a certain woman, which was diseased with an issue of blood twelve years, and had suffered many things of many physicians, and had spent all that she had, and was nothing bettered, neither could be healed of any, but rather grew worse, when she had heard of Jesus, came in the press behind, and touched the hem of his garment; for she said within herself, If I may but touch his garment, I shall be whole. And straightway the fountain of her blood was dried up; and she felt in her body that she was healed of that plague. And Jesus, immediately knowing in himself that virtue had gone out of him, turned him about in the press, and said, Who touched me? When all denied, Peter and they that were with him said, Master, thou seest the multitude throng thee and press thee, and sayest thou, Who touched me? And Jesus said, Somebody hath touched me; for I perceive that virtue is gone out of me. And he looked round about to see her that had done this thing; and when the woman saw that she was

L 8, 42
M 9, 19
L 8, 42
K 5, 25
M 9, 20
K 5, 26
L 8, 43
K 5, 26
— 27
M 9, 20
— 21
K 5, 29
— 30
L 8, 45
— 46
K 5, 32
L 8, 47

Jan. 17. Apl. 18.	July 18. Oct. 17.

The Four Gospels arranged

L 8, 47	not hid, she came trembling, and falling down before him, she declared unto him before all the people for what cause she had touched him, and how she was healed immediately.
— 48	And he said unto her, Daughter, be of good comfort: thy faith hath made thee whole; go
M 9, 22	in peace. And the woman was made whole from that hour.
L 8, 49	While he yet spake, there came one from the ruler of the synagogue's house, saying to him, Thy daughter is dead; trouble not the
— 50	Master. But when Jesus heard it, he answered
K 5, 36	him, saying unto the ruler of the synagogue,
L 8, 50	Fear not; believe only, and she shall be made
— 51	whole. And when he came into the house, he suffered no man to go in, save Peter, and
K 5, 37 L 8, 52	James, and John the brother of James. And all wept, and bewailed her; but he said, Weep
— 53	not; she is not dead, but sleepeth. And they laughed him to scorn, knowing that she was
M 9, 23	dead. And when he saw the minstrels and
L 8, 54	the people making a noise he put them all out,
K 5, 40	and took the father and mother of the damsel and them that were with him, and entering in
L 8, 54	where the damsel was lying, he took her by
K 5, 41	the hand, and called, saying, Talitha-cumi; which is, being interpreted, Damsel, I say
L 8, 55	unto thee, Arise. And her spirit came again,

| Jan. 18. Apl. 19. | in one Continuous Narrative. | July 19. Oct. 18. |

and she arose straightway, and walked; and he commanded to give her meat. K 5, 42
L 8, 55

And her parents were astonished with a great astonishment; but he charged them straitly that they should tell no man what was done. But the fame hereof went abroad into all that land. — 56
K 5, 43
L 8, 56
M 9, 26

XVIII.

Jan. 18. Apl. 19. July 19. Oct. 18.

The blind receive their sight, the dumb speak, and the diseased are cured. Christ chooses his twelve apostles.

AND when Jesus departed thence, two blind men followed him, crying, and saying, Thou son of David, have mercy on us. And when he was come into the house, the blind men came to him; and Jesus said unto them, Believe ye that I am able to do this? They said unto him, Yea, Lord. Then touched he their eyes, saying, According to your faith be it unto you. And their eyes were opened; and Jesus straitly charged them, saying, See that no man know it. But they, when they were departed, spread abroad his fame in all that country.

As they went out, behold, they brought to him a dumb man possessed with a devil, and

M 9, 27
— 28
— 29
— 30
— 31
— 32
— 33

Jan. 18. Apl. 19.	July 19. Oct. 18.

The Four Gospels arranged

M 9,33 — when the devil was cast out, the dumb spake; and the multitudes marvelled, saying, It was
— 34 never so seen in Israel. But the Pharisees said, He casteth out devils through the prince of the devils.

K 6, 1 And he went out from thence, and came into his own country; and his disciples followed
— 2 him. And when the sabbath day was come, he began to teach in the synagogue; and many hearing him were astonished, saying, Whence hath this man these things? and what wisdom is this which is given unto him, that even such
— 3 mighty works are wrought by his hands? Is not this the carpenter, the son of Mary, the brother of James, and Joses, and of Judas, and Simon? and are not his sisters here with us?
— 4 And they were offended at him. But Jesus said unto them, A prophet is not without honour, but in his own country, and among his
— 5 own kin, and in his own house. And he could
M 13,58 there do no mighty work, because of their un-
K 6, 5 belief; save that he laid his hands upon a few
— 6 sick folk and healed them. And he marvelled because of their unbelief.

M 9,35 And Jesus went about all the cities and villages, teaching in their synagogues, and preaching the gospel of the kingdom, and healing every sickness and every disease among

	Jan. 18. Apl. 19.	in one Continuous Narrative.	July 19. Oct. 18.

the people. But when he saw the multitudes, he was moved with compassion on them, because they fainted, and were scattered abroad, as sheep having no shepherd. Then said he unto his disciples, The harvest truly is plenteous, but the labourers are few; pray ye therefore the Lord of the harvest, that he will send forth labourers into his harvest.	M 9, 36 — 37 — 38
And it came to pass in those days, that he went out into a mountain to pray, and continued all night in prayer to God. And when it was day, he called unto him his disciples, whom he would; and they came unto him; and of them he chose twelve, whom also he named apostles; that they should be with him, and that he might send them forth to preach, and to have power to heal sicknesses, and to cast out devils.	L 6, 12 — 13 K 3, 13 L 6, 13 K 3, 14 — 15
Now the names of the twelve apostles are these: The first, Simon, whom Christ surnamed Peter, and Andrew his brother; James the son of Zebedee, and John his brother; and he surnamed them Boanerges, which is, The sons of thunder; Philip, and Bartholomew; Thomas, called Didymus; and Levi, surnamed Matthew the publican, and James, the sons of Alphæus; and Judas the brother of James, named also Lebbæus, whose surname was	M 10, 2 K 3, 16 M 10, 2 K 3, 17 M 10, 3 J 11, 16 L 5, 27 M 10, 3 K 2, 14 L 6, 16 M 10, 3

| Jan. 19. Apl. 20. | The Four Gospels arranged | July 20. Oct. 19. |

L 6, 15 M 10, 4	Thaddæus; Simon the Canaanite, called Zelotes; and Judas Iscariot, who also betrayed him.
L 6, 17	And he came down, and stood in the plain with them, and the company of his disciples, and a great multitude of people out of all Judæa and Jerusalem; and from the sea coast of Tyre and Sidon, which came to hear him,
— 18	and to be healed of their diseases, and they that were vexed with unclean spirits; and they
— 19	were healed. And the whole multitude sought to touch him; for there went virtue out of him, and healed them all.

XIX.

JAN. 19. APL. 20. JULY 20. OCT. 19.

Christ's sermon on the mount.

M 5, 1	AND seeing the multitudes, Jesus went up into a mountain; and when he was sat,
— 2	his disciples came unto him; and he opened his mouth, and taught them, saying,
— 3	Blessed are the poor in spirit; for theirs is the kingdom of heaven.
— 4	Blessed are they that mourn; for they shall be comforted.
— 5	Blessed are the meek; for they shall inherit the earth.

| Jan. 19. Apl. 20. | in one Continuous Narrative. | July 20. Oct. 19. |

Blessed are they which do hunger and thirst after righteousness; for they shall be filled. — M 5, 6

Blessed are the merciful; for they shall obtain mercy. — — 7

Blessed are the pure in heart; for they shall see God. — — 8

Blessed are the peacemakers; for they shall be called the children of God. — — 9

Blessed are they which are persecuted for righteousness' sake; for theirs is the kingdom of heaven. — — 10

Blessed are ye, when men shall revile you, and persecute you, and shall separate you from their company, and shall say all manner of evil against you falsely, for my sake. Rejoice, and be exceeding glad; for great is your reward in heaven: for so persecuted their fathers the prophets which were before you. — — 11 / L 6, 22 / M 5, 11 / — 12 / L 6, 23 / M 5, 12

But woe unto you that are rich! for ye have received your consolation. — L 6, 24

Woe unto you that are full! for ye shall hunger. — — 25

Woe unto you that laugh now! for ye shall mourn and weep.

Woe unto you, when all men shall speak well of you! for so did their fathers to the false prophets. — — 26

Salt is good: ye are the salt of the earth; — K 9, 50 / M 5, 13

| Jan. 19. | The Four Gospels arranged | July 20. |
| Apl. 20. | | Oct. 19. |

M 5, 13
L 14, 35
M 5, 13
K 9, 50
— 49

but if the salt have lost its savour, wherewith shall it be salted? It is thenceforth good for nothing; it is fit neither for the land, nor yet for the dunghill; but to be cast out, and to be trodden under foot of men. Have salt in yourselves, and have peace one with another. For every one shall be salted with fire, and every sacrifice shall be salted with salt.

M 5, 14
L 8, 16

Ye are the light of the world. A city that is set on a hill cannot be hid. No man, when he hath lighted a candle, covereth it with a vessel, or putteth it under a bed; but setteth it on a candlestick, that they which enter in

M 5, 16

may see the light. Let your light so shine before men, that they may see your good works, and glorify your Father which is in heaven.

— 17
— 18
— 19
— 20

Think not that I am come to destroy the law, or the prophets; I am not come to destroy, but to fulfil; for, Verily, I say unto you, till heaven and earth pass, one jot or one tittle shall in no wise pass from the law, till all be fulfilled. Whosoever therefore shall break one of these least commandments, and shall teach men so, he shall be called the least in the kingdom of heaven; but whosoever shall do and teach them, the same shall be called great in the kingdom of heaven. For I say unto

| Jan. 20. Apl. 21. | in one Continuous Narrative. | July 21. Oct. 20. |

you, that except your righteousness shall exceed the righteousness of the scribes and Pharisees, ye shall in no case enter into the kingdom of heaven.   M 5, 20

XX.

Jan. 20. Apl. 21. July 21. Oct. 20.

Christ's sermon on the mount continued.

YE have heard that it was said by them of old time,* Thou shalt not kill; and whosoever shall kill shall be in danger of the judgment; but I, Jesus, say unto you, that whosoever is angry with his brother without a cause shall be in danger of the judgment; and whosoever shall say to his brother, Raca, shall be in danger of the council; but whosoever shall say, Thou fool, shall be in danger of hell fire. Therefore if thou bring thy gift to the altar, and there remember that thy brother hath aught against thee; leave there thy gift before the altar, and go thy way; first be reconciled to thy brother, and then come and offer thy gift. When thou goest with thine adversary to the magistrate, as thou art in the way, give diligence that thou mayest be

M 5, 21

— 22

— 23

— 24

L 12, 58

* Ex. xx, 13. Deut. xix, 11-13.

| Jan. 20. | | July 21. |
| Apl. 21. | The Four Gospels arranged | Oct. 20. |

L 12, 58

M 5, 26

delivered from him; lest he hale thee to the judge, and the judge deliver thee to the officer, and the officer cast thee into prison. Verily, I say unto thee, thou shalt by no means come out thence, till thou hast paid the uttermost farthing.

— 27

— 28

L 11, 34

— 36

— 34

— 35

M 6, 23

Ye have heard that it was said by them of old time,* Thou shalt not commit adultery; but I say unto you, that whosoever looketh on a woman to lust after her hath committed adultery with her already in his heart. The light of the body is the eye; therefore when thine eye is single, thy whole body also is full of light; and if thy whole body therefore be full of light, having no part dark, the whole shall be full of light, as when the bright shining of a candle doth give thee light. But when thine eye is evil, thy body also is full of darkness. Take heed therefore that the light which is in thee be not darkness; for if the light that is in thee be darkness, how great is that darkness!

M 5, 29

K 9, 48

If thy right eye offend thee, pluck it out, and cast it from thee; for it is profitable for thee that one of thy members should perish, and not that thy whole body should be cast into hell, where their worm dieth not, and the

* Ex. xx. 14.

| Jan. 20. Apl. 21. | in one Continuous Narrative. | July 21. Oct. 20. |

fire is not quenched. And if thy right hand offend thee, cut it off, and cast it from thee; for it is profitable for thee that one of thy members should perish, and not that thy whole body should be cast into hell, into the fire that never shall be quenched, where their worm dieth not, and the fire is not quenched. And if thy foot offend thee, cut it off; it is better for thee to enter halt into life, than having two feet to be cast into hell, into the fire that never shall be quenched, where their worm dieth not, and the fire is not quenched.

Again, ye have heard that it hath been said by them of old time,* Thou shalt not forswear thyself, but shalt perform unto the Lord thine oaths; but I say unto you, Swear not at all; neither by heaven, for he that shall swear by heaven, sweareth by the throne of God, and by him that sitteth thereon; nor by the earth, for it is his footstool; neither by Jerusalem, for it is the city of the great King; neither shalt thou swear by thy head, because thou canst not make one hair white or black. But let your communication be, Yea, yea; Nay, nay; for whatsoever is more than these cometh of evil.

* Num. xxx, 2.

Margin references:
M 5, 30
K 9, 43
— 44
— 45
— 46
M 5, 33
— 34
M 23, 22
M 5, 35
— 36
— 37

XXI.

Jan. 21. Apl. 22. July 22. Oct. 21.

Christ's sermon on the mount continued.

M 5, 38 — YE have heard that it hath been said,* An eye for an eye, and a tooth for a tooth;
— 39 — but I, Jesus, say unto you, that ye resist not evil; but whosoever shall smite thee on thy
— 40 — right cheek, turn to him the other also. And if any man will sue thee at the law, and take away thy coat, let him have thy cloak also.
— 41 — And whosoever shall compel thee to go a mile,
L 6, 30 — go with him twain; and of him that taketh
M 5, 42 — away thy goods ask them not again; and from him that would borrow of thee, turn thou not away.
— 43 — Ye have heard that it hath been said,† Thou shalt love thy neighbour, and hate thine enemy;
— 44 — but I say unto you, Love your enemies, bless them that curse you, do good to them that hate you, and pray for them that despitefully
L 6, 32 — use you, and persecute you; for if ye love
M 5, 46 — them that love you, what thank have ye? do
L 6, 32 — not even the publicans the same? for sinners also love those that love them. And if ye
M 5, 47 — salute your brethren only, what do ye more

* Lev. xxiv, 20.   † Lev. xix, 18. Deut, xxiii, 6.

than others? do not even the publicans so? And if ye do good to them that do good to you, what thank have ye? for sinners also do even the same. And if ye lend to them of whom ye hope to receive, what thank have ye? for sinners also lend to sinners, to receive as much again. But love ye your enemies, and do good, and lend, hoping for nothing again ; and your reward shall be great, and ye shall be the children of the Highest : for he is kind unto the unthankful and to the evil : he maketh his sun to rise on the evil and on the good, and sendeth rain on the just and on the unjust. Be ye therefore merciful, as your Father also is merciful. And all things whatsoever ye would that men should do to you, do ye even so to them : for this is the law and the prophets.*

Take heed that ye do not your alms before men, to be seen of them ; otherwise ye have no reward of your Father which is in heaven. Therefore when thou doest thine alms, do not sound a trumpet before thee, as the hypocrites do in the synagogues and in the streets, that they may have glory of men. Verily, I say unto you, they have their reward. But when

* Lev. xix, 18. Isa. i, 17. Jer. vii, 5, 6. Ezek. xviii, 7, 8. Micah vi, 8. Zech. vii, 9, 10 ; viii, 16. Mal. iii, 5.

| Jan. 22. Apl. 23. | The Four Gospels arranged | July 23. Oct. 22. |

M 6, 3	thou doest alms, let not thy left hand know
— 4	what thy right hand doeth; that thine alms may be in secret; and thy Father which seeth in secret himself shall reward thee openly.
— 5	And when thou prayest, thou shalt not be as the hypocrites are; for they love to pray standing in the synagogues and at the corners of the streets, that they may be seen of men. Verily, I say unto you, they have their reward.
— 6	But thou, when thou prayest, enter into thy closet, and when thou hast shut thy door, pray to thy Father which is in secret; and thy Father which seeth in secret shall reward
— 7	thee openly. But when ye pray, use not vain repetitions, as the heathen do; for they think that they shall be heard for their much speak-
— 8	ing. Be not ye therefore like unto them; for your Father knoweth what things ye have need of, before ye ask him.

XXII.

JAN. 22.   APL. 23.   JULY 23.   OCT. 22.

Christ's sermon on the mount continued.

M 6, 16	MOREOVER, said Jesus, when ye fast, be not, as the hypocrites, of a sad countenance; for they disfigure their faces, that they

| Jan. 22. Apl. 23. | in one Continuous Narrative. | July 23. Oct. 22. |

may appear unto men to fast. Verily, I say unto you, they have their reward. But thou, when thou fastest, anoint thy head, and wash thy face; that thou appear not unto men to fast, but unto thy Father which is in secret; and thy Father, which seeth in secret, shall reward thee openly. — M 6, 16 / — 17 / — 18

Judge not, and ye shall not be judged; condemn not, and ye shall not be condemned; forgive, and ye shall be forgiven. Give to every man that asketh of thee; give, and it shall be given unto you; good measure, pressed down, shaken together, and running over, shall men give into your bosom; for with what judgment ye judge, ye shall be judged; and with the same measure that ye mete withal it shall be measured to you again. — L 6, 37 / — 30 / — 38 / M 7, 2 / L 6, 38

And why beholdest thou the mote that is in thy brother's eye, but perceivest not the beam that is in thine own eye? Either how canst thou say to thy brother, Brother, let me pull out the mote that is in thine eye, when thou thyself beholdest not the beam that is in thine own eye? Thou hypocrite, cast out first the beam out of thine own eye, and then shalt thou see clearly to pull out the mote that is in thy brother's eye. — 41 / — 42

Beware of false prophets, which come to you — M 7, 1

| Jan. 22. Apl. 23. | The Four Gospels arranged | July 23. Oct. 22. |

M 7,15	in sheep's clothing, but inwardly are ravening
— 16	wolves. Ye shall know them by their fruits,
L 6,44	as every tree is known by its own fruit. For of thorns men do not gather figs, nor of a
— 43	bramble bush gather they grapes. A good tree bringeth not forth corrupt fruit; neither doth a corrupt tree bring forth good fruit.
— 45	A good man out of the good treasure of his heart bringeth forth that which is good; and an evil man out of the evil treasure of his heart bringeth forth that which is evil; for of the abundance of the heart his mouth speaketh.
— 46	And why call ye me, Lord, Lord, and do not
M 7,21	the things which I say? Not every one that saith unto me, Lord, Lord, shall enter into the kingdom of heaven; but he that doeth the will of my Father which is in heaven.
L 6,47	Whosoever cometh to me, and heareth my sayings, and doeth them, I will show you to
— 48	whom he is like: he is like a man which built a house, and digged deep, and laid the foun-
M 7,25	dation on a rock; and the rain descended, and
L 6,48	the floods came, and the winds blew; and when the flood arose, the stream beat vehemently
— 49	upon that house, and could not shake it; for it was founded upon a rock. But he that heareth, and doeth not, is like a man that without a foundation built a house upon the

| Jan. 23. Apl. 24. | in one Continuous Narrative. | July 24. Oct. 23. |

earth; against which the stream did beat vehemently, and immediately it fell; and the ruin of that house was great.   L 6, 49

XXIII.

Jan. 23. Apl. 24. July 24. Oct. 23.

Christ heals the centurion's servant, and raises the widow's son.

NOW when Jesus had ended all his sayings in the audience of the people, he came down from the mountain, and great multitudes followed him; and he entered into Capernaum. And a certain centurion's servant, who was dear unto him, was sick of the palsy, grievously tormented, and ready to die. And when he heard of Jesus, he sent unto him the elders of the Jews, beseeching him that he would come and heal his servant. And when they came to Jesus, they besought him instantly, saying, that he was worthy for whom he should do this; for he loveth our nation, and he hath built us a synagogue. Then Jesus went with them. And when he was now not far from the house, the centurion sent friends to him, saying unto him, Lord, trouble not thyself; for I am not worthy that thou shouldest enter under my roof; wherefore neither thought I myself worthy to come

L 7, 21
M 8, 1

L 7, 1
— 2
M , 6
L , 2
— 3

— 4

— 5

— 6

— 7

| | Jan. 23.
Apl. 24. | The Four Gospels arranged | July 24.
Oct. 23. |

L 7, 7 — 8	unto thee; but say in a word, and my servant shall be healed. For I also am a man set under authority, having under me soldiers, and I say unto one, Go, and he goeth; and to another, Come, and he cometh; and to my
— 9	servant, Do this, and he doeth it. When Jesus heard these things, he marvelled at him, and turned him about, and said unto the people that followed him, I say unto you, I have not
M 8, 13	found so great faith, no, not in Israel. And Jesus said unto the centurion by his messengers, Go thy way, and as thou hast believed, so be it done unto thee. And his servant was
L 7, 10	healed in the self-same hour. And they that were sent, returning to the house, found the servant whole that had been sick.
— 11	And it came to pass the day after, that he went into a city called Nain; and many of his disciples went with him, and much people.
— 12	Now when he came nigh to the gate of the city, behold, there was a dead man carried out, the only son of his mother, and she was a widow; and much people of the city was
— 13	with her. And when the Lord saw her, he had compassion on her, and said unto her,
— 14	Weep not. And he came and touched the bier; and they that bare him stood still. And he said, Young man, I say unto thee,

| Jan. 24. Apl. 25. | in one Continuous Narrative. | July 25. Oct. 24. |

Arise. And he that was dead sat up, and began to speak. And he delivered him to his mother. And there came a fear on all; and they glorified God, saying, that a great prophet is risen up among us; and, that God hath visited his people. And this rumour of him went forth throughout all Judæa, and throughout all the region round about.

	L 7, 15
	— 16
	— 17

XXIV.
Jan. 24. Apl. 25. July 25. Oct. 24.
Christ's testimony to John the Baptist. John the Baptist beheaded.

A ND the disciples of John showed him in the prison the works of Christ. And John calling unto him two of his disciples sent them to Jesus, saying, Art thou he that should come?* or look we for another? When the men were come unto him, they said, John Baptist hath sent us unto thee, saying, Art thou he that should come? or look we for another? And in that same hour he cured many of their infirmities and plagues, and of evil spirits; and unto many that were blind he gave sight. Then Jesus answering said unto them, Go your way, and tell John what things ye have seen and heard; how that the blind

	L 7, 18
	M 11, 2
	L 7, 19
	— 20
	— 21
	— 22

* Isa. xxxv, 4-6.

| | Jan. 24. | The Four Gospels arranged | July 25. |
| | Apl. 25. | | Oct. 24. |

L 7, 22

— 23

see, the lame walk, the lepers are cleansed, the deaf hear, the dead are raised, to the poor the gospel is preached ; and blessed is he, whosoever shall not be offended in me.

— 24

— 25

— 26

— 27

K 1, 2

M 11, 14

L 7, 28

L 16, 16

M 11, 12

And when the messengers of John were departed, he began to say unto the people concerning John, What went ye out into the wilderness to see? A reed shaken with the wind? But what went ye out to see? A man clothed in soft raiment? Behold, they which are gorgeously apparelled, and live delicately, are in kings' courts. But what went ye out to see? A prophet? Yea, I say unto you, and much more than a prophet. This is he, of whom it is written in the prophets,* Behold, I send my messenger before thy face, which shall prepare thy way before thee. And if ye will receive it, this is Elijah, which was to come.† Verily, I say unto you, among those that are born of women there is not a greater prophet than John the Baptist ; but he that is least in the kingdom of God is greater than he. The law and the prophets were until John ; since that time the kingdom of God is preached, and every man presseth into it ; it suffereth violence, and the violent take it by force. He that hath ears to hear, let him hear.

* Mal. iii, 1. † Mal. iv, 5, 6.

| Jan. 24. Apl. 25. | in one Continuous Narrative. | July 25. Oct. 24. |

And all the people that heard him, and the publicans,* justified God, being baptized with the baptism of John. But the Pharisees and lawyers† rejected the counsel of God against themselves, being not baptized of him.

And the Lord said, Whereunto then shall I liken the men of this generation? and to what are they like? They are like unto children sitting in the market-place, and calling one to another, and saying, We have piped unto you, and ye have not danced; we have mourned to you, and ye have not wept. For John the Baptist came neither eating bread nor drinking wine; and ye say, He hath a devil. The Son of man is come eating and drinking; and ye say, Behold a gluttonous man, and a winebibber, a friend of publicans and sinners! But wisdom is justified of all her children.

And when a convenient day was come, that King Herod on his birthday made a supper to his lords, high captains, and chief estates of Galilee; and when the daughter of the said Herodias came in, and danced, and pleased Herod and them that sat with him, the king said unto the damsel, Ask of me whatsoever thou wilt, and I will give it thee. And he

L 7, 29
— 30
— 31
— 32
— 33
— 34
— 35
K 6, 21
— 14
— 21
— 22
— 23

* Publicans—collectors of the *public* taxes.
† Lawyers—expounders of the *law* of Moses.

| Jan. 24. | The Four Gospels arranged | July 25. |
| ApL 25. | | Oct. 24. |

K 6, 23
— 24
— 25

— 26
— 27

— 28

— 29

M 14, 12
L 9, 7
K 6, 14
L 9, 7
M 14, 2

L 9, 8

sware unto her, Whatsoever thou shalt ask of me, I will give it thee, unto the half of my kingdom. And she went forth, and said unto her mother, What shall I ask? And she said, The head of John the Baptist. And she came in straightway with haste unto the king, and asked, saying, I will that thou give me by and by in a charger the head of John the Baptist. And the king was exceedingly sorry; yet for his oath's sake, and for their sakes which sat with him, he would not reject her. And immediately the king sent an executioner, and commanded his head to be brought; and he went and beheaded him in the prison, and brought his head in a charger, and gave it to the damsel; and the damsel gave it to her mother. And when his disciples heard of it, they came and took up his corpse, and laid it in a tomb, and went and told Jesus.

Now Herod the tetrarch heard of all that was done by Jesus, for his name was spread abroad; and he was perplexed, because that it was said by some, that this is John the Baptist; he is risen from the dead; and therefore mighty works do show forth themselves in him; and by some, that Elijah had appeared;* and by others, that one of the old prophets was

* Mal. iv, 5.

risen again. And Herod said, John have I beheaded; but who is this, of whom I hear such things? And he desired to see him.

L 9, 9

XXV.

Jan. 25. Apl. 26. July 26. Oct. 25.

A woman bathes Christ's feet with her tears.

AND one of the Pharisees desired Jesus that he would eat with him. And he went into the Pharisee's house, and sat down to meat. And, behold, a woman in the city, who was a sinner, when she knew that Jesus sat at meat in the Pharisee's house, brought an alabaster box of ointment, and stood at his feet behind him weeping, and began to wash his feet with tears, and did wipe them with the hairs of her head, and kissed his feet, and anointed them with the ointment. Now when the Pharisee which had bidden him saw it, he spake within himself, saying, This man, if he were a prophet, would have known who and what manner of woman this is that toucheth him; for she is a sinner. And Jesus answering said unto him, Simon, I have somewhat to say unto thee. And he said, Master, say on. There was a certain creditor which had two debtors: the one owed five hundred pence,

L 7, 36

— 37

— 38

— 39

— 40

— 41

| Jan. 25. | The Four Gospels arranged | July 26. |
| ApL 26. | | Oct. 25. |

L 7,42 and the other fifty; and when they had nothing wherewith to pay, he frankly forgave them both. Tell me therefore, which
— 43 of them will love him most? Simon answered and said, I suppose that he to whom he forgave most. And he said unto him,
— 44 Thou hast rightly judged. And he turned to the woman, and said unto Simon, Seest thou this woman? I entered into thy house, thou gavest me no water for my feet; but she hath washed my feet with tears, and wiped
— 45 them with the hairs of her head. Thou gavest me no kiss; but this woman since the time I
— 46 came in hath not ceased to kiss my feet. My head with oil thou didst not anoint; but this woman hath anointed my feet with ointment.
— 47 Wherefore I say unto thee, Her sins, which are many, are forgiven; for she loved much; but to whom little is forgiven, the same loveth
— 48 little. And he said unto her, Thy sins are
— 49 forgiven. And they that sat at meat with him began to say within themselves, Who is this that
— 50 forgiveth sins also? And he said to the woman, Thy faith hath saved thee; go in peace.

M 11, 20 Then began he to upbraid the cities wherein most of his mighty works were done, because
— 21 they repented not: Woe unto thee, Chorazin! woe unto thee, Bethsaida! for if the mighty

| Jan. 26. Apl. 27. | in one Continuous Narrative. | July 27. Oct. 26. |

works, which were done in you, had been done in Tyre and Sidon, they would have repented long ago in sackcloth and ashes. But I say unto you, It shall be more tolerable for Tyre and Sidon at the day of judgment than for you. And thou, Capernaum, which art exalted unto heaven, shalt be thrust down to hell: for if the mighty works, which have been done in thee, had been done in Sodom, it would have remained until this day.* But I say unto you, that it shall be more tolerable for the land of Sodom in the day of judgment, than for thee.

M 11, 21
— 22

L 10, 15
M 11, 23

— 24
•

XXVI.

Jan. 26. Apl. 27. July 27. Oct. 26.

The impotent man at the pool of Bethesda. Christ's oneness with the Father.

AFTER this there was a feast of the Jews; and Jesus went up to Jerusalem.

Now there is at Jerusalem by the sheep market a pool, which is called in the Hebrew tongue Bethesda, having five porches. In these lay a great multitude of impotent folk, of blind, halt, withered, waiting for the moving of the water. For an angel went down at a certain season into the pool, and troubled the water;

J 5, 1
— 2
— 3
— 4

* Gen. xix, 24, 25.

Jan. 26. Apl. 27.	July 27. Oct. 26.

The Four Gospels arranged

J 5, 4	whosoever then first after the troubling of the water stepped in was made whole of whatsoever disease he had.
— 5	And a certain man was there, which had
— 6	had an infirmity thirty and eight years. When Jesus saw him lie, and knew that he had been then a long time in that case, he said unto him,
— 7	Wilt thou be made whole? The impotent man answered him, Sir, I have no man, when the water is troubled, to put me into the pool; but while I am coming, another steppeth down
— 8	before me. Jesus said unto him, Rise, take up
— 9	thy bed, and walk. And immediately the man was made whole, and took up his bed, and walked; and on the same day was the sabbath.
— 10	The Jews therefore said unto him that was cured, It is the sabbath day; it is not lawful
— 11	for thee to carry thy bed.* He answered them, He that made me whole, the same said unto
— 12	me, Take up thy bed, and walk. Then asked they him, What man is that which said unto
— 13	thee, Take up thy bed, and walk? And he that was healed wist not who it was; for Jesus had conveyed himself away, a multitude
— 14	being in that place. Afterward Jesus found him in the temple, and said unto him, Behold, thou art made whole; sin no more, lest a worse

* Ex. xx, 10.

| Jan. 26. Apl. 27. | in one Continuous Narrative. | July 27. Oct. 26. |

thing come unto thee. The man departed, and told the Jews that it was Jesus, which had made him whole. And therefore did the Jews persecute Jesus, and sought to slay him, because he had done these things on the sabbath day. But Jesus answered them, My Father worketh hitherto, and I work. Therefore the Jews sought the more to kill him, because he not only had broken the sabbath, but said also that God was his Father, making himself equal with God.

Then answered Jesus and said unto them, Verily, verily, I say unto you, the Son can do nothing of himself, but what he seeth the Father do: for what things soever he doeth, these also doeth the Son likewise. For the Father loveth the Son, and showeth him all things that himself doeth; and he will show him greater works than these, that ye may marvel. For as the Father raiseth up the dead, and quickeneth them; even so the Son quickeneth whom he will. For the Father judgeth no man, but hath committed all judgment unto the Son; that all men should honour the Son, even as they honour the Father. He that honoureth not the Son, honoureth not the Father which hath sent him.

Verily, verily, I say unto you, he that

J 5, 15
— 16
— 17
— 18
— 19
— 20
— 21
— 22
— 23
— 24

J 5, 24	heareth my word, and believeth on him that sent me, hath everlasting life, and shall not come into condemnation; but is passed from death
— 25	unto life. Verily, verily, I say unto you, the hour is coming, and now is, when the dead shall hear the voice of the Son of God; and they
— 26	that hear shall live. For as the Father hath life in himself, so hath he given to the Son to
— 27	have life in himself; and hath given him authority to execute judgment also, because he
— 28	is the Son of man. Marvel not at this; for the hour is coming, in the which all that are in the
— 29	graves shall hear his voice, and shall come forth; they that have done good, unto the resurrection of life; and they that have done evil, unto the resurrection of damnation.*
— 30	I can of mine own self do nothing: as I hear, I judge; and my judgment is just; because I seek not mine own will, but the will of
— 31	the Father which hath sent me. If I bear witness of myself, my witness is not true.
— 32	There is another that beareth witness of me; and I know that the witness which he wit-
— 33	nesseth of me is true. Ye sent unto John, and
— 34	he bare witness unto the truth. But I receive not testimony from man; but these things I
— 35	say, that ye might be saved. He was a burning

* Dan. xii, 2, 3.

| Jan. 27. Apl. 28. | in one Continuous Narrative. | July 28. Oct. 27. |

and a shining light ; and ye were willing for a season to rejoice in his light. But I have greater witness than that of John ; for the works which the Father hath given me to finish, the same works that I do bear witness of me, that the Father hath sent me. And the Father himself, which hath sent me, hath borne witness of me. Ye have neither heard his voice at any time, nor seen his shape. And ye have not his word abiding in you ; for whom he hath sent, him ye believe not.

J 5, 35
— 36

— 37

— 38

XXVII.
Jan. 27. Apl. 28. July 28. Oct. 27.
Christ's testimony to the Scriptures. On keeping the sabbath day.

SEARCH the scriptures,* said Christ, for in them ye think ye have eternal life ; and they are they which testify of me ; and ye will not come to me, that ye might have life.

I receive not honour from men. But I know you, that ye have not the love of God in you. I am come in my Father's name, and ye receive me not ; if another shall come in his own name, him ye will receive. How can ye believe, which receive honour one of another, and seek not the honour that cometh from God only ?

J 5, 39
— 40

— 41
— 42
— 43

— 44

* *I. e.*, the Old Testament ; the New had not then been written.

Jan. 27.		July 28.
Apl. 28.	The Four Gospels arranged	Oct. 27.

J 5, 45   Do not think that I will accuse you to the Father; there is one that accuseth you, even
— 46   Moses, in whom ye trust. For had ye believed Moses, ye would have believed me; for he
— 47   wrote of me.* But if ye believe not his writings, how shall ye believe my words?

L 6, 1   And it came to pass on the second sabbath after the first, that he went through the corn
M 12, 1   fields; and his disciples were a hungered, and
L 6, 1   plucked the ears of corn, and did eat, rubbing
— 2   them in their hands. And certain of the Pharisees said unto them, Why do ye that which is
— 3   not lawful to do on the sabbath days? And Jesus answering them said, Have ye not read
K 2, 25   so much as this,† what David did, when he
L 6, 3   had need, and himself was a hungered, and
K 2, 26   they which were with him; how he went into the house of God in the days of Abiathar the high priest, and did eat the show-bread, which it is not lawful to eat but for the priests,‡ and
M 12, 5   gave also to them which were with him? Or have ye not read in the law,§ how that on the sabbath days the priests in the temple profane
— 6   the sabbath, and are blameless? But I say unto you, that in this place is one greater than
— 7   the temple. But if ye had known what this

* Gen. iii, 15; xxviii, 14; xlix, 10. Num. xxi, 8; xxiv, 17. Deut. xviii, 15, 18, 19.
† 1 Sam. xxi, 1, 6.   ‡ Lev. xxiv, 9.   § Num. xxviii, 9.

| Jan. 27. Apl. 28. | in one Continuous Narrative. | July 28. Oct. 27. |

meaneth,* I will have mercy, and not sacrifice, ye would not have condemned the guiltless. And he said unto them, The sabbath was made for man,† and not man for the sabbath; therefore the Son of man is Lord also of the sabbath.

And when he was departed thence it came to pass also on another sabbath, that he entered into the synagogue and taught; and there was a man whose right hand was withered. And the scribes and Pharisees watched him, whether he would heal on the sabbath day; that they might find an accusation against him. But he knew their thoughts, and said to the man which had the withered hand, Rise up, and stand forth in the midst. And he arose and stood forth. Then said Jesus unto them, I will ask you one thing; Is it lawful on the sabbath days to do good or to do evil? to save life, or to destroy it? But they held their peace. And he said unto them, What man shall there be among you, that shall have one sheep, and if it fall into a pit on the sabbath day, will not lay hold on it, and lift it out? How much then is a man better than a sheep! Wherefore it is lawful to do well on the sabbath days. And when he had looked round about

M 12, 7

K 2, 27
— 28

M 12, 9
L 6, 6
— 7

— 8

— 9

K 3, 4
M 12, 11

— 12

K 3, 5

* Hosea vi, 6.   † Ex. xxiii, 12.

| Jan. 29. | | July 29. |
| Apl. 29. | The Four Gospels arranged | Oct. 28. |

K 3, 5 — on them with anger, being grieved for the hardness of their hearts, he said unto the man, Stretch forth thy hand. And he stretched it out: and his hand was restored whole as the other.

L 6, 11 — And the Pharisees were filled with madness;
K 3, 6 — and went forth, and straightway took counsel with the Herodians against him, how they might destroy him.

M 12, 15 — But when Jesus knew it he withdrew him-
K 3, 7 — self with his disciples to the sea; and a great
— 8 — multitude from Galilee followed him, and from Judæa, and from Jerusalem, and from Idumæa, and from beyond Jordan.

XXVIII.

JAN. 28. APL. 29. JULY 29. OCT. 28.

Christ followed by multitudes. On blasphemy against the Holy Ghost.

K 3, 8 — AND they about Tyre and Sidon, a great multitude, when they had heard what
— 9 — great things Jesus did, came unto him. And he spake to his disciples, that a small ship should wait on him because of the multitude,
— 10 — lest they should throng him; for he had healed many; insomuch that they pressed upon him
— 11 — to touch him, as many as had plagues; and unclean spirits, when they saw him, fell down

| Jan. 28. Apl. 29. | in one Continuous Narrative. | July 29. Oct. 28. |

before him, and cried, saying, Thou art the Son of God. And he straitly charged them that they should not make him known; that it might be fulfilled which was spoken by Isaiah the prophet,* saying, Behold my servant, whom I have chosen; my beloved, in whom my soul is well pleased; I will put my spirit upon him, and he shall show judgment to the Gentiles. He shall not strive, nor cry; neither shall any man hear his voice in the streets. A bruised reed shall he not break, and smoking flax shall he not·quench, till he send forth judgment unto victory. And in his name shall the Gentiles trust.

K 8, 11
— 12
M 12, 17
— 18
— 19
— 20
— 21

And it came to pass afterward, that he went throughout every city and village, preaching and showing the glad tidings of the kingdom of God; and the twelve were with him, and certain women, which had been healed of evil spirits and infirmities, Mary called Magdalene, out of whom went seven devils, and Joanna the wife of Chuza, Herod's steward, and Susanna, and many others, which ministered unto him of their substance.

L 8, 1
— 2
— 3

And they went into a house, and the multitude came together again, so that they could not so much as eat bread. And when his

K 8, 19
— 20
— 21

* Isa. xlii, 1-3.

Jan. 28. Apl. 29.	July 29. Oct. 28.

The Four Gospels arranged

K 3, 21 — friends heard of it, they went out to lay hold on him; for they said, He is beside himself.

M 12, 22 — Then was brought unto him one possessed with a devil, blind, and dumb; and he healed him, insomuch that the blind and dumb both saw

— 23 and spake. And all the people were amazed, and said, Is not this the son of David?

— 24
K 3, 22 — But when the Pharisees and the scribes which came down from Jerusalem heard it,

M 12, 24
K 3, 22 — they said, This fellow hath Beelzebub, and by the prince of the devils casteth he out devils.

M 12, 25
K 3, 23 — And Jesus knew their thoughts, and called them unto him, and said unto them, in para-

M 12, 25 — bles, How can Satan cast out Satan? Every kingdom divided against itself is brought to desolation; and every city or house divided

— 26 against itself shall not stand: and if Satan cast out Satan, he is divided against himself;

— 27 how shall then his kingdom stand? And if I by Beelzebub cast out devils, by whom do your children cast them out? therefore they shall be

— 28 your judges. But if I cast out devils by the Spirit of God, then the kingdom of God is come

K 3, 27 — unto you. No man can enter into a strong man's house, and spoil his goods, except he first bind the strong man, and then he will spoil his

L 11, 21 — house. When a strong man armed keepeth his

— 22 palace, his goods are in peace; but when a

| Jan. 29. Apl. 30. | in one Continuous Narrative. | July 30. Oct. 29. |

stronger than he cometh upon him, and overcometh him, he taketh from him all his armour wherein he trusted, and divideth his spoils. — L 11, 22

Wherefore I say unto you, All manner of sins and blasphemies wherewith soever they shall blaspheme shall be forgiven unto men; but the blasphemy against the Holy Ghost shall not be forgiven unto men. And whosoever speaketh a word against the Son of man, it shall be forgiven him; but whosoever speaketh against the Holy Ghost, it shall not be forgiven him, neither in this world, neither in the world to come; but he is in danger of eternal damnation; because they said, He hath an unclean spirit. — M 12, 31; K 3, 28; M 12, 32; K 3, 29; — 30

O generation of vipers, how can ye, being evil, speak good things? But I say unto you, that every idle word that men shall speak, they shall give account thereof in the day of judgment; for by thy words thou shalt be justified, and by thy words thou shalt be condemned. — M 12, 34; — 36; — 37

XXIX.

Jan. 29. Apl. 30. July 30. Oct. 29.

The scribes and Pharisees seek a sign from heaven. Christ shows wherein true blessedness consists.

WHEN the people were gathered thick together, then certain of the scribes — L 11, 29; M 12, 38; L 11, 16

Jan. 29. Apl. 30.	July 30. Oct. 29.

The Four Gospels arranged

M 12, 38
L 11, 16
M 12, 39
L 11, 29

— 30

M 12, 40

L 11, 32

— 31

— 24

— 25
M 12, 45

and of the Pharisees, tempting Jesus, answered, saying, Master, we would see a sign from heaven from thee. But he answered and said unto them, This is an evil generation; they seek a sign; and there shall no sign be given it, but the sign of Jonah the prophet:* for as Jonah was a sign unto the Ninevites, so shall also the Son of man be to this generation. For as Jonah was three days and three nights in the whale's belly, so shall the Son of man be three days and three nights in the heart of the earth. The men of Nineveh shall rise up in the judgment with this generation, and shall condemn it; for they repented at the preaching of Jonah;† and, behold, a greater than Jonah is here. The queen of the south shall rise up in the judgment with the men of this generation, and condemn them; for she came from the utmost parts of the earth to hear the wisdom of Solomon;‡ and, behold, a greater than Solomon is here. When the unclean spirit is gone out of a man, he walketh through dry places, seeking rest, and finding none, he saith, I will return into my house whence I came out; and when he is come, he findeth it empty, swept, and garnished. Then goeth he, and taketh with himself seven other

* Jonah i, 17.   † Jonah iii, 5-10.   ‡ 1 Kings x, 1-13.

| Jan. 29. Apl. 30. | in one Continuous Narrative. | July 30. Oct. 29. |

spirits more wicked than himself, and they enter in and dwell there; and the last state of that man is worse than the first. Even so shall it be also unto this wicked generation. — M 12, 45

And it came to pass, as he spake these things, that a certain woman of the company lifted up her voice, and said unto him, Blessed is the womb that bare thee, and the paps which thou hast sucked. But he said, Yea rather, blessed are they that hear the word of God, and keep it. — L 11, 27 / — 28

While he yet talked to the people, behold, his mother and his brethren stood without, desiring to speak with him, and could not come at him for the press, and sent unto him calling him. — M 12, 46 / L 8, 19 / K 3, 31

Then one said unto him, Behold, thy mother and thy brethren stand without, desiring to speak with thee. But he answered and said unto him that told him, Who is my mother? and who are my brethren? My mother and my brethren are these which hear the word of God, and do it. And he stretched forth his hand toward his disciples, and said, Behold my mother and my brethren! For whosoever shall do the will of my Father which is in heaven, the same is my brother, and sister, and mother. — M 12, 47 / — 48 / L 8, 21 / M 12, 49 / — 50

Jan. 30. May 1.	The Four Gospels arranged	July 31. Oct. 30.

XXX.

Jan. 30.   May 1.   July 31.   Oct. 30.

Christ's condemnation of hypocrisy and covetousness.

L 11, 37 — AND as Jesus spake, a certain Pharisee besought him to dine with him; and he
— 38 — went in, and sat down to meat. And when the Pharisee saw it, he marvelled that he had
— 39 — not first washed before dinner. And the Lord said unto him, Now do ye Pharisees make clean the outside of the cup and the platter; but your inward part is full of ravening and
— 40 — wickedness. Ye fools, did not he that made that which is without make that which is
— 41 — within also? But rather give alms of such
M 23, 26 — things as ye have within the cup and platter;
L 11, 41 — and, behold, all things are clean unto you.

M 23, 23
L 11, 42
M 23, 23
L 11, 42
M 23, 23 — Woe unto you, scribes and Pharisees, hypocrites! for ye tithe mint, and rue, and anise, and cummin, and all manner of herbs, and pass over the weightier matters of the law,
L 11, 42 — judgment, mercy, and faith, and the love of God: these ought ye to have done,* and not
M 23, 24 — to leave the other undone.† Ye blind guides, which strain at a gnat and swallow a camel.
L 11, 44 — Woe unto you, scribes and Pharisees, hypo-

* Micah vi, 8.   † Deut. xiv, 22.   Mal. iii, 10.

| Jan. 30. May 1. | in one Continuous Narrative. | July 31. Oct. 30. |

crites! for ye are as graves which appear not, and the men that walk over them are not aware of them. Ye are like unto whited sepulchres, which indeed appear beautiful outward, but within are full of dead men's bones, and of all uncleanness. Even so ye also outwardly appear righteous unto men, but within ye are full of hypocrisy and iniquity.

Then answered one of the lawyers, and said unto him, Master, thus saying, thou reproachest us also. And he said, Woe unto you also, ye lawyers! for ye lade men with burdens grievous to be borne, and ye yourselves touch not the burdens with one of your fingers. Woe unto you, lawyers! for ye have taken away the key of knowledge, and shut up the kingdom of heaven against men: ye entered not in yourselves, and them that were entering in ye hindered.

And as he said these things unto them, the scribes and the Pharisees began to urge him vehemently, and to provoke him to speak of many things; laying wait for him, and seeking to catch something out of his mouth, that they might accuse him.

In the mean time, when there was gathered together an innumerable multitude of people, insomuch that they trode one upon another, he

L 11, 44
M 23, 27
— 28
L 11, 45
— 46
— 52
M 23, 13
L 11, 52
— 53
— 54
L 12, 1

| Jan. 31. | | Aug. 1. |
| May 2. | The Four Gospels arranged | Oct. 31. |

L 12, 1 began to say unto his disciples first of all, Beware ye of the leaven of the Pharisees, which is
— 2 hypocrisy; for there is nothing covered, that shall not be revealed; neither hid, that shall
L 8, 17
L 12, 3 not be known and come abroad. Therefore whatsoever ye have spoken in darkness shall be heard in the light; and that which ye have spoken in the ear in closets shall be proclaimed upon the housetops.

XXXI.

JAN. 31.   MAY 2.   AUG. 1.   OCT. 31.

Undue anxiety condemned.

L 12, 13 AND one of the company said unto Jesus, Master, speak to my brother, that he
— 14 divide the inheritance with me. And he said unto him, Man, who made me a judge or a
— 15 divider over you? And he said unto them, Take heed, and beware of covetousness; for a man's life consisteth not in the abundance of the things which he possesseth.
— 16 And he spake a parable unto them, saying, The ground of a certain rich man brought forth
— 17 plentifully; and he thought within himself, saying, What shall I do, because I have no
— 18 room where to bestow my fruits? And he said, This will I do; I will pull down my barns, and

| Jan. 31. May 2. | in one Continuous Narrative. | Aug. 1. Oct. 31. |

build greater ; and there will I bestow all my fruits and my goods. And I will say to my soul, Soul, thou hast much goods laid up for many years ; take thine ease, eat, drink, and be merry. But God said unto him, Thou fool, this night thy soul shall be required of thee ; then whose shall those things be, which thou hast provided? So is he that layeth up treasure for himself, and is not rich toward God.

    Sell that ye have, and give alms ; lay not up for yourselves treasures upon earth, where moth and rust corrupt, and where thieves break through and steal; provide yourselves with bags which wax not old, a treasure in the heavens that faileth not, where no thief approacheth, neither moth nor rust doth corrupt, and where thieves do not break through nor steal ; for where your treasure is, there will your heart be also.

    Therefore I say unto you, Take no thought for your life, what ye shall eat, or what ye shall drink ; nor yet for your body, what ye shall put on. Is not the life more than meat, and the body than raiment? Behold the fowls of the air; for they sow not, neither do they reap, nor gather into barns; yet your heavenly Father feedeth them. Are ye not much better than they? Are not five sparrows sold for two farthings, and not one of them is forgotten before

Side references: L 12, 18 — 19 — 20 — 21 — 33 M 6, 19 L 12, 33 M 6, 20 — 21 — 25 — 26 L 12, 6

| | Jan. 31.
May 2. | The Four Gospels arranged | Aug. 1.
Oct. 31. |

M 10, 29	God? One of them shall not fall on the ground
L 12, 7	without your Father. Fear not, therefore; ye are of more value than many sparrows; even the very hairs of your head are all numbered;
L 21, 18 L 12, 25	there shall not a hair of your head perish. And which of you with taking thought can add to
— 26	his stature one cubit? If ye then are not able to do that thing which is least, why take ye
M 6, 28	thought for the rest? And why take ye thought for raiment? Consider the lilies of the field, how they grow; they toil not, neither do they
— 29	spin; and yet I say unto you, that even Solomon in all his glory was not arrayed like one
— 30	of these. Wherefore, if God so clothe the grass,
L 12, 28	which is to-day in the field, and to-morrow is
M 6, 30	cast into the oven, shall he not much more
— 31	clothe you, O ye of little faith? Therefore take no thought, saying, What shall we eat? or, What shall we drink? or, Wherewithal
— 32	shall we be clothed? (for after all these things do these Gentiles seek:) for your heavenly Father knoweth that ye have need of all these
— 33	things. But seek ye first the kingdom of God, and his righteousness; and all these things
— 34	shall be added unto you. Take therefore no thought for the morrow; for the morrow shall take thought for the things of itself. Sufficient unto the day is the evil thereof.

XXXII.

Feb. 1. May 3. Aug. 2. Nov. 1.

Repentance urged. The parable of the fig tree, of the sower, and of the tares and the wheat.

THERE were present at that season some that told Jesus of the Galilæans, whose blood Pilate had mingled with their sacrifices. And Jesus answering said unto them, Suppose ye that these Galilæans were sinners above all the Galilæans, because they suffered such things? I tell you, Nay; but, except ye repent, ye shall all likewise perish. Or those eighteen, upon whom the tower in Siloam fell, and slew them, think ye that they were sinners above all men that dwelt in Jerusalem? I tell you, Nay; but, except ye repent, ye shall all likewise perish.

He spake also this parable; A certain man had a fig tree planted in his vineyard; and he came and sought fruit thereon, and found none. Then said he unto the dresser of his vineyard, Behold, these three years I come seeking fruit on this fig tree, and find none; cut it down; why cumbereth it the ground? And he answering said unto him, Lord, let it alone this year also, till I shall dig about it, and dung it;

L 13, 1
— 2
— 3
— 4
— 5
— 6
— 7
—

| Feb. 1. | | Aug. 2. |
| May 8. | **The Four Gospels arranged** | Nov. 1. |

L 13, 9 — and if it bear fruit, well; and if not, then after that thou shalt cut it down.

M 13, 1
K 4, 1 — The same day went Jesus out of the house, and began again to teach by the sea side; and there was gathered unto him a great multitude

L 8, 4
K 4, 1 — out of every city, so that he entered into a ship, and sat in the sea; and the whole multi-

— 2 — tude was by the sea on the land. And he taught them many things by parables, and said

— 3 — unto them in his doctrine, Hearken; behold,

L 8, 5 — there went out a sower to sow his seed; and it

K 4, 4
M 13, 4 — came to pass, as he sowed, that some seeds fell

L 8, 5 — by the way side, and were trodden down, and

M 13, 4 — the fowls came and devoured them up; some

— 5 — fell upon stony places, where they had not much earth; and forthwith they sprang up

K 4, 5 — because they had no depth of earth; but when

M 13, 6 — the sun was up, they were scorched; and be-

L 8, 6 — cause they had no root, and lacked moisture,

M 13, 6 — they withered away. And some fell among thorns; and the thorns sprang up, and choked

— 7
K 4, 7
M 13, 8
K 4, 8
M 13, 8 — them, and they yielded no fruit. But other fell into good ground, and sprang up and increased, and brought forth fruit, some a hundredfold, some sixtyfold, and some thirty-

L 8, 8 — fold. And when he had said these things, he cried, He that hath ears to hear, let him hear.

M 13, 24 — Another parable put he forth unto them,

| Feb. 1. May 3. | in one Continuous Narrative. | Aug. 2. Nov. 1. |

saying, The kingdom of heaven is likened unto a man which sowed good seed in his field; but while men slept, his enemy came and sowed tares among the wheat, and went his way. But when the blade was sprung up, and brought forth fruit, then appeared the tares also. So the servants of the householder came and said unto him, Sir, didst not thou sow good seed in thy field? whence then hath it tares? He said unto them, An enemy hath done this. The servants said unto him, Wilt thou then that we go and gather them up? But he said, Nay; lest while ye gather up the tares, ye root up also the wheat with them. Let both grow together until the harvest; and in the time of harvest I will say to the reapers, Gather ye together first the tares, and bind them in bundles to burn them; but gather the wheat into my barn.

And he said, So is the kingdom of God, as if a man should cast seed into the ground; and should sleep, and rise night and day, and the seed should spring and grow up, he knoweth not how. For the earth bringeth forth fruit of itself; first the blade, then the ear, after that the full corn in the ear. But when the fruit is brought forth, immediately he putteth in the sickle, because the harvest is come.

M 13, 24
— 25
— 26
— 27
— 28
— 29
— 30

K 4, 26
— 27
— 28
— 29

XXXIII.

Feb. 2. May 4. Aug. 3. Nov. 2.

The parables of the grain of mustard seed, and of leaven; also the parable of the sower.

M 13, 31 L 13, 18	ANOTHER parable put Jesus forth unto them, saying, Unto what is the kingdom of God like? and whereunto shall I resemble it? It is like the least of all seeds, a grain of mustard seed, which a man took, and cast into his garden; and it grew, and became the greatest among herbs, and waxed a great tree; and the fowls of the air lodged in the branches of it, and under the shadow of it.
— 19 M 13, 32 L 13, 19	
M 13, 32	
K 4, 32	
L 13, 20 — 21	And again he said, Whereunto shall I liken the kingdom of God? It is like leaven, which a woman took and hid in three measures of meal, till the whole was leavened.
M 13, 34 K 4, 33 M 13, 34 K 4, 33 M 13, 34 — 35	All these and many such things spake Jesus unto the multitude in parables, as they were able to hear it; and without a parable spake he not unto them; that it might be fulfilled which was spoken by the prophet,* saying, I will open my mouth in parables; I will utter things which have been kept secret from the foundation of the world.

* Psa. lxxviii, 2.

| Feb. 2. | in one Continuous Narrative. | Aug. 8. |
| May 4. | | Nov. 2. |

Then Jesus sent the multitude away, and went into the house; and when they were alone, he expounded all things to his disciples. M 13, 36 / K 4, 34

And they that were about him with the twelve came, and said unto him, Why speakest thou unto them in parables? He answered and said unto them, Because it is given unto you to know the mysteries of the kingdom of heaven; but to them that are without, it is not given. Therefore speak I to them in parables; because they seeing see not, and hearing they hear not, neither do they understand. And in them is fulfilled the prophecy of Isaiah,* which saith, By hearing ye shall hear, and shall not understand; and seeing ye shall see, and shall not perceive; for this people's heart is waxed gross, and their ears are dull of hearing, and their eyes they have closed; lest at any time they should see with their eyes, and hear with their ears, and should understand with their heart, and should be converted, and I should heal them, and their sins should be forgiven them. — 10 / M 13, 10 / — 11 / K 4, 11 / M 13, 11 / — 13 / — 14 / — 15 / K 4, 12

And he turned him unto his disciples, and said privately, Blessed are the eyes which see the things that ye see; and blessed are your ears, for they hear; for I tell you, that many L 10, 23 / M 13, 16 / L 10, 24

* Isa. vi. 9, 10.

| Feb. 2. | The Four Gospels arranged | Aug. 3. |
| May 4. | | Nov. 2. |

M 13, 17
L 10, 24

prophets and righteous men and kings have desired to see those things which ye see, and have not seen them ; and to hear those things which ye hear, and have not heard them.

K 4, 13

And he said unto them, Know ye not this parable? and how then will ye know all par-

M 13, 18
L 8, 11
K 4, 14
L 8, 12
M 13, 19

ables? Hear ye therefore the parable of the sower. The seed is the word of God ; the sower soweth the word ; those by the way side are they that hear ; when any one heareth the word of the kingdom, and understandeth it not, then cometh the wicked one, and catcheth

L 8, 12
M 13, 20

away that which was sown in his heart, lest he should believe and be saved. But he that received the seed into stony places, the same is he that heareth the word, and anon with joy

— 21

receiveth it ; yet hath he not root in himself, but dureth for a while ; for when tribulation or persecution ariseth because of the word, by and

L 8, 13
M 13, 22

by he is offended, and in time of temptation falleth away. He also that received seed among the thorns is he that heareth the word

L 8, 14
K 4, 19
L 8, 14
M 13, 23

and goeth forth, and the cares and riches and pleasures of this life, and the lusts of other things entering in, choke the word, and he bringeth no fruit to perfection. But he that received seed into the good ground is he that

K 4, 20

heareth the word, and receiveth it in an honest

| Feb. 3. May 5. | in one Continuous Narrative. | Aug. 4. Nov. 3. |

and good heart, and understandeth it; which also beareth fruit with patience, and bringeth forth, some a hundredfold, some sixty, and some thirty. Take heed therefore how ye hear.

L 8, 15
M 13, 23
L 8, 15
M 13, 23
L 8, 18

XXXIV.

Feb. 3. May 5. Aug. 4. Nov. 3.

Explanation of the parable of the tares and the wheat; the kingdom of heaven likened unto a net, a treasure, and a pearl of great price. All must be forsaken for Christ.

AND Jesus' disciples came unto him, saying, Declare unto us the parable of the tares of the field. He answered and said unto them, He that soweth the good seed is the Son of man; the field is the world; the good seeds are the children of the kingdom; but the tares are the children of the wicked one; the enemy that sowed them is the devil; the harvest is the end of the world; and the reapers are the angels. As therefore the tares are gathered and burned in the fire; so shall it be in the end of this world. The Son of man shall send forth his angels, and they shall gather out of his kingdom all things that offend, and them which do iniquity; and shall cast them into a furnace of fire; there shall be wailing and gnashing of teeth. Then shall the righteous shine forth

M 13, 36
— 37
— 38
— 39
— 40
— 41
— 42
— 43

Feb. 3. May 5.	𝕮𝖍𝖊 𝖋𝖔𝖚𝖗 𝕲𝖔𝖘𝖕𝖊𝖑𝖘 𝖆𝖗𝖗𝖆𝖓𝖌𝖊𝖉 Aug. 4. Nov. 3.

M 13, 43   as the sun in the kingdom of their Father. Who hath ears to hear, let him hear.

— 47   Again, the kingdom of heaven is like unto a net, that was cast into the sea, and gathered of
— 48   every kind; which, when it was full, they drew to shore, and sat down, and gathered the good
— 49   into vessels, but cast the bad away. So shall it be at the end of the world; the angels shall come forth, and sever the wicked from among
— 50   the just, and shall cast them into the furnace of fire; there shall be wailing and gnashing of teeth.

— 44   Again, the kingdom of heaven is like unto treasure hid in a field; the which, when a man hath found, he hideth, and for joy thereof goeth and selleth all that he hath, and buyeth that field.

— 45   Again, the kingdom of heaven is like unto
— 46   a merchant-man, seeking goodly pearls; who, when he had found one pearl of great price, went and sold all that he had, and bought it.

— 51   Jesus said unto them, Have ye understood all these things? They said unto him, Yea, Lord.
— 52   Then said he unto them, Therefore every scribe which is instructed unto the kingdom of heaven is like unto a man that is a householder, which bringeth forth out of his treasure things new and old.

— 53   And it came to pass that when Jesus had finished these parables he departed thence.

| Feb. 3. | | Aug. 4. |
| May 5. | in one Continuous Narrative. | Nov. 3. |

And the same day, when the even was come, when Jesus saw great multitudes about him, he went into a ship with his disciples; and he said unto them, Let us go over unto the other side of the lake. And a certain scribe came, and said unto him, Master, I will follow thee whithersoever thou goest. And Jesus said unto him, The foxes have holes, and the birds of the air have nests; but the Son of man hath not where to lay his head.	K 4, 35 M 8, 18 L 8, 22 M 8, 19 — 20
And he said unto another, Follow me. But he said, Lord, suffer me first to go and bury my father. But Jesus said unto him, Follow me; and let the dead bury their dead; but go thou and preach the kingdom of God.	L 9, 59 M 8, 22 L 9, 60
And another also said, Lord, I will follow thee; but let me first go bid them farewell which are at home at my house. And Jesus said unto him, No man, having put his hand to the plough, and looking back, is fit for the kingdom of God. Which of you, intending to build a tower, sitteth not down first, and counteth the cost, whether he has sufficient to finish it? Lest haply, after he hath laid the foundation, and is not able to finish it, all that behold it begin to mock him, saying, This man began to build, and was not able to finish. Or what king, going to make war against another	— 61 — 62 L 14, 28 — 29 — 30 — 31

| Feb. 4. | **The Four Gospels arranged** | Aug. 5. |
| May 6. | | Nov. 4. |

L 14, 31	king, sitteth not down first, and consulteth whether he is able with ten thousand to meet him that cometh against him with twenty thousand?
— 32	Or else, while the other is yet a great way off, he sendeth an ambassage, and desireth conditions
— 33	of peace. So likewise, whosoever he is of you that forsaketh not all that he hath, he cannot
— 35	be my disciple. He that hath ears to hear, let him hear.

XXXV.

Feb. 4. May 6. Aug. 5. Nov. 4.

The storm on the lake: Christ stills the wind and the waves. The devils sent into a herd of swine.

K 4, 36 L 8, 22 K 4, 36 L 8, 23	AND when they had sent away the multitude, they launched forth. And there were also with Jesus other little ships. But as they sailed he fell asleep; and there came
K 4, 37	down a great storm of wind on the lake; and the waves beat into the ship, so that it was
L 8, 23 K 4, 38	now full, and they were in jeopardy. And he was in the hinder part of the ship, asleep on
L 8, 24	a pillow: and they came to him, and awoke
M 8, 25	him, saying, Master, master, save us; we
K 4, 39	perish. Then he arose, and rebuked the wind, and said unto the sea, Peace, be still! And the wind ceased, and there was a great

| Feb. 4. | | Aug. 5. |
| May 6. | in one Continuous Narrative. | Nov. 4. |

calm. And he said unto them, Why are ye so fearful? Where is your faith? And they feared exceedingly, and said one to another, What manner of man is this, that even the wind and the sea obey him?

And they came over unto the other side of the sea, into the country of the Gadarenes, which is over against Galilee. And when he went forth to land, there met him two possessed with devils, coming out of the tombs, exceedingly fierce, so that no man might pass by that way. One with an unclean spirit ware no clothes, neither abode in any house, but had his dwelling among the tombs; and no man could bind him, no, not with chains; because that he had been often bound with fetters and chains, and the chains had been plucked asunder by him, and the fetters broken in pieces; neither could any man tame him: he brake the bands, and was driven by the devil into the wilderness. And always, night and day, he was in the mountains, and in the tombs, crying, and cutting himself with stones. But when he saw Jesus afar off, he ran and fell down before him, and worshipped him, and cried with a loud voice, and said, What have I to do with thee, Jesus, thou Son of the most high God? I adjure thee

K 4, 4)
L 8, 25
K 4, 41

K 5, 1
L 8, 26
— 27
M 8, 28

K 5, 2
L 8, 27
K 5, 3
— 4

L 8, 22
K 5, 5

— 6
L 8, 28
K 5, 7

| Feb. 4. | | Aug. 5. |
| May 6. | The Four Gospels arranged | Nov. 4. |

M 8, 29
K 5, 8

L 8, 30

M 8, 30
K 5, 11
— 18
— 12
— 10
L 8, 31

M 8, 31
— 32

K 5, 13

L 8, 34

M 8, 34

L 8, 35

K 5, 15

L 8, 36
K 5, 16

by God, that thou torment me not, before the time. For he had said unto him, Come out of the man, thou unclean spirit. And Jesus asked him, saying, What is thy name? And he said, Legion; because many devils were entered into him.

And there was a good way off from them, nigh unto the mountains, a great herd of swine feeding, about two thousand. And all the devils besought him much that he would not send them away out of the country, into the deep, saying, If thou cast us out, suffer us to go away into the herd of swine. And he said unto them, Go. And the unclean spirits went out, and entered into the swine; and the whole herd ran violently down a steep place into the sea, and were choked.

When they that fed them saw what was done, they fled, and went and told everything in the city and in the country. And, behold, the whole city came out to meet Jesus; and to see what it was that was done. And when they came to Jesus, and found the man, out of whom the devils were departed, sitting at the feet of Jesus, clothed, and in his right mind, they were afraid. And they that saw it told them how it befell to him that was possessed with the devils, and was healed, and

104

	in one Continuous Narrative.	
Feb. 5. May 7.		Aug. 6. Nov. 5.

also concerning the swine. Then the whole multitude of the country of the Gadarenes round about besought him to depart from them out of their coasts; for they were taken with great fear: and he went up into the ship, and returned back again.

And when he was come into the ship, he that had been possessed with the devils prayed him that he might be with him. Howbeit Jesus suffered him not, but said unto him, Go home to thy friends, and tell them how great things the Lord hath done for thee, and hath had compassion on thee. And he departed, and began to publish in Decapolis how great things Jesus had done for him; and all men did marvel. And it came to pass, that, when Jesus was returned by ship unto the other side, the people gladly received him, for they were all waiting for him; and he came into his own city.

L 8, 37

K 5, 17
L 8, 37

K 5, 18

— 19

— 20

L 8, 40
K 5, 21
L 8, 40
M 9, 1

XXXVI.

Feb. 5. May 7. Aug. 6. Nov. 5.

*Christ sends forth his twelve apostles to preach,
and to heal the sick.*

AND when Jesus had called unto him his twelve disciples, he began to send them forth by two and two; and gave them power

M 10, 1
K 6, 7
M 10, 1

| | Feb. 5. May 7. | The Four Gospels arranged | Aug. 6. Nov. 5 |

M 10, 1	against unclean spirits, to cast them out, and to heal all manner of sickness and all manner of disease.
— 5	These twelve Jesus sent forth, to preach the
L 9, 2	kingdom of God, and to heal the sick, and
M 10, 5	commanded them, saying, Go not into the way of the Gentiles, and into any city of
— 6	the Samaritans enter ye not; but go rather to the lost sheep of the house of Israel.
— 7	And as ye go, preach, saying, The kingdom
— 8	of heaven is at hand. Heal the sick, cleanse the lepers, raise the dead, cast out devils;
K 6, 8	freely ye have received, freely give. Take nothing for your journey, save a staff only; no scrip, no bread, no money in your purse,
M 10, 9 L 9, 3 K 6, 9	neither gold, nor silver, nor brass; neither two coats apiece; neither shoes, but be shod with
L 10, 4	sandals; and salute no man by the way. And
M 10, 11	into whatsoever house or city or town ye shall
L 9, 4	enter, inquire who in it is worthy; and there
L 10, 7	abide till ye go thence. Go not from house
— 8 M 10, 10	to house; and eat such things as are set before you, for the workman is worthy of his meat.
L 10, 5	And into whatsoever house ye enter, first say,
— 6	Peace be to this house. And if the son of peace be there, your peace shall rest upon it; if not, it shall turn to you again.
L 10, 10	But into whatsoever city or house ye enter,

| Feb. 5. May 7. | in one Continuous Narrative. | Aug. 6. Nov. 5. |

and they receive you not, nor hear your words, when ye depart out of that house or city, shake off the very dust from your feet for a testimony against them, and say, Even the very dust of your city which cleaveth on us we do wipe off against you: notwithstanding, be ye sure of this, that the kingdom of God is come nigh unto you. Verily, I say unto you, it shall be more tolerable for the land of Sodom and Gomorrha in the day of judgment, than for that city. He that receiveth you receiveth me; and he that receiveth me receiveth him that sent me; he that heareth you heareth me; and he that despiseth you despiseth me; and he that despiseth me despiseth him that sent me. He that receiveth a prophet in the name of a prophet shall receive a prophet's reward; and he that receiveth a righteous man in the name of a righteous man shall receive a righteous man's reward. And whosoever shall give you a cup of water to drink in my name, because ye belong to Christ, verily, I say unto you, he shall not lose his reward.

And it came to pass, when Jesus had made an end of commanding his twelve disciples, that he departed thence to teach and to preach in their cities. And they went out, through the towns, preaching that men should repent.

M 10, 14
L 9, 5
L 10, 11

M 10, 15

— 40

L 9, 16

M 10, 41

K 9, 41

M 11, 1

K 6, 12
L 9, 6
K 6, 12

K 6, 13	And they cast out many devils, and anointed with oil many that were sick, and healed them.

XXXVII.

Feb. 6. May 8. Aug. 7. Nov. 6.

Christ miraculously feeds the multitude with five barley loaves and two fishes.

J 6, 4 K 6, 30	AND the passover, a feast of the Jews, was nigh; and the apostles gathered themselves together unto Jesus, and told him all things, both what they had done, and what
— 31	they had taught. And he said unto them, Come ye yourselves apart into a desert place, and rest awhile; for there were many coming and going, and they had no leisure so much
— 32 J 6, 1 M 14, 13	as to eat. And they departed over the sea of Galilee, which is the sea of Tiberias, by ship
L 9, 10	privately into a desert place belonging to the
K 6, 33	city called Bethsaida. And the people saw them departing, and many knew him, and ran afoot thither out of all cities, and outwent them,
J 6, 2	and came together unto him, because they saw his miracles which he did on them that were
K 6, 34	diseased. And Jesus, when he came out, saw much people, and was moved with compassion toward them, because they were as sheep not
J 6, 3	having a shepherd. And he went up into a mountain, and there he sat with his disciples;

| Feb. 6. / May 8. | in one Continuous Narrative. | Aug. 7. / Nov. 6. |

and he began to teach them many things of the kingdom of God, and healed them that had need of healing.

And when the day was then far spent, his disciples came unto him, and said, This is a desert place, and now the time is far passed; send them away, that they may go into the towns and country round about, and lodge, and get victuals; for we are here in a desert place, and they have nothing to eat. But Jesus said unto them, They need not depart; give ye them to eat. And they said unto him, Shall we go and buy two hundred pennyworth of bread, and give them to eat? He said unto Philip, Whence shall we buy bread, that these may eat? And this he said to prove him: for he himself knew what he would do. Philip answered him, Two hundred pennyworth of bread is not sufficient for them, that every one of them may take a little. He said unto them, How many loaves have ye? go and see. One of his disciples, Andrew, Simon Peter's brother, said unto him, There is a lad here, which hath five barley loaves and two small fishes; but what are they among so many? We have no more; except we should go and buy meat for all this people.

He said, Bring them hither to me. And he commanded the multitude to sit down by com-

K 6, 34
L 9, 11

K 6, 35

— 36
L 9, 12

K 6, 36
M 14, 16
K 6, 37

J 6, 5

— 6
— 7

K 6, 38
J 6, 8

— 9

L 9, 13
M 14, 18
— 19
K 6, 39

| | Feb. 7.
May 9. | The Four Gospels arranged | Aug. 8.
Nov. 7. |

K 6, 40	panies upon the green grass. And they sat down in ranks, by hundreds, and by fifties.
— 41	And when he had taken the five loaves and the two fishes, he looked up to heaven, and blessed, and brake the loaves, and gave them to his dis-
L 9, 16	ciples to set before the multitude; and the two
K 6, 41 J 6, 11	fishes divided he among them all, as much as
K 6, 42	they would. And they did all eat, and when
J 6, 12	they were filled, he said unto his disciples, Gather up the fragments that remain, that
— 13	nothing be lost. Therefore they gathered them together, and filled twelve baskets with the frag-
K 6, 43	ments of the five barley loaves, and of the fishes,
J 6, 13	which remained over and above unto them that
M 14, 21	had eaten. And they that had eaten were about five thousand men, beside women and children.
J 6, 14	Then those men, when they had seen the miracle that Jesus did, said, This is of a truth that prophet that should come into the world.*

XXXVIII.

Feb. 7. May 9. Aug. 8. Nov. 7.

Christ walks on the sea.

J 6, 15	WHEN Jesus therefore perceived that they would come and take him by force, to
M 14, 22	make him a king, he straightway constrained

* Deut. xviii. 15, 18.

| Feb. 7. May 9. | in one Continuous Narrative. | Aug. 8. Nov. 7. |

his disciples to get into a ship, and to go before him unto the other side, to Bethsaida, while he sent the multitudes away. And when the evening was come, his disciples went down unto the sea, and entered into a ship, and went over the sea toward Capernaum. And when he had sent the multitudes away, he went up into a mountain apart to pray. And it was now dark, and he was there alone on the land. But the ship was in the midst of the sea, tossed with waves; for the wind was contrary. And he saw them toiling in rowing; and in the fourth watch of the night, when they had rowed about five and twenty or thirty furlongs, Jesus went unto them, walking on the sea, and would have passed by them. But when they saw him walking upon the sea, they supposed it to be a spirit, and cried out; for they all saw him, and were afraid. But straightway Jesus spake unto them, saying, Be of good cheer; it is I; be not afraid. And Peter answered him and said, Lord, if it is thou, bid me come unto thee on the water. And he said, Come. And when Peter was come down out of the ship, he walked on the water, to go to Jesus. But when he saw the wind boisterous, he was afraid; and beginning to sink, he cried, saying, Lord, save me! And immediately Jesus stretched forth his hand, and	M 14, 22 K 6, 45 M 14, 22 — 23 J 6, 16 — 17 M 14, 23 J 6, 17 K 6, 47 M 14, 24 K 6, 48 M 14, 25 J 6, 19 M 14, 25 K 6, 48 — 49 — 50 J 6, 19 M 14, 27 — 28 — 29 — 30 — 31

Feb. 7. May 9.	**The Four Gospels arranged** Aug. 8. Nov. 7.

M 14, 31
— 32

J 6, 21

M 14, 33
K 6, 51
— 52

M 14, 33

K 6, 53

— 54
— 55

— 56

M 14, 36
J 6, 22

caught him, and said unto him, O thou of little faith, wherefore didst thou doubt? And when they were come into the ship, the wind ceased, and immediately the ship was at the land whither they went.

Then they that were in the ship were sore amazed in themselves beyond measure, and wondered. For they considered not the miracle of the loaves; for their heart was hardened: and they came and worshipped him, saying, Of a truth thou art the Son of God.

And when they had passed over, they came into the land of Gennesaret, and drew to the shore. And when they were come out of the ship, straightway they knew him, and ran through that whole region round about, and began to carry about in beds those that were sick, where they heard he was. And whithersoever he entered, into villages, or cities, or country, they laid the sick in the streets, and besought him that they might touch if it were but the border of his garment; and as many as touched him were made perfectly whole.

The day following, when the people which stood on the other side of the sea saw that there was none other boat there, save that one whereinto his disciples were entered, and that Jesus went not with his disciples into the boat, but that his disciples were gone away alone; (howbeit there came other boats from Tiberias nigh unto the place where they did eat bread, after that the Lord had given thanks:) when the people therefore saw that Jesus was not there, neither his disciples, they also took shipping, and came to Capernaum, seeking for Jesus. And when they had found him on the other side of the sea, they said unto him, Rabbi, when camest thou hither? Jesus answered them and said, Verily, verily, I say unto you, ye seek me, not because ye saw the miracles, but because ye did eat of the loaves, and were filled.

J 6,22
— 23
— 24
— 25
— 26

XXXIX.

Feb. 8. May 10. Aug. 9. Nov. 8.

Christ speaks of himself under the similitude of the bread of life.

LABOUR not, said Jesus, for the meat which perisheth, but for that meat which endureth unto everlasting life, which the Son of man shall give unto you; for him hath God the Father sealed.

Then said they unto him, What shall we do, that we might work the works of God? Jesus answered and said unto them, This is the work

J 6,27
— 28
— 29

Feb. 8. May 10.	The Four Gospels arranged	Aug. 9. Nov. 8.

J 6, 29
— 30
— 31
— 32

— 33

— 34
— 35

— 36

— 37

— 38

— 39

— 40

of God, that ye believe on him whom he hath sent. They said therefore unto him, What sign shewest thou then, that we may see, and believe thee? what dost thou work? Our fathers did eat manna in the desert; as it is written,* He gave them bread from heaven to eat. Then Jesus said unto them, Verily, verily, I say unto you, Moses gave you not that bread from heaven; but my Father giveth you the true bread from heaven. For the bread of God is he which cometh down from heaven, and giveth life unto the world. Then said they unto him, Lord, evermore give us this bread. And Jesus said unto them, I am the bread of life; he that cometh to me shall never hunger, and he that believeth on me shall never thirst. But I said unto you, that ye also have seen me, and believe not.

All that the Father giveth me shall come to me; and him that cometh to me I will in no wise cast out. For I came down from heaven, not to do mine own will, but the will of him that sent me.† And this is the Father's will which hath sent me, that of all which he hath given me I should lose nothing, but should raise it up again at the last day. And this is the will of him that sent me, that every one which seeth the Son, and believeth on him,

* Neh. ix, 15.   † Psa. xl, 7, 8.

| Feb. 8. May 10. | in one Continuous Narrative. | Aug. 9. Nov. 8. |

may have everlasting life; and I will raise him up at the last day. J 6, 40

The Jews then murmured at him, because he said, I am the bread which came down from heaven. And they said, Is not this Jesus, the son of Joseph, whose father and mother we know? how is it then that he saith, I came down from heaven? Jesus therefore answered and said unto them, Murmur not among yourselves. No man can come to me, except the Father which hath sent me draw him; and I will raise him up at the last day. It is written in the prophets,* And they shall be all taught of God. Every man therefore that hath heard, and hath learned of the Father, cometh unto me. Not that any man hath seen the Father, save he which is of God, he hath seen the Father. — 41 — 42 — 43 — 44 — 45 — 46

Verily, verily, I say unto you, he that believeth on me hath everlasting life. I am that bread of life. Your fathers did eat manna in the wilderness, and are dead. This is the bread which cometh down from heaven, that a man may eat thereof, and not die. I am the living bread which came down from heaven; if any man eat of this bread, he shall live for ever; and the bread that I will give is my flesh, which I will give for the life of the world. — 47 — 48 — 49 — 50 — 51

* Isa. liv, 13.

| | Feb. 8.
May 10. | The Four Gospels arranged | Aug. 9.
Nov. 8. |

J 6, 52	The Jews therefore strove among themselves, saying, How can this man give us his flesh to
— 53	eat? Then Jesus said unto them, Verily, verily, I say unto you, except ye eat the flesh of the Son of man, and drink his blood, ye have
— 54	no life in you. Whoso eateth my flesh, and drinketh my blood, hath eternal life; and I
— 55	will raise him up at the last day; for my flesh is meat indeed, and my blood is drink indeed.
— 56	He that eateth my flesh, and drinketh my blood,
— 57	dwelleth in me, and I in him. As the living Father hath sent me, and I live by the Father; so he that eateth me, even he shall live by
— 58	me. This is that bread which came down from heaven; not as your fathers did eat manna, and are dead; he that eateth of this bread shall live for ever.
— 59	These things said he in the synagogue, as he
— 60	taught in Capernaum. Many therefore of his disciples, when they had heard this, said, This
— 61	is a hard saying; who can hear it? When Jesus knew in himself that his disciples murmured at it, he said unto them, Doth this
— 62	offend you? What if ye shall see the Son of
— 63	man ascend up where he was before? It is the spirit that quickeneth; the flesh profiteth nothing: the words that I speak unto you,
— 64	they are spirit, and they are life. But there

Feb. 9. May 11.	in one Continuous Narrative.	Aug. 10. Nov. 9.

are some of you that believe not. For Jesus knew from the beginning who they were that believed not, and who should betray him. And he said, Therefore said I unto you, that no man can come unto me, except it were given unto him by my Father.

From that time many of his disciples went back, and walked no more with him. Then said Jesus unto the twelve, Will ye also go away? Then Simon Peter answered him, Lord, to whom shall we go? thou hast the words of eternal life; and we believe and are sure that thou art that Christ, the son of the living God. Jesus answered them, Have not I chosen you twelve, and one of you is a devil? He spake of Judas Iscariot the son of Simon; for he it was that should betray him, being one of the twelve.

J 6, 64
— 65
— 66
— 67
— 68
— 69
— 70
— 71

XL.

Feb. 9. May 11. Aug. 10. Nov. 9.

The word of God, rather than tradition, is to be followed.

AFTER these things Jesus walked in Galilee; for he would not walk in Jewry, because the Jews sought to kill him.

Then came together unto him the Pharisees, and certain of the scribes, which came from

J 7, 1

7, 1

| Feb. 9.
May 11. | **The Four Gospels arranged** | Aug. 10.
Nov. 9. |

K 7, 2   Jerusalem. And when they saw some of his disciples eat bread with defiled, that is to say,
— 3   with unwashen, hands, they found fault. For the Pharisees, and all the Jews, except they wash their hands oft, eat not, holding the tra-
— 4   dition of the elders. And when they come from the market, except they wash, they eat not. And many other things there are, which they have received to hold, as the washing of cups, and pots, brasen vessels, and of tables.
— 5   Then the Pharisees and scribes asked him, Why walk not thy disciples according to the tradition of the elders, but eat bread with un-
— 6   washen hands? He answered and said unto
M 15, 7   them, Ye hypocrites, well did Isaiah prophesy
— 8   of you, saying,* This people draw nigh unto me with their mouth, and honour me with their lips; but their heart is far from me.
— 9   But in vain they do worship me, teaching for
K 7, 8   doctrines the commandments of men. For, laying aside the commandment of God, ye hold the tradition of men, as the washing of pots and cups; and many other such like
— 9   things do ye. And he said unto them, Full well ye reject the commandment of God, that
M 15, 4   ye may keep your own tradition. For God commanded, saying, † Honour thy father and

         * Isa. xxix, 13.   † Ex. xx, 12.

| Feb. 9. May 11. | in one Continuous Narrative. | Aug. 10. Nov. 9. |

thy mother; and, *Whoso curseth father or mother, let him die the death; but ye say, If a man shall say to his father or mother, It is Corban, that is to say, a gift, by whatsoever thou mightest be profited by me, and honour not his father or his mother, he shall be free. And ye suffer him no more to do aught for his father or his mother; making the word of God of none effect through your tradition, which ye have delivered; and many such like things do ye.

And when he had called all the people unto him, he said unto them, Hearken unto me every one of you, and understand: there is nothing from without a man, that entering into him can defile him; but the things which come out of him, those are they that defile the man. If any man have ears to hear, let him hear.

Then came his disciples, and said unto him, Knowest thou that the Pharisees were offended, after they heard this saying? But he answered and said, Every plant, which my heavenly Father hath not planted, shall be rooted up. Let them alone; they are blind leaders of the blind. And if the blind lead the blind, both shall fall into the ditch.

And when he was entered into the house

* Ex. xxi, 17.

M 15, 4
K 7, 11

M 15, 6
K 7, 12
— 13

— 14
— 15

— 16

M 15, 12
— 13

— 14

K 7, 17

Feb. 10. May 12.	Aug. 11. Nov. 10.

The Four Gospels arranged

M 15, 15
K 7, 18   from the people, Peter said unto him, Declare unto us this parable. And he said unto them, Are ye so without understanding also? Do ye not perceive, that whatsoever thing from without entereth into the man, it cannot defile him,

— 19   because it entereth not into his heart, but into the belly, and goeth out into the draught, purg-

M 15, 18   ing all meats? But those things which proceed out of the mouth come forth from the heart,

K 7, 21   and they defile the man. For from within, out of the heart of men, proceed evil thoughts,

M 15, 19
K 7, 22   adulteries, fornications, murders, false witness, thefts, covetousness, wickedness, deceit, lasciviousness, an evil eye, blasphemy, pride, foolish-

— 23   ness: all these evil things come from within,

M 15, 20   and these are the things which defile a man; but to eat with unwashen hands defileth not a man.

XLI.

Feb. 10.   May 12.   Aug. 11.   Nov. 10.

The Syrophœnician woman's faith, and consequent importunity rewarded. The deaf and dumb healed.

M 15, 21
K 7, 24   THEN Jesus went thence, and departed into the coasts of Tyre and Sidon, and entered into a house, and would have no man know it; but he could not be hid.

| Feb. 10.
May 12. | in one Continuous Narrative. | Aug. 11.
Nov. 10. |

And, behold, a woman of Canaan, a Greek, a Syrophœnician by nation, whose young daughter had an unclean spirit, heard of him, and came out of the same coasts, and fell at his feet and besought him, saying, Have mercy on me, O Lord, thou son of David; my daughter is grievously vexed with a devil. But he answered her not a word. And his disciples came and besought him, saying, Send her away; for she crieth after us. But he answered and said, I am not sent but unto the lost sheep of the house of Israel. Then came she and worshipped him, saying, Lord, help me. But he answered and said, Let the children first be filled; for it is not meet to take the children's bread, and to cast it unto the dogs. And she answered and said unto him, Truth, Lord; yet the dogs under the table eat of the children's crumbs. Then Jesus answered and said unto her, O woman, great is thy faith; for this saying go thy way; and be it unto thee even as thou willest: the devil is gone out of thy daughter. And her daughter was made whole from that very hour. And when she was come to her house, she found the devil gone out, and her daughter laid upon the bed.	M 15, 22 K 7, 26 — 25 M 15, 22 K 7, 25 M 15, 22 — 23 — 24 — 25 K 7, 27 M 15, 26 K 7, 28 M 15, 27 K 7, 28 M 15, 28 K 7, 29 M 15, 28 K 7, 29 M 15, 28 K 7, 30
And again, departing from the coasts of Tyre and Sidon, he came nigh unto the sea of	— 31 M 15, 29

| Feb. 10. May 12. | The Four Gospels arranged | Aug. 11. Nov. 10. |

K 7, 31
M 15, 29

— 33

— 34

— 35

— 36

— 37

M 15, 30

— 31

Galilee, through the midst of the coasts of Decapolis; and went up into a mountain, and sat down there.

And they brought unto him one that was deaf, and had an impediment in his speech; and they besought him to put his hand upon him. And he took him aside from the multitude, and put his fingers into his ears, and he spat, and touched his tongue; and looking up to heaven, he sighed, and said unto him, Ephphatha, that is, Be opened. And straightway his ears were opened, and the string of his tongue was loosed, and he spake plainly. And he charged them that they should tell no man; but the more he charged them, so much the more a great deal they published it; and were beyond measure astonished, saying, He hath done all things well; he maketh both the deaf to hear, and the dumb to speak.

And great multitudes came unto him, having with them those that were lame, blind, dumb, maimed, and many others, and cast them down at Jesus' feet; and he healed them; insomuch that the multitude wondered, when they saw the dumb to speak, the maimed to be whole, the lame to walk, and the blind to see; and they glorified the God of Israel.

| Feb. 11. May 13. | in one Continuous Narrative. | Aug. 12. Nov. 11. |

XLII.

Feb. 11. May 13. Aug. 12. Nov. 11.

The multitude miraculously fed with seven loaves and a few small fishes. The Pharisees and Sadducees seek a sign from heaven. Christ gives sight to a blind man.

IN those days the multitude being very great, and having nothing to eat, Jesus called his disciples unto him, and said unto them, I have compassion on the multitude, because they have now been with me three days, and have nothing to eat; and if I send them away fasting to their own houses, they will faint by the way; for divers of them came from far. And his disciples answered him, Whence can a man satisfy so great a multitude with bread here in the wilderness? And he asked them, How many loaves have ye? And they said, Seven. And he commanded the people to sit down on the ground; and he took the seven loaves, and gave thanks, and brake, and gave to his disciples to set before them; and they did set them before the people. And they had a few small fishes: and he blessed, and commanded to set them also before them. And they did all eat, and were filled; and they took up of the broken meat that was left seven

K 8, 1
— 2
— 3
— 4
M 15, 33
K 8, 4
— 5
— 6
— 7
M 15, 37

| | Feb. 11. May 13. | The Four Gospels arranged | Aug. 12. Nov. 11. |

M 15, 38	baskets full. And they that did eat were four thousand men, beside women and children.
— 39	And he sent away the multitude, and straight-
K 8, 10	way entered into a ship with his disciples, and
M 15, 39	came into the coasts of Magdala, the parts of
K 8, 10	Dalmanutha.
M 16, 1	The Pharisees also with the Sadducees came
K 8, 11	forth, and began to question with him, and
M 16, 1	tempting, desired him that he would show
— 2	them a sign from heaven. He answered and said unto them, When it is evening, ye say, It will be fair weather; for the sky is red. And
— 3	in the morning, It will be foul weather to-day; for the sky is red and lowring. When ye see
L 12, 54	a cloud rise out of the west, straightway ye say, There cometh a shower; and so it is.
— 55	And when ye see the south wind blow, ye say, There will be heat; and it cometh to
— 56	pass. Ye hypocrites, ye can discern the face of the sky and of the earth; but how is it
M 16, 3	that ye do not discern the signs of this time?
L 12, 57	Yea, and why even of yourselves judge ye not what is right?
K 8, 12	And he sighed deeply in his spirit, and said,
M 16, 4	A wicked and adulterous generation seeketh after a sign; and there shall no sign be given unto it, but the sign of the prophet Jonah.*

* Jonah, i, 17.

| Feb. 11. May 13. | in one Continuous Narrative. | Aug. 12. Nov. 11. |

And he left them, and entering into the ship again, departed to the other side.   K 8, 13

Now the disciples had forgotten to take bread, neither had they in the ship with them more than one loaf. Then Jesus said unto them, Take heed and beware of the leaven of the Pharisees and of the Sadducees, and of the leaven of Herod. And they reasoned among themselves, saying, It is because we have no bread. Which when Jesus perceived, he said unto them, O ye of little faith, why reason ye among yourselves, because ye have brought no bread? Perceive ye not yet, neither understand? Have ye your heart yet hardened? Having eyes, see ye not? and having ears, hear ye not? and do ye not remember? Do ye not yet understand, neither remember the five loaves of the five thousand, and how many baskets ye took up? They said unto him, Twelve. Neither the seven loaves of the four thousand, and how many baskets ye took up? And they said, Seven. And he said unto them, How is it that ye do not understand that I spake it not to you concerning bread, that ye should beware of the leaven of the Pharisees and of the Sadducees? Then understood they how that he bade them not beware of the leaven of bread,

Marginal references:
— 14
M 16, 6
K 8, 15
— 16
M 16, 8
K 8, 17
— 18
M 16, 9
K 8, 19
M 16, 10
K 8, 20
M 16, 11
— 12

| | Feb. 12. | The Four Gospels arranged | Aug. 13. |
| | May 14. | | Nov. 12. |

M 16, 12 — but of the doctrine of the Pharisees and of the Sadducees.

K 8, 22 — And he came to Bethsaida; and they brought a blind man unto him, and besought him to touch

— 23 — him. And he took the blind man by the hand, and led him out of the town; and when he had spit on his eyes, and put his hands upon him,

— 24 — he asked him if he saw aught. And he looked

— 25 — up, and said, I see men as trees, walking. After that he put his hands again upon his eyes, and made him look up: and he was restored, and

— 26 — saw every man clearly. And he sent him away to his house, saying, Neither go into the town, nor tell it to any in the town.

XLIII.

FEB. 12. MAY 14. AUG. 13. NOV. 12.

Simon Peter acknowledges Jesus to be the Christ. Peter rebuked by Christ. Self-denial enjoined.

K 8, 27 — AND Jesus went out, and his disciples, into the towns of Cæsarea Philippi; and by

L 9, 18 — the way it came to pass, that as he was alone praying, his disciples were with him; and he

M 16, 13 — asked them, saying, Who do men say that I,

— 14 — the Son of man, am? And they said, Some say that thou art John the Baptist; some,

L 9, 19 — Elijah; and others, Jeremiah, or that one of

| Feb. 12. May 14. | in one Continuous Narrative. | Aug. 13. Nov. 12. |

the old prophets is risen again. He said unto them, But who say ye that I am? And Simon Peter answered and said, Thou art the Christ, the Son of the living God. And Jesus answered and said unto him, Blessed art thou, Simon Bar-jona; for flesh and blood hath not revealed it unto thee, but my Father which is in heaven. And I say also unto thee, that thou art Peter, and upon this rock I will build my church; and the gates of hell shall not prevail against it. And I will give unto thee the keys of the kingdom of heaven; and whatsoever thou shalt bind on earth shall be bound in heaven; and whatsoever thou shalt loose on earth shall be loosed in heaven.
    Then charged he his disciples that they should tell no man that he was Jesus the Christ.
    From that time forth began Jesus to show unto his disciples, how that he must go unto Jerusalem, and suffer many things, and be rejected by the elders and chief priests and scribes, and be killed, and be raised again the third day. And he spake that saying openly. Then Peter took him, and began to rebuke him, saying, Be it far from thee, Lord; this shall not be unto thee. But when he had turned about and looked on his disciples, he rebuked Peter,
	M 16, 15
	— 16
	
	— 17
	
	— 18
	
	— 19
	
	— 20
	
	— 21
	
	K 8, 31
	M 16, 21
	
	K 8, 32
	M 16, 22
	
	K 8, 33

| Feb. 12. | | Aug. 13. |
| May 14. | The Four Gospels arranged | Nov. 12. |

M 16, 23 — saying, Get thee behind me, Satan; for thou art an offence unto me; for thou savourest not the things that are of God, but those that are of men.

L 14, 25
K 8, 34
L 9, 23 — And there went great multitudes with him; and when he had called the people unto him, with his disciples also, he said unto them all, If any man will come after me, let him deny himself, and take up his cross daily, and follow

M 10, 38
L 14, 27 — me. He that taketh not his cross, and followeth after me, is not worthy of me. And whosoever doth not bear his cross, and come

M 10, 37 — after me, cannot be my disciple. He that loveth father or mother more than me, is not worthy of me; and he that loveth son or daughter more than me is not worthy of me,

L 9, 24 — for whosoever will save his life shall lose it;

K 8, 35 — but whosoever will lose his life for my sake, and the gospel's, the same shall save it, and
J 12, 25 — shall keep it unto life eternal. For what
K 8, 36 — shall it profit a man, if he shall gain the
L 9, 25 — whole world and lose his own soul, or be
K 8, 37 — cast away? Or what shall a man give in exchange for his soul?

L 18, 28
M 19, 27 — Then Peter said, Lo, we have left all, and followed thee, what shall we have therefore?
L 18, 29 — And he said unto them, Verily, I say unto you, there is no man that hath left house, or

Feb. 13. May 15.	in one Continuous Narrative.	Aug. 14. Nov. 13.

brethren, or sisters, or father, or mother, or wife, or children, or lands, for my name's sake, and the gospel's, who shall not receive manifold more in this present time, houses, and brethren, and sisters, and mothers, and children, and lands, with persecutions; and in the world to come inherit everlasting life.	M 19, 29 K 10, 29 L 18, 30 K 10, 30 M 19, 29

XLIV.

Feb. 13. May 15. Aug. 14. Nov. 13.

Faith in Christ is to be openly confessed.
The Transfiguration of Christ.

WHOSOEVER shall confess me before men, said Jesus, him will I confess also before my Father which is in heaven, and before the angels of God; but whosoever shall deny me before men, or be ashamed of me and of my words in this adulterous and sinful generation; of him also shall the Son of man be ashamed, when he shall come in his own glory, and in his Father's, and of the holy angels; and him will I also deny before my Father which is in heaven, and before the angels of God. For the Son of man shall come in the glory of his Father with his angels; and then he shall reward every man according to his works.	M 10, 32 L 12, 8 M 10, 33 K 8, 38 L 9, 26 M 10, 33 L 12, 9 M 16, 27

| Feb. 13. | | Aug. 14. |
| May 15. | The Four Gospels arranged | Nov. 13. |

J 12, 26

M 19, 28

L 9, 27

K 9, 1
M 17, 1
K 9, 2
L 9, 28
— 29
M 17, 2

K 9, 3

M 17, 2
L 9, 29
— 30
— 31

— 32

— 33

If any man serve me, let him follow me; and where I am, there shall also my servant be; if any man serve me, him will my Father honour. Verily, I say unto you, ye which have followed me, in the regeneration when the Son of man shall sit on the throne of his glory, ye also shall sit upon twelve thrones, judging the twelve tribes of Israel. But I tell you of a truth, that there are some of them that stand here, which shall not taste of death, till they have seen the kingdom of God come with power.

And after six days Jesus took Peter, James, and John his brother, and led them up into a high mountain apart by themselves to pray. And as he prayed, the fashion of his countenance was altered, and he was transfigured before them; and his face did shine as the sun, and his raiment became shining, exceeding white as snow, so as no fuller on earth can white them; white as the light, and glistering. And, behold, there talked with him two men, which were Moses and Elijah; who appeared in glory, and spake of his decease which he should accomplish at Jerusalem.

But Peter and they that were with him were heavy with sleep; and when they were awake, they saw his glory, and the two men that stood with him. And it came to pass, as they de-

| Feb. 13. May 15. | in one Continuous Narrative. | Aug. 14. Nov. 13. |

parted from him, Peter said unto Jesus, Master, it is good for us to be here; and let us make three tabernacles; one for thee, and one for Moses, and one for Elijah; for he wist not what to say; for they were sore afraid.

While he yet spake, behold, a bright cloud overshadowed them; and they feared as they entered into the cloud. And there came a voice out of the cloud, saying, This is my beloved Son, in whom I am well pleased; hear ye him. And when the disciples heard it, they fell on their face, and were sore afraid. And when the voice was past, Jesus came and touched them, and said, Arise, and be not afraid. And suddenly, when they had looked round about, they saw no man any more, save Jesus only with themselves.

And as they came down from the mountain, Jesus charged them, saying, Tell the vision to no man, until the Son of man is risen again from the dead. And they kept it close, and told no man in those days any of those things which they had seen; questioning one with another what the rising from the dead could mean.

And his disciples asked him, saying, Why then say the scribes that Elijah must first come? And Jesus answered and said unto them, Elijah truly shall first come, and re-

L 9, 33
K 9, 6
M 17, 5
L 9, 34
— 35
M 17, 5
— 6
L 9, 36
M 17, 7
K 9, 8
M 17, 9
L 9, 36
K 9, 10
M 17, 10
— 11

Feb. 14. May 16.	**The Four Gospels arranged** Aug. 15. Nov. 14.

M 17, 12   store all things. But I say unto you, That Elijah is come already, and they knew him not, but have done unto him whatsoever they listed. Likewise shall also the Son of man
K 9, 12   suffer many things of them, and be set at
— 13
M 17, 13   naught, as it is written of him.* Then the disciples understood that he spake unto them of
L 1, 17   John the Baptist, who should go before him in the spirit and power of Elijah.

XLV.

FEB. 14. MAY 16. AUG. 15. NOV. 14.

A deaf and dumb spirit exorcised from a child.

L 9, 17   AND it came to pass, that on the next day, when Jesus and the three apostles were
K 9, 14   come down from the hill to his disciples, he saw a great multitude about them, and the
— 15   scribes questioning with them. And straightway all the people, when they beheld him, were greatly amazed, and running to him sa-
— 16   luted him. And he asked the scribes, What
— 17   question ye with them? And one of the
M 17, 14   multitude, kneeling down to him, cried out,
L 9, 38   saying, Master, I beseech thee, look upon
K 9, 17   my son; for he is mine only child, and hath
M 17, 15   a dumb spirit and is lunatic and sore vexed.
L 9, 39   And, lo, a spirit taketh him, and he suddenly

* Isa. liii, 8.

| Feb. 14. | | Aug. 15. |
| May 16. | in one Continuous Narrative. | Nov. 14. |

crieth out; and it teareth him that he foameth again, and gnasheth with his teeth, and pineth away, and, bruising him, hardly departeth from him. And I besought thy disciples to cast him out; and they could not.

And Jesus answering said, O faithless and perverse generation, how long shall I be with you, and suffer you? Bring thy son hither to me. And as he was yet a coming, the devil threw him down, and tare him; and he fell on the ground, and wallowed foaming. And Jesus asked his father, How long is it ago since this came unto him? And he said, Of a child. And ofttimes it hath cast him into the fire, and into the waters, to destroy him; but if thou canst do anything, have compassion on us, and help us. Jesus said unto him, If thou canst believe, all things are possible to him that believeth. And straightway the father of the child cried out, and said with tears, Lord, I believe; help thou mine unbelief.

When Jesus saw that the people came running together, he rebuked the foul spirit, saying unto him, Thou dumb and deaf spirit, I charge thee, come out of him, and enter no more into him. And the spirit cried, and rent him sore, and came out of him; and he was as one dead; insomuch that many said, He is

L 9, 39
K 9, 18
L 9, 39
— 40

— 41

— 42
K 9, 20
— 21

— 22

— 23

— 24

— 25

— 26

| Feb. 14. May 16. | The Four Gospels arranged | Aug. 15. Nov. 14. |

L 9, 42	dead. But Jesus rebuked the unclean spirit,
K 9, 27	and healed the child, and took him by the
L 9, 42	hand and lifted him up, and delivered him
M 17, 18	again to his father; and the child was cured
L 9, 43	from that very hour. And they were all amazed at the mighty power of God.
K 9, 28	And when he was come into the house, his disciples asked him privately, Why could not
M 17, 20	we cast him out? And Jesus said unto them,
L 17, 5	Because of your unbelief. And the apostles
— 6	said unto the Lord, Increase our faith. And the Lord said, If ye had faith as a grain of mustard seed, ye might say unto this sycamine tree, Be thou plucked up by the root, and be thou planted in the sea; and it should obey
M 17, 20	you. Or ye might say unto this mountain, Remove hence to yonder place; and it should remove; and nothing should be impossible
— 21	unto you. Howbeit this kind goeth not out but by prayer and fasting.
K 9, 38	And John answered him, saying, Master, we saw one casting out devils in thy name, and he followeth not us; and we forbad him, because
— 39	he followeth not us. But Jesus said, Forbid him not; for there is no man which shall do a miracle in my name, that can lightly speak
— 40	evil of me. For he that is not against us is on our part.

| Feb. 15. May 17. | in one Continuous Narrative. | Aug. 16. Nov. 15. |

XLVI.
FEB. 15. MAY 17. AUG. 16. NOV. 15.
Christ foretells his sufferings; pays tribute; and discourses on true greatness.

AND they departed thence, and passed through Galilee; and Jesus would not that any man should know it. But while they wondered every one at all things which Jesus did, he said unto his disciples, Let these sayings sink down into your ears; for the Son of man shall be delivered into the hands of men. But they understood not that saying, and it was hid from them, that they perceived it not; and they feared to ask him of that saying.

And they were in the way going up to Jerusalem, and Jesus went before them; and they were amazed; and as they followed, they were afraid. And he took the twelve disciples apart in the way, and began to tell them what things should happen unto him, saying, Behold, we go up to Jerusalem; and all things that are written by the prophets concerning the Son of man shall be accomplished.* For the Son of man shall be delivered unto the chief priests, and unto the scribes; and they shall condemn him to death, and shall deliver him to the Gentiles; and they shall mock him, and spitefully

K 9, 30
L 9, 43
— 44
— 45

K 10, 32
M 20, 17
K 10, 32
— 33
L 18, 31
K 10, 33
— 34
L 18, 32

* Psa. xxii. Isa. liii.

| Feb. 15. | The Four Gospels arranged | Aug. 16. |
| May 17. | | Nov. 15. |

K 10, 34
M 20, 19
K 9, 31
M 17, 23

treat him, and shall scourge him, and shall spit upon him, and shall crucify him; and they shall kill him; and after that he is killed, he shall rise the third day. And they were exceedingly sorry.

— 24

And when they were come to Capernaum, they that received tribute money came to Peter, and said, Doth not your master pay tribute? He said, Yes. And when he was come into the house, Jesus anticipated him, saying, What thinkest thou, Simon? of whom do the kings of the earth take custom or tribute? of their own children, or of strangers? Peter said unto him, Of strangers. Jesus said unto him, Then are the children free. Notwithstanding, lest we should offend them, go thou to the sea, and cast a hook, and take the fish that first cometh up; and when thou hast opened his mouth, thou shalt find a piece of money; that take, and give unto them for me and thee.

— 25

— 26

— 27

M 18, 1

K 9, 33

— 34

L 22, 24

At the same time came the disciples unto Jesus, saying, Who is the greatest in the kingdom of heaven? and being in the house he asked them, What was it that ye disputed among yourselves by the way? But they held their peace; for by the way they had disputed among themselves, which of them should be accounted the greatest.

| Feb. 15. May 17. | in one Continuous Narrative. | Aug. 16. Nov. 15. |

And Jesus, perceiving the thought of their heart, sat down, and called the twelve, and said unto them, If any man desire to be first, the same shall be last of all, and servant of all; and he that is least among you all, the same shall be great. And whosoever shall exalt himself shall be abased; and he that shall humble himself shall be exalted. L 9, 47 / K 9, 35 / L 9, 48 / M 23, 12

And he said unto them, The kings of the Gentiles exercise lordship over them; and they that exercise authority over them are called benefactors. But ye shall not be so; but he that is greatest among you, let him be as the younger; and he that is chief, as he that doth serve. For whether is greater, he that sitteth at meat, or he that serveth? is not he that sitteth at meat? but I am among you as he that serveth. Ye are they which have continued with me in my temptations; and I appoint unto you a kingdom, as my Father hath appointed unto me; that ye may eat and drink at my table in my kingdom, and sit on thrones judging the twelve tribes of Israel. L 22, 25 / — 26 / — 27 / — 28 / — 29 / — 30

And he took a child, and set him in the midst of them; and when he had taken him in his arms, he said unto them, Verily, I say unto you, except ye be converted, and become as little children, ye shall not enter into the K 9, 36 / M 18, 3

| Feb. 16. | | Aug. 17. |
| May 18. | The Four Gospels arranged | Nov. 16. |

M 18, 4

K 9, 37

kingdom of heaven. Whosoever therefore shall humble himself as this little child, the same is greatest in the kingdom of heaven. Whosoever shall receive one of such children in my name, receiveth me ; and whosoever shall receive me, receiveth not me, but him that sent me.

XLVII.
FEB. 16. MAY 18. AUG. 17. NOV. 16.

A forgiving spirit necessary to salvation.

L 17, 1
M 18, 7
L 17, 1

— 2

M 18, 6
L 17, 2
M 18, 6
— 10

— 15
L 17, 3
M 18, 15

L 17, 3
M 18, 16

THEN said Jesus unto the disciples, Woe unto the world because of offences ! It is impossible but that offences will come ; but woe unto him through whom they come ! It were better for him that a millstone were hanged about his neck, and he drowned in the depth of the sea, than that he should offend one of these little ones that believe in me. Take heed that ye despise not one of these little ones ; for I say unto you, that in heaven their angels do always behold the face of my Father which is in heaven.

Moreover, take heed to yourselves ; if thy brother trespass against thee, go and tell him his fault between thee and him alone ; if he shall hear thee, thou hast gained thy brother ; and if he repent, forgive him. But if he will not hear thee, then take with thee one or two

| Feb. 16.
May 18. | in one Continuous Narrative. | Aug. 17.
Nov. 16. |

more, that in the mouth of two or three witnesses every word may be established. And if he shall neglect to hear them, tell it unto the church ; but if he neglect to hear the church, let him be unto thee as a heathen man and a publican.

Then came Peter to him, and said, Lord, how oft shall my brother sin against me, and I forgive him ? till seven times in a day ? Jesus said unto him, I say not unto thee, Until seven times ; but, Until seventy times seven. Therefore is the kingdom of heaven likened unto a certain king, which would take account of his servants. And when he had begun to reckon, one was brought unto him, which owed him ten thousand talents. But forasmuch as he had not wherewith to pay, his lord commanded him to be sold, and his wife, and children, and all that he had, and payment to be made. The servant therefore fell down, and worshipped him, saying, Lord, have patience with me, and I will pay thee all. Then the lord of that servant was moved with compassion, and loosed him, and forgave him the debt. But the same servant went out, and found one of his fellowservants, which owed him a hundred pence ; and he laid hands on him, and took him by the throat, saying, Pay

M 18, 16
— 17

— 21

L 17, 4
M 18, 22

— 23

— 24

— 25

— 26

— 27

— 28

Feb. 17. May 19.   The Four Gospels arranged   Aug. 18. Nov. 17.

M 18, 29 — me that thou owest. And his fellowservant fell down at his feet, and besought him, saying, Have patience with me, and I will pay thee all.
— 30 And he would not; but went and cast him into
— 31 prison, till he should pay the debt. So when his fellowservants saw what was done, they were very sorry, and came and told unto their
— 32 lord all that was done. Then his lord, after that he had called him, said unto him, O thou wicked servant, I forgave thee all that debt,
— 33 because thou desiredst me; shouldest not thou also have had compassion on thy fellowservant,
— 34 even as I had pity on thee? And his lord was wrath, and delivered him to the tormentors, till he should pay all that was due unto him.
— 35 So likewise shall my heavenly Father do also unto you, if ye from your hearts forgive not every one his brother his trespasses.

XLVIII.

FEB. 17. MAY 19. AUG. 18. NOV. 17.

The seventy sent forth. Christ's brethren do not believe in him. James and John's revengeful spirit reproved.

L 10, 1 AFTER these things the Lord appointed other seventy also, and sent them two and two before his face into every city and
— 2 place, whither he himself would go. Then

| Feb. 17. May 19. | in one Continuous Narrative. | Aug. 18. Nov. 17. |

said he unto them, Go your ways; behold, I send you forth as sheep in the midst of wolves; be ye therefore wise as serpents, and harmless as doves. Give not that which is holy unto the dogs, lest they turn again and rend you; neither cast ye your pearls before swine, lest they trample them under their feet. But when they persecute you in this city, flee ye into another; for verily, I say unto you, ye shall not have gone over the cities of Israel, till the Son of man be come. The disciple is not above his master, nor the servant above his lord, neither he that is sent, greater than he that sent him. It is enough for the disciple that is perfect, that he be as his master, and the servant as his lord. If they have called the master of the house Beelzebub, how much more shall they call them of his household? Fear them not therefore.

Now the Jews' feast of tabernacles was at hand. His brethren therefore said unto him, Depart hence, and go into Judæa, that thy disciples also may see the works that thou doest; for there is no man that doeth any thing in secret, and he himself seeketh to be known openly. If thou doest these things, show thyself to the world. For neither did his brethren believe in him. Then Jesus said

L 10, 3
M 10, 16

M 7, 6

M 10, 23

— 24
J 13, 16
M 10, 25
L 6, 40
M 10, 25

— 26
J 7, 2
— 3

— 4

— 5
— 6

| Feb. 17. | | Aug. 18. |
| May 19. | The Four Gospels arranged | Nov. 17. |

J 7, 6	unto them, My time is not yet come; but your
— 7	time is alway ready. The world cannot hate you; but me it hateth, because I testify of it,
— 8	that the works thereof are evil. Go ye up unto this feast; I go not up yet unto this feast;
— 9	for my time is not yet fully come. When he had said these words unto them, he abode still
— 10	in Galilee. But when his brethren were gone
M 19, 1	up, and he had finished these sayings, he de-
K 10, 1	parted from Galilee, and came into the coasts
M 19, 2	of Judæa by the farther side of Jordan; and great multitudes followed him; and he healed
K 10, 1	them there; and, as he was wont, he taught
J 7, 10	them again. Then went he also up unto the feast, not openly, but as it were in secret.
L 9, 51	And it came to pass, when the time was come that he should be received up, he stead-
— 52	fastly set his face to go to Jerusalem, and sent messengers before his face; and they went, and entered into a village of the Samaritans,
— 53	to make ready for him. And they did not receive him, because his face was as if he
— 54	would go to Jerusalem. And when his dis- ciples James and John saw this, they said, Lord, wilt thou that we command fire to come down from heaven, and consume them, even
— 55	as Elijah did?* But he turned, and rebuked

* 2 Kings, 1, 10, 12.

| Feb. 18. May 20. | in one Continuous Narrative. | Aug. 19. Nov. 18. |

them, and said, Ye know not what manner of spirit ye are of. For the Son of man is not come to destroy men's lives, but to save them. And they went to another village.

XLIX.

Feb. 18. May 20. Aug. 19. Nov. 18.

Ten lepers cleansed. Christ at the feast of tabernacles.

AND it came to pass, as Jesus went to Jerusalem, that he passed through the midst of Samaria and Galilee. And as he entered into a certain village, there met him ten men that were lepers, which stood afar off; and they lifted up their voices, and said, Jesus, Master, have mercy on us. And when he saw them, he said unto them, Go show yourselves unto the priests. And it came to pass, that, as they went, they were cleansed. And one of them, when he saw that he was healed, turned back, and with a loud voice glorified God, and fell down on his face at Jesus's feet, giving him thanks; and he was a Samaritan. And Jesus answering said, Were there not ten cleansed? but where are the nine? There are not found that returned to give glory to God, save this stranger. And

L 9, 55
— 56

L 17, 11
— 12
— 13
— 14
— 15
— 16
— 17
— 18
— 19

Feb. 18. May 20.	The Four Gospels arranged	Aug. 19. Nov. 18.

L 17, 19 — he said unto him, Arise, go thy way; thy faith hath made thee whole.

J 7, 11 — Then the Jews sought him at the feast, and
— 12 — said, Where is he? And there was much murmuring among the people concerning him; for some said, He is a good man; others said,
— 13 — Nay; but he deceiveth the people. Howbeit no man spake openly of him for fear of the Jews.
— 14 — Now about the midst of the feast Jesus
— 15 — went up into the temple, and taught. And the Jews marvelled, saying, How knoweth this
— 16 — man letters, having never learned? Jesus answered them, and said, My doctrine is not
— 17 — mine, but his that sent me. If any man will do his will, he shall know of the doctrine, whether it is of God, or whether I speak of
— 18 — myself. He that speaketh of himself seeketh his own glory; but he that seeketh his glory that sent him, the same is true, and no un-
— 19 — righteousness is in him. Did not Moses give you the law,* and yet none of you keepeth the
— 20 — law? Why go ye about to kill me? The people answered and said, Thou hast a devil; who
— 21 — goeth about to kill thee? Jesus answered and said unto them, I have done one work, and
— 22 — ye all marvel. Moses gave unto you circum-

* Deut. xxx, 19.

| Feb. 18. May 20. | in one Continuous Narrative. | Aug 19. Nov. 18. |

cision;* (not because it is of Moses, but of the fathers;)† and ye on the sabbath day circumcise a man. If a man on the sabbath day receive circumcision, that the law of Moses should not be broken; are ye angry at me, because I have made a man every whit whole on the sabbath day? Judge not according to the appearance, but judge righteous judgment.

Then said some of them of Jerusalem, Is not this he whom they seek to kill? But, lo, he speaketh boldly, and they say nothing unto him. Do the rulers know indeed that this is the very Christ? Howbeit we know this man whence he is; but when Christ cometh, no man knoweth whence he is.

Then cried Jesus in the temple as he taught, saying, Ye both know me, and ye know whence I am; and I am not come of myself, but he that sent me is true, whom ye know not. But I know him; for I am from him, and he hath sent me.

Then they sought to take him; but no man laid hands on him, because his hour was not yet come. And many of the people believed on him, and said, When Christ cometh, will he do more miracles than these which this man hath done?

J 7, 22
— 23
— 24
— 25
— 26
— 27
— 28
— 29
— 30
— 31

* Lev. xii, 3.   † Gen. xvii, 12.

L.

Feb. 19. May 21. Aug. 20. Nov. 19.

The Pharisees and chief priests send officers to take Christ.

J 7, 32 — THE Pharisees heard that the people murmured such things concerning Jesus; and the Pharisees and the chief priests sent

— 33 — officers to take him. Then said Jesus unto them, Yet a little while am I with you, and

— 34 — then I go unto him that sent me. Ye shall seek me, and shall not find me; and where I am, thither ye cannot come.

— 35 — Then said the Jews among themselves, Whither will he go, that we shall not find him? will he go unto the dispersed among

— 36 — the Gentiles,* and teach the Gentiles? What manner of saying is this that he said, Ye shall seek me, and shall not find me; and where I

J 8, 21 — am, thither ye cannot come? Then said Jesus again unto them, I go my way, and ye shall seek me, and shall die in your sins; whither I

— 22 — go, ye cannot come. Then said the Jews, Will he kill himself? because he saith, Whither I go, ye cannot come.

— 23 — And he said unto them, Ye are from beneath; I am from above: ye are of this world; I am

* 2 Kings, xvii, 23.

| Feb. 19. May 21. | in one Continuous Narrative. | Aug. 20. Nov. 19. |

not of this world. I said therefore unto you, that ye shall die in your sins ; for if ye believe not that I am he, ye shall die in your sins.   J 8, 24

Then said they unto him, Who art thou? And Jesus said unto them, Even the same that I said unto you from the beginning. I have many things to say and to judge of you; but he that sent me is true ; and I speak to the world those things which I have heard of him. They understood not that he spake to them of the Father. Then said Jesus unto them, When ye have lifted up the Son of man, then shall ye know that I am he, and that I do nothing of myself; but as my Father hath taught me, I speak these things. And he that sent me is with me ; the Father hath not left me alone ; for I do always those things that please him. As he spake these words, many believed on him.   — 25, — 26, — 27, — 28, — 29, — 30

In the last day, that great day of the feast, Jesus stood and cried, saying, If any man thirst, let him come unto me, and drink. He that believeth on me, as the scripture hath said, out of his belly shall flow rivers of living water.* (But this spake he of the Spirit, which they that believe on him should receive; for the Holy Ghost was not yet given; because   J 7, 37, — 38, — 39

* Isa. lviii, 11.

M 11, 28	that Jesus was not yet glorified.) Come unto me, all ye that labour and are heavy laden, and
— 29	I will give you rest. Take my yoke upon you, and learn of me; for I am meek and lowly in heart; and ye shall find rest unto your souls.
— 30	For my yoke is easy, and my burden is light.
J 7, 40	Many of the people therefore, when they heard this saying, said, Of a truth this is the Pro-
— 41	phet.* Others said, This is the Christ. But some said, Shall Christ come out of Galilee?
— 42	Hath not the scripture said, that Christ cometh of the seed of David,† and out of the town of
— 43	Bethlehem,‡ where David was? So there was a division among the people because of him.
— 44	And some of them would have taken him; but no man laid hands on him.
— 45	Then came the officers to the chief priests and Pharisees; and they said unto them, Why
— 46	have ye not brought him? The officers an-
— 47	swered, Never man spake like this man. Then answered them the Pharisees, Are ye also de-
— 48	ceived? Have any of the rulers or of the Pha-
— 49	risees believed on him? But this people who
— 50	know not the law are cursed. Nicodemus said unto them, (he that came to Jesus by night,
— 51	being one of them,) Doth our law judge any man before it heareth him, and knoweth what

* Deut. xviii, 15, 18.   † Jer. xxiii, 5.   ‡ Micah v, 2.

he doeth?* They answered and said unto him, Art thou also of Galilee? Search, and look; for out of Galilee ariseth no prophet.† And every man went unto his own house.

J 7, 52
— 53

LI.

FEB. 20. MAY 22. AUG. 21. NOV. 20.

The woman taken in adultery. Christ bears record of himself.

JESUS went unto the mount of Olives. And early in the morning he came again into the temple, and all the people came unto him; and he sat down, and taught them. And the scribes and Pharisees brought unto him a woman taken in adultery; and when they had set her in the midst, they said unto him, Master, this woman was taken in adultery, in the very act. Now Moses in the law commanded us, that such should be stoned;‡ but what sayest thou? This they said, tempting him, that they might have to accuse him. But Jesus stooped down, and with his finger wrote on the ground, as if he heard them not. So when they continued asking him, he lifted up himself, and said unto them, He that is without sin among you, let him first cast a stone at

J 8, 1
— 2
— 3
— 4
— 5
— 6
— 7

* Deut. xix, 16-19.   † Isa. ix, 1, 2.   ‡ Deut. xxii, 24.

| Feb. 20. | | Aug. 21. |
| May 22. | The Four Gospels arranged | Nov. 20. |

J 8, 8 — her. And again he stooped down, and wrote
— 9 on the ground. And they which heard it, being convicted by their own conscience, went out one by one, beginning at the eldest, even unto the last; and Jesus was left alone, and the
— 10 woman standing in the midst. When Jesus had lifted up himself, and saw none but the woman, he said unto her, Woman, where are those thine accusers? hath no man condemned
— 11 thee? She said, No man, Lord. And Jesus said unto her, Neither do I condemn thee; go, and sin no more.

— 12 Then spake Jesus again unto them, in the
— 20 treasury, as he taught in the temple; saying,
— 12 I am the light of the world; he that followeth me shall not walk in darkness, but shall have
— 13 the light of life. The Pharisees therefore said unto him, Thou bearest record of thyself; thy
— 14 record is not true. Jesus answered and said unto them, Though I bear record of myself, yet my record is true; for I know whence I came, and whither I go: but ye cannot tell
— 15 whence I came, and whither I go. Ye judge
— 16 after the flesh; I judge no man. And yet if I judge, my judgment is true; for I am not alone, but I and the Father that sent me.
— 17 It is also written in your law,* that the tes-

* Deut. xvii, 6.

timony of two men is true. I am one that bear witness of myself, and the Father that sent me beareth witness of me. Then said they unto him, Where is thy Father? Jesus answered, Ye neither know me, nor my Father; if ye had known me, ye would have known my Father also.

These words spake Jesus, and no man laid hands on him; for his hour was not yet come.

LII.

FEB. 21. MAY 23. AUG. 22. NOV. 21.

Obedience to Christ, and its blessedness.

THEN said Jesus to those Jews which believed on him, If ye continue in my word, then are ye my disciples indeed; and ye shall know the truth, and the truth shall make you free. They answered him, We are Abraham's seed, and were never in bondage to any man: how sayest thou, Ye shall be made free? Jesus answered them, Verily, verily, I say unto you, whosoever committeth sin is the servant of sin. And the servant abideth not in the house for ever; but the Son abideth ever. If the Son therefore shall make you free, ye shall be free indeed. I know that ye are Abraham's seed; but ye seek to kill me, because my word hath

J 8, 18
— 19

— 20

J 8, 31
— 32
— 33
— 34
— 35
— 36
— 37

| Feb. 21. | | Aug. 22. |
| May 23. | The Four Gospels arranged | Nov. 21. |

J 8, 38 — no place in you. I speak that which I have seen with my Father; and ye do that which ye
— 39 have seen with your father. They answered and said unto him, Abraham is our father. Jesus said unto them, If ye were Abraham's children, ye would do the works of Abraham.
— 40 But now ye seek to kill me, a man that hath told you the truth, which I have heard of God;
— 41 this did not Abraham. Ye do the deeds of your father. Then said they to him, We are not born of fornication; we have one Father,
— 42 even God. Jesus said unto them, If God were your Father, ye would love me; for I proceeded forth and came from God; neither
— 43 came I of myself, but he sent me. Why do ye not understand my speech? even because ye
— 44 cannot hear my word. Ye are of your father the devil, and the lusts of your father ye will do. He was a murderer from the beginning, and abode not in the truth, because there is no truth in him. When he speaketh a lie, he speaketh of his own; for he is a liar, and the
— 45 father of it. And because I tell you the truth,
— 46 ye believe me not. Which of you convicteth me of sin? And if I say the truth, why do ye
— 47 not believe me? He that is of God heareth God's words; ye therefore hear them not, be-
— 48 cause ye are not of God. Then answered the

| Feb. 21. | | Aug. 22. |
| May 23. | in one Continuous Narrative. | Nov. 21. |

Jews, and said unto him, Say we not well that thou art a Samaritan, and hast a devil? Jesus answered, I have not a devil; but I honour my Father, and ye do dishonour me. And I seek not mine own glory; there is one that seeketh and judgeth. Verily, verily, I say unto you, if a man keep my saying, he shall never see death. Then said the Jews unto him, Now we know that thou hast a devil. Abraham is dead, and the prophets;* and thou sayest, If a man keep my saying, he shall never taste of death. Art thou greater than our father Abraham, which is dead; and the prophets which are dead? whom makest thou thyself? Jesus answered, If I honour myself, my honour is nothing; it is my Father that honoureth me, of whom ye say, that he is your God: yet ye have not known him; but I know him; and if I should say, I know him not, I should be a liar like unto you; but I know him, and keep his saying. Your father Abraham rejoiced to see my day; and he saw it and was glad.† Then said the Jews unto him, Thou art not yet fifty years old, and hast thou seen Abraham? Jesus said unto them, Verily, verily, I say unto you, before Abraham was, I am. Then took they up stones to cast at him; but Jesus hid him-

J 8, 49
— 50
— 51
— 52
— 53
— 54
— 55
— 56
— 57
— 58
— 59

* Zech. i, 5.   † Gen. xxii, 13, 14.

| J 8,59 | self, and went out of the temple, going through the midst of them, and so passed by.
| L 10,17 | And the seventy returned with joy, saying, Lord, even the devils are subject unto us
| — 18 | through thy name. And he said unto them, I beheld Satan as lightning fall from heaven.*
| — 20 | Notwithstanding in this rejoice not, that the spirits are subject unto you; but rather rejoice because your names are written in heaven.
| — 21 | In that hour Jesus rejoiced in spirit, and said, I thank thee, O Father, Lord of heaven and earth, that thou hast hid these things from the wise and prudent, and hast revealed them unto babes: even so, Father; for so it seemed
| — 22 | good in thy sight. All things are delivered to me of my Father; and no man knoweth who the Son is, but the Father; and who the Father is, but the Son, and he to whom the Son will reveal him.

LIII.

FEB. 22. MAY 24. AUG. 23. NOV. 22.

The man who fell among thieves. Mary and her sister Martha. Christ's teaching respecting prayer.

| L 10,25 | AND, behold, a certain lawyer stood up, and tempted Jesus, saying, Master, what
| — 26 | shall I do to inherit eternal life? He said unto

* Isa. xiv, 12.

| Feb. 22. May 24. | in one Continuous Narrative. | Aug. 23. Nov. 22. |

him, What is written in the law? how readest thou? And he answering said, Thou shalt love the Lord thy God with all thy heart, and with all thy soul, and with all thy strength, and with all thy mind;* and thy neighbour as thyself.† And he said unto him, Thou hast answered right; this do, and thou shalt live. But he, willing to justify himself, said unto Jesus, And who is my neighbour? And Jesus answering said, A certain man went down from Jerusalem to Jericho, and fell among thieves, which stripped him of his raiment, and wounded him, and departed, leaving him half dead. And by chance there came down a certain priest that way; and when he saw him, he passed by on the other side. And likewise a Levite, when he was at the place, came and looked on him, and passed by on the other side. But a certain Samaritan, as he journeyed, came where he was; and when he saw him, he had compassion on him, and went to him, and bound up his wounds, pouring in oil and wine, and sat him on his own beast, and brought him to an inn, and took care of him. And on the morrow when he departed, he took out two pence, and gave them to the host, and said unto him, Take care of him; and whatsoever	L 10, 27 — 28 — 29 — 30 — 31 — 32 — 33 — 34 — 35

* Deut. vi, 5.   † Lev. xix, 18.

| | Feb. 22. May 24. | The Four Gospels arranged | Aug. 23. Nov. 22. |

L 10, 35 — thou spendest more, when I come again I will repay thee.

— 36 — Which now of these three, thinkest thou, was neighbour unto him that fell among the

— 37 — thieves? And he said, He that showed mercy on him. Then said Jesus unto him, Go, and do thou likewise.

— 38 — Now it came to pass, as they went, that he entered into a certain village; and a certain woman named Martha received him into her

— 39 — house. And she had a sister called Mary, which also sat at Jesus' feet, and heard his

— 40 — word. But Martha was cumbered about much serving, and came to him, and said, Lord, dost thou not care that my sister hath left me to serve

— 41 — alone? bid her therefore that she help me. And Jesus answered and said unto her, Martha, Martha, thou art careful and troubled about

— 42 — many things; but one thing is needful; and Mary hath chosen that good part, which shall not be taken away from her.

L 11, 1 — And it came to pass, that, as he was praying in a certain place, when he ceased, one of his disciples said unto him, Lord, teach us to pray,

— 2 — as John also taught his disciples. And he said

M 6, 9 — unto them, After this manner pray ye;—Our Father who art in heaven, hallowed be thy

— 10 — name. Thy kingdom come. Thy will be

| Feb. 22. May 24. | in one Continuous Narrative. | Aug. 23. Nov. 22. |

done on earth as it is in heaven. Give us this day our daily bread. And forgive us our debts; for we also forgive every one that is indebted to us. And lead us not into temptation; but deliver us from evil. For thine are the kingdom, and the power, and the glory, for ever. Amen.

And when ye stand praying, forgive, if ye have aught against any; that your Father also which is in heaven may forgive you your trespasses. For if ye forgive men their trespasses, your heavenly Father will also forgive you; but if ye do not forgive, neither will your Father which is in heaven forgive your trespasses.

And he said unto them, Which of you shall have a friend, and shall go unto him at midnight, and say unto him, Friend, lend me three loaves; for a friend of mine in his journey is come to me, and I have nothing to set before him; and he from within shall answer and say, Trouble me not: the door is now shut, and my children are with me in bed; I cannot rise and give thee? I say unto you, Though he will not rise and give him because he is his friend, yet because of his importunity he will rise and give him as many as he needeth. And I say unto you, Ask, and it shall be given you; seek, and ye shall find; knock, and it shall be

M 6, 11
— 12
L 11, 4
M 6, 12
— 13

K 11, 25

M 6, 14
K 11, 26

L 11, 5

— 6

— 7

— 8

— 9

Feb. 23. May 25.	The Four Gospels arranged	Aug. 24. Nov. 23.

L 11, 10 opened unto you. For, every one that asketh receiveth; and he that seeketh findeth; and to
— 11 him that knocketh it shall be opened. If a son shall ask bread of any of you that is a father, will he give him a stone? or if he ask a
— 12 fish, will he for a fish give him a serpent? Or if he shall ask an egg, will he offer him a scor-
— 13 pion? If ye then, being evil, know how to give good gifts unto your children, how much more shall your heavenly Father give the Holy Spirit to them that ask him!

LIV.

FEB. 23. MAY 25. AUG. 24. NOV. 23.

Christ gives sight to a blind man. Worldly trouble not the necessary consequence of sin.

J 9, 1 AND as Jesus passed by, he saw a man
— 2 which was blind from his birth. And his disciples asked him, saying, Master, who did sin, this man, or his parents, that he was
— 3 born blind? Jesus answered, Neither because this man sinned, nor his parents; but that the works of God should be made manifest in him.
— 4 I must work the works of him that sent me, while it is day; the night cometh, when no
— 5 man can work. As long as I am in the world,
— 6 I am the light of the world. When he had

| Feb. 23. May 25. | in one Continuous Narrative. | Aug. 24. Nov. 23. |

thus spoken, he spat on the ground, and made clay of the spittle, and he anointed the eyes of the blind man with the clay, and said unto him, Go, wash in the pool of Siloam, (which is by interpretation, Sent.) He went his way therefore, and washed, and came seeing. The neighbours therefore, and they which before had seen him that he was blind, said, Is not this he that sat and begged? Some said, This is he; others said, He is like him; but he said, I am he. Therefore said they unto him, How were thine eyes opened? He answered and said, A man that is called Jesus made clay, and anointed mine eyes, and said unto me, Go to the pool of Siloam, and wash; and I went and washed, and I received sight. Then said they unto him, Where is he? He said, I know not. They brought to the Pharisees him that aforetime was blind. And it was the sabbath day when Jesus made the clay, and opened his eyes. Then again the Pharisees also asked him how he had received his sight. He said unto them, He put clay upon mine eyes, and I washed, and do see.

Therefore said some of the Pharisees, This man is not of God, because he keepeth not the sabbath day. Others said, How can a man that is a sinner do such miracles? And there

J 9, 6
— 7
— 8
— 9
— 10
— 11
— 12
— 13
— 14
— 15
— 16

| Feb. 23. May 25. | The Four Gospels arranged | Aug. 24. Nov. 23. |

J 9,17 was a division among them. They said unto the blind man again, What sayest thou of him, that he hath opened thine eyes? He said, He
— 18 is a prophet. But the Jews did not believe concerning him, that he had been blind, and received his sight, until they had called the parents of him that had received his sight.
— 19 And they asked them, saying, Is this your son, who ye say was born blind? how then
— 20 doth he now see? His parents answered them and said, We know that this is our son, and
— 21 that he was born blind; but by what means he now seeth, we know not; or who hath opened his eyes, we know not; he is of age, ask him;
— 22 he shall speak for himself. These words spake his parents, because they feared the Jews; for the Jews had agreed already, that if any man did confess that he was Christ, he should be
— 23 put out of the synagogue. Therefore said his parents, He is of age, ask him.
— 24 Then again called they the man that had been blind, and said unto him, Give God the praise; we know that this man is a sinner.
— 25 He answered and said, Whether he is a sinner or not, I know not; one thing I know,
— 26 that, whereas I was blind, now I see. Then said they to him again, What did he to
— 27 thee; how opened he thine eyes? He an-

| Feb 23. May 25. | in one Continuous Narrative. | Aug. 24. Nov. 23. |

swered them, I have told you already, and   J 9, 27
ye did not hear; wherefore would ye hear
it again? will ye also be his disciples? Then   — 28
they reviled him, and said, Thou art his disciple; but we are Moses' disciples. We know   — 29
that God spake unto Moses;* as for this fellow,
we know not whence he is. The man answered   — 30
and said unto them, Why herein is a marvellous
thing, that ye know not whence he is, and yet
he hath opened mine eyes. Now we know   — 31
that God heareth not sinners; but if any man
is a worshipper of God, and doeth his will,
him he heareth. Since the world began was   — 32
it not heard that any man opened the eyes of
one that was born blind. If this man were not   — 33
of God, he could do nothing.

They answered and said unto him, Thou   — 34
wast altogether born in sins, and dost thou
teach us! And they cast him out.

Jesus heard that they had cast him out; and   — 35
when he had found him, he said unto him,
Dost thou believe on the Son of God? He   — 36
answered and said, Who is he, Lord, that I
might believe on him? And Jesus said unto   — 37
him, Thou hast both seen him, and it is he
that talketh with thee. And he said, Lord, I   — 38
believe. And he worshipped him.

         * Ex. iii, 4, 15.

J 9, 39	And Jesus said, For judgment I am come into this world, that they which see not might see; and that they which see might be made
— 40	blind. And some of the Pharisees which were with him heard these words, and said unto
— 41	him, Are we blind also? Jesus said unto them, If ye were blind, ye would have no sin; but now ye say, We see; therefore your sin remaineth.

LV.

Feb. 24.   May 26.   Aug. 25.   Nov. 24.

Christ the good shepherd. Christ affirms his oneness with the Father.

J 10, 1	VERILY, verily, I say unto you, said Jesus, he that entereth not by the door into the sheepfold, but climbeth up some other way,
— 2	the same is a thief and a robber. But he that entereth in by the door is the shepherd of the
— 3	sheep. To him the porter openeth; and the sheep hear his voice; and he calleth his own
— 4	sheep by name, and leadeth them out. And when he putteth forth his own sheep, he goeth before them, and the sheep follow him; for they
— 5	know his voice. And a stranger will they not follow, but will flee from him; for they know
— 6	not the voice of strangers. This parable spake Jesus unto them; but they understood not what

| Feb. 24. May 26. | in one Continuous Narrative. | Aug. 25. Nov. 24. |

things they were which he spake unto them. Then said Jesus unto them again, Verily, verily, I say unto you, I am the door of the sheep. All that ever came before me were thieves and robbers; but the sheep did not hear them. I am the door; by me if any man enter in, he shall be saved, and shall go in and out, and find pasture. The thief cometh not, but to steal, to kill, and to destroy; I am come that they might have life, and that they might have it more abundantly. I am the good shepherd; the good shepherd giveth his life for the sheep. But he that is a hireling, and not the shepherd, whose own the sheep are not, seeth the wolf coming, and leaveth the sheep, and fleeth; and the wolf catcheth them, and scattereth the sheep. The hireling fleeth, because he is a hireling, and careth not for the sheep. I am the good shepherd, and know my sheep, and am known of mine. As the Father knoweth me, even so know I the Father; and I lay down my life for the sheep. And other sheep I have, which are not of this fold;* them also I must bring, and they shall hear my voice; and there shall be one fold, and one shepherd. Therefore doth my Father love me, because I lay down my life, that I might take it again.

J 10, 6
— 7
— 8
— 9
— 10
— 11
— 12
— 13
— 14
— 15
— 16
— 17

* Isa. xlix, 6.

| Feb. 24. May 26. | The Four Gospels arranged | Aug. 25. Nov. 24. |

J 10, 18	No man taketh it from me, but I lay it down of myself. I have power to lay it down, and I have power to take it again. This commandment have I received of my Father.
— 19	There was a division therefore again among
— 20	the Jews for these sayings. And many of them said, He hath a devil, and is mad; why
— 21	hear ye him? Others said, These are not the words of him that hath a devil. Can a devil open the eyes of the blind?
— 22	And it was at Jerusalem, the feast of the
— 23	dedication, and it was winter. And Jesus walked in the temple in Solomon's porch.
— 24	Then came the Jews round about him, and said unto him, How long dost thou make us to doubt? If thou art the Christ, tell us
— 25	plainly. Jesus answered them, I told you, and ye believed not: the works that I do in my Father's name, they bear witness of me.
— 26	But ye believe not, because ye are not of my
— 27	sheep, as I said unto you. My sheep hear my voice, and I know them, and they follow me;
— 28	and I give unto them eternal life; and they shall never perish, neither shall any man pluck
— 29	them out of my hand. My Father, which gave them me, is greater than all; and no man is
— 30	able to pluck them out of my Father's hand. I and my Father are one.

Then the Jews took up stones again to stone him. Jesus answered them, Many good works have I showed you from my Father; for which of those works do ye stone me? The Jews answered him, saying, For a good work we stone thee not; but for blasphemy; and because that thou, being a man, makest thyself God. Jesus answered them, Is it not written in your law,* I said, Ye are gods? If he called them gods, unto whom the word of God came, and the scripture cannot be broken; say ye of him, whom the Father hath sanctified, and sent into the world, Thou blasphemest; because I said, I am the Son of God? If I do not the works of my Father, believe me not. But if I do, though ye believe not me, believe the works; that ye may know, and believe, that the Father is in me, and I in him.

Therefore they sought again to take him; but he escaped out of their hand, and went away again beyond Jordan into the place where John at first baptized; and there he abode. And many resorted unto him, and said, John did no miracle; but all things that John spake of this man were true. And many believed on him there.

* Psa. lxxxii, 6.

LVI.

FEB. 25. MAY 27. AUG. 26. NOV. 25.
Christ raises Lazarus from the dead.

J 11, 1	NOW a certain man was sick, named Lazarus, of Bethany, the town of Mary
— 2	and her sister Martha. (It was that Mary which anointed the Lord with ointment, and wiped his feet with her hair, whose brother Lazarus was
— 3	sick.) Therefore his sisters sent unto him, saying, Lord, behold, he whom thou lovest is sick.
— 4	When Jesus heard that, he said, This sickness is not unto death, but for the glory of God, that the Son of God might be glorified thereby.
— 5	Now Jesus loved Martha, and her sister,
— 6	and Lazarus. When he had heard therefore that he was sick, he abode two days still in the
— 7	same place where he was. Then after that said he to his disciples, Let us go into Judæa
— 8	again. His disciples said unto him, Master, the Jews of late sought to stone thee; and
— 9	goest thou thither again? Jesus answered, Are there not twelve hours in the day? If any man walk in the day, he stumbleth not,
— 10	because he seeth the light of this world. But if a man walk in the night, he stumbleth,
— 11	because there is no light in him. These things said he; and after that he said unto them, Our

| Feb. 25. May 27. | in one Continuous Narrative. | Aug. 26. Nov. 25. |

friend Lazarus sleepeth; but I go, that I may		J 11, 11
awake him out of sleep. Then said his disci-		— 12
ples, Lord, if he sleepeth, he will do well.		
Howbeit Jesus spake of his death: but they		— 13
thought that he had spoken of taking rest in		
sleep. Then said Jesus unto them plainly,		— 14
Lazarus is dead. And I am glad for your		— 15
sakes that I was not there, to the intent ye may		
believe; nevertheless let us go unto him. Then		— 16
said Thomas, which is called Didymus, unto his		
fellow-disciples, Let us also go, that we may die		
with him. Then when Jesus came, he found that		— 17
he had lain in the grave four days already.		
Now Bethany was nigh unto Jerusalem,		— 18
about fifteen furlongs off; and many of the		— 19
Jews came to Martha and Mary, to comfort		
them concerning their brother. Then Martha,		— 20
as soon as she heard that Jesus was coming,		
went and met him; but Mary sat still in the		
house. Then said Martha unto Jesus, Lord,		— 21
if thou hadst been here, my brother had not		
died. But I know, that even now, whatso-		— 22
ever thou wilt ask of God, God will give it		
thee. Jesus said unto her, Thy brother shall		— 23
rise again. Martha said unto him, I know		— 24
that he shall rise again in the resurrection at		
the last day. Jesus said unto her, I am the		— 25
resurrection, and the life; he that believeth in		

| Feb. 25. | The Four Gospels arranged | Aug. 6. |
| May 27. | | Nov. 25. |

J 11, 25 me, though he were dead, yet shall he live;
— 26 and whosoever liveth and believeth in me shall
— 27 never die. Believest thou this? She said
unto him, Yea, Lord; I believe that thou art
the Christ, the Son of God, which should come
— 28 into the world.* And when she had so said,
she went her way, and called Mary her sister
secretly, saying, The Master is come, and
— 29 calleth for thee. As soon as she heard that,
she arose quickly, and came unto him.
— 30 Now Jesus was not yet come into the town,
but was in that place where Martha met him.
— 31 The Jews then which were with her in the
house, and comforted her, when they saw
Mary, that she rose up hastily and went out,
followed her, saying, She goeth unto the grave
— 32 to weep there. Then when Mary was come
where Jesus was, and saw him, she fell down
at his feet, saying unto him, Lord, if thou
hadst been here, my brother had not died.
— 33 When Jesus therefore saw her weeping, and
the Jews also weeping which came with her,
he groaned in the spirit, and was troubled,
— 34 and said, Where have ye laid him? They
— 35 said unto him, Lord, come and see. Jesus
— 36 wept. Then said the Jews, Behold how he
— 37 loved him! And some of them said, Could

* Mal. iii, 1.

| Feb. 25. May 27. | in one Continuous Narrative. | Aug. 26. Nov. 25. |

not this man, which opened the eyes of the blind, have caused that even this man should not have died? Jesus therefore again groaning in himself came to the grave. It was a cave, and a stone lay upon it. Jesus said, Take ye away the stone. Martha, the sister of him that was dead, said unto him, Lord, by this time he stinketh; for he hath been dead four days. Jesus said unto her, Said I not unto thee, that if thou wouldest believe, thou shouldest see the glory of God? Then they took away the stone from the place where the dead was laid. And Jesus lifted up his eyes, and said, Father, I thank thee that thou hast heard me. And I knew that thou hearest me always; but because of the people which stand by I said it, that they may believe that thou hast sent me. And when he had thus spoken, he cried with a loud voice, Lazarus, come forth! And he that was dead came forth, bound hand and foot with graveclothes; and his face was bound about with a napkin. Jesus said unto them, Loose him, and let him go.

Then many of the Jews which came to Mary, and had seen the things which Jesus did, believed on him. But some of them went their ways to the Pharisees, and told them what things Jesus had done.

J 11, 37
— 38
— 39
— 40
— 41
— 42
— 43
— 44
— 45
— 46

Feb. 26.
May 28.

The Four Gospels arranged

Aug. 27.
Nov. 26.

LVII.

FEB. 26. MAY 28. AUG. 27. NOV. 26.

Caiaphas prophesies that Christ should die for the people. Christ heals a woman who had been bowed together eighteen years. Salvation is something to be striven for. The Pharisees caution Christ against Herod.

J 11, 47 — THEN gathered the chief priests and the Pharisees a council, and said, What do
— 48 we? for this man doeth many miracles. If we let him thus alone, all men will believe on him;
and the Romans will come and take away both
— 49 our place and nation. And one of them, named Caiaphas, being the high priest that same year, said unto them, Ye know nothing
— 50 at all, nor consider that it is expedient for us, that one man should die for the people, that
— 51 the whole nation perish not. And this spake he not of himself; but being high priest that year, he prophesied that Jesus should die for
— 52 that nation; and not for that nation only, but that also he should gather together in one the children of God that were scattered abroad.
— 53 Then from that day forth they took counsel
— 54 together to put him to death. Jesus therefore walked no more openly among the Jews; but went thence unto a country near to the wilder-

| Feb. 26. May 28. | in one Continuous Narrative. | Aug. 27. Nov. 26. |

ness, into a city called Ephraim, and there continued with his disciples.   J 11, 54

And he was teaching in one of the synagogues on the sabbath. And, behold, there was a woman which had had a spirit of infirmity eighteen years, and was bowed together, and could in no wise lift up herself. And when Jesus saw her, he called her to him, and said unto her, Woman, thou art loosed from thine infirmity. And he laid his hands on her; and immediately she was made straight, and glorified God.

And the ruler of the synagogue answered with indignation, because that Jesus had healed on the sabbath day, and he said unto the people, There are six days in which men ought to work ; in them therefore come and be healed, and not on the sabbath day. The Lord then answered him, and said, Thou hypocrite, doth not each one of you on the sabbath loose his ox or his ass from the stall, and lead him away to watering? And ought not this woman, whom Satan hath bound, lo, these eighteen years, being a daughter of Abraham, to be loosed from this bond on the sabbath day? And when he had said these things, all his adversaries were ashamed ; and all the people rejoiced for all the glorious things that were done by him.

L 13, 10
— 11
— 12
— 13
— 14
— 15
— 16
— 17

| Feb. 26. | | Aug. 27. |
| May 28. | The Four Gospels arranged | Nov. 26. |

L 13, 22	And he went through the cities and villages, teaching, and journeying toward Jerusalem.
— 23	Then said one unto him, Lord, are there few
— 24	that be saved? And he said unto them, Strive
M 7, 13	to enter in at the strait gate; for wide is the gate, and broad is the way, that leadeth to destruction, and many there are which go in
— 14	thereat; because strait is the gate, and narrow is the way, which leadeth unto life, and few
L 13, 24	there are that find it; for many, I say unto you, will seek to enter in, and shall not be
— 25	able.* When once the master of the house is risen up, and hath shut to the door, and ye begin to stand without, and to knock at the door, saying, Lord, Lord, open unto us; and he shall answer and say unto you, I know you
— 26	not whence ye are; then shall ye begin to say, We have eaten and drunk in thy presence, and
M 7, 22	thou hast taught in our streets. Lord, Lord, have we not prophesied in thy name? and in thy name have cast out devils? and in thy name
L 13, 27	done many wonderful works? But he shall say, I tell you, I know you not whence ye are; depart from me, all ye workers of iniquity.
— 28	There shall be weeping and gnashing of teeth, when ye shall see Abraham, and Isaac, and Jacob, and all the prophets, in the kingdom

* Jer. xxix, 13.

| Feb. 27. May 29. | in one Continuous Narrative. | Aug. 28. Nov. 27. |

of God, and you yourselves thrust out. And they shall come from the east, and from the west, and from the north, and from the south, and shall sit down in the kingdom of God; but the children of the kingdom shall be cast out into outer darkness. And, behold, there are last which shall be first, and there are first which shall be last.   L 13, 29   M 8, 12   L 13, 30

The same day there came certain of the Pharisees, saying unto him, Get thee out, and depart hence; for Herod will kill thee. And he said unto them, Go ye, and tell that fox, Behold, I cast out devils, and I do cures to-day and to-morrow, and the third day I shall be perfected. Nevertheless I must walk to-day, and to-morrow, and the day following; for it cannot be that a prophet perish out of Jerusalem.   — 31   — 32   — 33

LVIII.

Feb. 27. May 29. Aug. 28. Nov. 27.

Christ heals on the sabbath day, and discourses on humility and beneficence. Christ likens the kingdom of heaven to a wedding feast, from attendance at which the invited guests beg to be excused.

AND it came to pass, as Jesus went into the house of one of the chief Pharisees to eat bread on the sabbath day, that they watched him. And, behold, there was a certain man   L 14, 1   — 2

L 14, 3	before him which had the dropsy. And Jesus answering spake unto the lawyers and Pharisees, saying, Is it lawful to heal on the sabbath
— 4	day? And they held their peace. And he took him, and healed him, and let him go;
— 5	and answered them, saying, Which of you shall have an ass or an ox fallen into a pit, and will not straightway pull him out on the
— 6	sabbath day? And they could not answer him again to those things.
— 7	And he put forth a parable to those which were bidden, when he marked how they chose
— 8	out the chief places; saying unto them, When thou art bidden of any man to a wedding, sit not down in the highest place; lest a more honourable man than thou be bidden of him;
— 9	and he that bade thee and him come and say to thee, Give this man place; and thou begin
— 10	with shame to take the lowest place. But when thou art bidden, go and sit down in the lowest place; that when he that bade thee cometh, he may say unto thee, Friend, go up higher; then shalt thou have worship in the presence of them
— 11	that sit at meat with thee. For whosoever exalteth himself shall be abased; and he that humbleth himself shall be exalted.
— 12	Then said he also to him that bade him, When thou makest a dinner or a supper, call

| Feb. 27. May 29. | in one Continuous Narrative. | Aug. 28. Nov. 27. |

not thy friends, nor thy brethren, neither thy kinsmen, nor thy rich neighbours; lest they also bid thee again, and a recompense be made thee. But when thou makest a feast, call the poor, the maimed, the lame, the blind; and thou shalt be blessed; for they cannot recompense thee; but thou shalt be recompensed at the resurrection of the just. And when one of them that sat at meat with him heard these things, he said unto him, Blessed is he that shall eat bread in the kingdom of God.   L 14, 12 — 13 — 14 — 15

And Jesus answered and spake unto them again by parables, and said, The kingdom of heaven is like unto a certain king, which made a marriage for his son, and made a great supper and bade many; and sent forth his servants at supper time to call them that were bidden to the wedding; and they would not come. Again, he sent forth other servants, saying, Tell them which are bidden, Behold, I have prepared my dinner: my oxen and my fatlings are killed, and all things are ready; come unto the marriage. But they all with one consent began to make excuse. The first said unto him, I have bought a piece of ground, and I must needs go and see it; I pray thee have me excused. And another said, I have bought five yoke of oxen, and I go to prove them; I pray thee have me   M 22, 1 — 2 L 14, 16 M 22, 3 L 14, 17 M 22, 3 — 4 L 14, 18 — 19

| | Feb. 27. | The Four Gospels arranged | Aug. 28. |
| May 29. | | Nov. 27. |

L 14, 20
M 22, 5

L 14, 21

M 22, 8
L 14, 21

M 22, 9
L 14, 21
— 22

—

— 24

M 22, 10

— 11

— 12

— 13

excused. And another said, I have married a wife, and therefore I cannot come. So they made light of it, and went their ways, one to his farm, another to his merchandise. And the servants came and told their lord those things. Then the master of the house being angry said to his servants, The wedding is ready, but they which were bidden were not worthy. Go ye therefore into the streets and lanes of the city, and bid to the marriage as many as ye shall find, the poor, and the maimed, and the halt, and the blind. And the servant said, Lord, it is done as thou hast commanded, and yet there is room. And the lord said unto the servants, Go out into the highways and hedges, and compel them to come in, that my house may be filled; for I say unto you, That none of those men which were bidden shall taste of my supper. So those servants went out into the highways, and gathered together all as many as they found, both bad and good; and the wedding was furnished with guests. And when the king came in to see the guests, he saw there a man which had not on a wedding garment; and he said unto him, Friend, how camest thou in hither, not having a wedding garment? And he was speechless. Then said the king to the servants, Bind him hand and foot, and take him away, and cast him into outer darkness; there shall be weeping and gnashing of teeth. And the remnant of those who were bidden took the king's servants and treated them spitefully, and slew them. But when the king heard thereof, he was wrath; and he sent forth his armies, and destroyed those murderers, and burned up their city.

M 22, 13
— 6
— 7

LIX.

Feb. 28. May 30. Aug. 29. Nov. 28.

The parables of the lost sheep, the lost piece of silver, and the prodigal son.

THEN drew near unto Jesus all the publicans and sinners to hear him. And the Pharisees and scribes murmured, saying, This man receiveth sinners, and eateth with them. And Jesus answered, The Son of man is come to seek and to save that which was lost.

L 15, 1
— 2

L 19, 10

And he spake this parable unto them, saying, What man of you, having a hundred sheep, if he loseth one of them, doth not leave the ninety and nine in the wilderness, and go into the mountains and seek that which is gone astray, until he findeth it? And when

L 15, 3
— 4

M 18, 12
L 15, 5

| Feb. 28. | | Aug. 29. |
| May 30. | **The Four Gospels arranged** | Nov. 28. |

L 15, 5 — he hath found it, he layeth it on his shoulders,
— 6 rejoicing. And when he cometh home, he calleth together his friends and neighbours, saying unto them, Rejoice with me; for I
M 18, 13 have found my sheep which was lost. Verily, I say unto you, he rejoiceth more over that sheep, than over the ninety and nine which went not
— 14 astray. Even so it is not the will of your Father which is in heaven, that one of these
L15, 7 little ones should perish; and I say unto you, that likewise joy shall be in heaven over one sinner that repenteth, more than over ninety and nine just persons, which need no repentance.

— 8 Either what woman having ten pieces of silver, if she loseth one piece, doth not light a candle, and sweep the house, and seek dili-
— 9 gently till she findeth it? And when she hath found it, she calleth her friends and her neighbours together, saying, Rejoice with me; for I
— 10 have found the piece which I had lost. Likewise, I say unto you, there is joy in the presence of the angels of God over one sinner that repenteth.

— 11 And he said, A certain man had two sons;
— 12 and the younger of them said to his father, Father, give me the portion of goods that falleth to me. And he divided unto them his

| Feb. 28. May 30. | in one Continuous Narrative. | Aug. 29. Nov. 28. |

living. And not many days after, the younger son gathered all together, and took his journey into a far country, and there wasted his substance with riotous living. And when he had spent all, there arose a mighty famine in that land; and he began to be in want. And he went and joined himself to a citizen of that country; and he sent him into his fields to feed swine. And he would fain have filled his belly with the husks that the swine did eat; and no man gave unto him. And when he came to himself, he said, How many hired servants of my father's have bread enough and to spare, and I perish with hunger! I will arise and go to my father, and will say unto him, Father, I have sinned against heaven and before thee, and am no more worthy to be called thy son; make me as one of thy hired servants. And he arose, and came to his father. But when he was yet a great way off, his father saw him, and had compassion, and ran, and fell on his neck, and kissed him. And the son said unto him, Father, I have sinned against heaven and in thy sight, and am no more worthy to be called thy son. But the father said to his servants, Bring forth the best robe, and put it on him; and put a ring on his hand, and	L 15, 13 — 14 — 15 — 16 — 17 — 18 — 19 — 20 — 21 — 22

| Feb. 28. May 30. | The Four Gospels arranged | Aug. 29. Nov. 28. |

L 15, 23	shoes on his feet; and bring hither the fatted calf, and kill it; and let us eat, and be merry;
— 24	for this my son was dead, and is alive again; he was lost, and is found. And they began to be merry.
— 25	Now his elder son was in the field; and as he came and drew nigh to the house, he heard
— 26	music and dancing. And he called one of the servants, and asked what these things meant.
— 27	And he said unto him, Thy brother is come; and thy father hath killed the fatted calf, because he hath received him safe and sound.
— 28	And he was angry, and would not go in; therefore came his father out, and intreated
— 29	him. And he answering said to his father, Lo, these many years do I serve thee, neither transgressed I at any time thy commandment; and yet thou never gavest me a kid, that I
— 30	might make merry with my friends; but as soon as this thy son was come, which hath devoured thy living with harlots, thou hast
— 31	killed for him the fatted calf. And he said unto him, Son, thou art ever with me, and all
— 32	that I have is thine. It was meet that we should make merry, and be glad; for this thy brother was dead, and is alive again and was lost, and is found.

LX.

For Feb. 29, Leap year, see Section XCIII. at the end of the book.

MAR. 1. MAY 31. AUG. 30. NOV. 29.

The parables of the unjust steward, and of the rich man and Lazarus.

AND Jesus said also unto his disciples, There was a certain rich man, which had a steward; and the same was accused unto him that he had wasted his goods. And he called him, and said unto him, How is it that I hear this of thee? give an account of thy stewardship; for thou mayest be no longer steward. Then the steward said within himself, What shall I do? for my lord taketh away from me the stewardship: I cannot dig; to beg I am ashamed. I am resolved what to do, that, when I am put out of the stewardship, they may receive me into their houses. So he called every one of his lord's debtors unto him, and said unto the first, How much owest thou unto my lord? And he said, A hundred measures of oil. And he said unto him, Take thy bill, and sit down quickly, and write fifty. Then said he to another, And how much owest thou? And he said, A hundred measures of wheat. And he said unto him, Take thy bill,

L 16, 1

— 2

— 3

— 4

— 5

— 6

— 7

| | Mar. 1.
May 31. | The Four Gospels arranged | Aug. 30.
Nov. 29. |

L 16, 8	and write fourscore. And his lord commended the unjust steward, because he had done wisely: for the children of this world are in their gene-
— 9	ration wiser than the children of light. And I say unto you, Make to yourselves friends of the mammon of unrighteousness; that, when ye fail, they may receive you into everlasting habi-
— 10	tations. He that is faithful in that which is least is faithful also in much; and he that is
— 11	unjust in the least is unjust also in much. If therefore ye have not been faithful in the un- righteous mammon, who will commit to your
— 12	trust the true riches? And if ye have not been faithful in that which is another man's, who
— 13	shall give you that which is your own? No servant can serve two masters; for either he will hate the one, and love the other; or else he will hold to the one, and despise the other.
L 11, 23	Ye cannot serve God and mammon. He that is not with me is against me; and he that gathereth not with me scattereth.
L 16, 14	And the Pharisees also, who were covetous, heard all these things; and they derided him.
— 15	And he said unto them, Ye are they which justify yourselves before men; but God knoweth your hearts; for that which is highly esteemed among men is abomination in the sight of God.

| Mar. 1. May 31. | in one Continuous Narrative. | Aug. 30. Nov. 29. |

There was a certain rich man, which was clothed in purple and fine linen, and fared sumptuously every day: and there was a certain beggar named Lazarus, which was laid at his gate, full of sores, and desiring to be fed with the crumbs which fell from the rich man's table; moreover the dogs came and licked his sores. And it came to pass, that the beggar died, and was carried by the angels into Abraham's bosom: the rich man also died, and was buried; and in hell he lifted up his eyes, being in torments, and saw Abraham afar off, and Lazarus in his bosom. And he cried and said, Father Abraham, have mercy on me, and send Lazarus, that he may dip the tip of his finger in water, and cool my tongue; for I am tormented in this flame. But Abraham said, Son, remember that thou in thy lifetime receivedst thy good things, and likewise Lazarus evil things; but now he is comforted, and thou art tormented. And beside all this, between us and you there is a great gulf fixed; so that they which would pass hence to you cannot; neither can they pass to us, that would come thence. Then he said, I pray thee therefore, father, that thou wouldest send him to my father's house; for I have five brethren; that he may testify unto them, lest they also come	L 16, 19 — 20 — 21 — 22 — 23 — 24 — 25 — 26 — 27 — 28

| Mar. 2. | 𝔗𝔥𝔢 𝔉𝔬𝔲𝔯 𝔊𝔬𝔰𝔭𝔢𝔩𝔰 arranged | Aug. 31. |
| June 1. | | Nov. 30. |

L 16, 29 — into this place of torment. Abraham said unto him, They have Moses and the prophets;* let
— 30 — them hear them. And he said, Nay, father Abraham; but if one went unto them from the
— 31 — dead, they would repent. And he said unto him, If they hear not Moses and the prophets, neither would they be persuaded, though one rose from the dead.

LXI.

MAR. 2. JUNE 1. AUG. 31. NOV. 30.

On perseverance in prayer. The self-righteous condemned. On divorce and marriage; and on a child-like spirit.

L 18, 1 — AND Jesus spake a parable unto them to this end, that men ought always to pray,
— 2 — and not to faint; saying, There was in a city a judge, which feared not God, neither regarded
— 3 — man: and there was a widow in that city; and she came unto him, saying, Avenge me of
— 4 — mine adversary. And he would not for a while; but afterward he said within himself,
— 5 — Though I fear not God, nor regard man; yet because this widow troubleth me, I will avenge her, lest by her continual coming she weary
— 6 — me. And the Lord said, Hear what the un-
— 7 — just judge saith. And shall not God avenge

* *i.e.* the books of the Old Testament.

| Mar. 2. June 1. | in one Continuous Narrative. | Aug. 31. Nov. 30. |

his own elect, which cry day and night unto him, though he bear long with them? I tell you that he will avenge them speedily. Nevertheless when the Son of man cometh, will he find faith on the earth?

And he spake this parable unto certain which trusted in themselves that they were righteous, and despised others: Two men went up into the temple to pray; the one a Pharisee, and the other a publican. The Pharisee stood and prayed thus with himself: God, I thank thee, that I am not as other men are, extortioners, unjust, adulterers, or even as this publican. I fast twice in the week, I give tithes of all that I possess. And the publican, standing afar off, would not lift up so much as his eyes unto heaven, but smote upon his breast, saying, God be merciful to me a sinner. I tell you, this man went down to his house justified rather than the other; for every one that exalteth himself shall be abased; and he that humbleth himself shall be exalted.

The Pharisees also came unto him, tempting him, and saying unto him, Is it lawful for a man to put away his wife for every cause? And he answered and said unto them, Have ye not read,* that he which made them at the

* Gen. i, 27.

L 18, 7
— 8

— 9
— 10
— 11
— 12
— 13
— 14

M 19, 3
— 4

| Mar. 2. June 1. | The Four Gospels arranged | Aug. 31. Nov. 30. |

M 19, 5	beginning made them male and female, and said,* For this cause shall a man leave father and mother, and shall cleave to his wife; and
— 6	they twain shall be one flesh? Wherefore they are no more twain, but one flesh. What therefore God hath joined together, let no man put
— 7	asunder. They said unto him, Why did Moses then command to give a writing of divorce-
— 8	ment, and to put her away?† He said unto them, Moses, because of the hardness of your
K 10, 5	hearts, wrote you this precept and suffered you
M 19, 8	to put away your wives; but from the begin-
— 9	ning it was not so. And I say unto you, Whosoever shall put away his wife, except it be for fornication, and shall marry another, com-
M 5, 32	mitteth adultery, and causeth her to commit adultery; and whosoever shall marry her that
K 10, 12	is divorced committeth adultery. And if a woman shall put away her husband, and be married to another, she committeth adultery.
— 10	And in the house his disciples asked him again of the same matter, saying unto him,
M 19, 10	If the case of the man is so with his wife,
— 11	it is not good to marry. But he said unto them, All men cannot receive this saying, save
— 12	they to whom it is given. For there are some eunuchs, which were so born from their

* Gen. ii, 24. † Deut. xxiv, 1.

mother's womb; and there are some eunuchs, which were made eunuchs of men; and there are eunuchs, which have made themselves eunuchs for the kingdom of heaven's sake. He that is able to receive it, let him receive it.

And they brought young children to him, that he should put his hands on them and pray; and the disciples rebuked those that brought them. But when Jesus saw it, he was much displeased, and called them unto him, and said, Suffer little children to come unto me, and forbid them not; for of such is the kingdom of God. Verily, I say unto you, whosoever shall not receive the kingdom of God as a little child, he shall in no wise enter therein. And he took them up in his arms, put his hands upon them, and blessed them, and departed thence.

LXII.

MAR. 3. JUNE 2. SEP. 1. DEC. 1.

The danger of riches. The parable of the labourers in the vineyard. Works of supererogation impossible.

AND when Jesus was gone forth into the way, there came a certain ruler running, and kneeled to him, and asked him, Good Master, what good thing shall I do to inherit

| | Mar. 3.
June 2. | The Four Gospels arranged | Sep. 1.
Dec. 1. |

K 10, 18	eternal life? And Jesus said unto him, Why callest thou me good? There is none good
M 19, 17	but one, that is, God: but if thou wilt enter
— 18	into life, keep the commandments. He said unto him, Which? Jesus said, Thou shalt do no murder, Thou shalt not commit adultery, Thou shalt not steal, Thou shalt not bear false
K 10, 19 M 19, 19	witness, Defraud not, Honour thy father and thy mother, and, Thou shalt love thy neighbour
— 20 K 10, 20	as thyself. The young man answered and said unto him, Master, all these have I observed
M 19, 20	from my youth up: what lack I yet? Then
K 10, 21	Jesus beholding him loved him, and said unto
M 19, 21	him, One thing thou lackest: if thou wilt be
K 10, 21	perfect, go thy way, sell whatsoever thou hast, and give to the poor, and thou shalt have treasure in heaven; and come, take up the
— 22	cross, and follow me. And he was sad at that saying, and went away grieved; for he had
L 18, 24	great possessions. And when Jesus saw that
K 10, 23	he was very sorrowful, he looked round about, and said unto his disciples, How hardly shall they that have riches enter into the kingdom of
— 24	God! And the disciples were astonished at his words. But Jesus answered again, and said unto them, Children, how hard is it for them that trust in riches to enter into the king-
— 25	dom of God! It is easier for a camel to go

| Mar. 3. June 2. | in one Continuous Narrative. | Sep. 1. Dec. 1. |

through the eye of a needle,* than for a rich man to enter into the kingdom of God. And they were astonished out of measure, saying among themselves, Who then can be saved? And Jesus looking upon them said, With men it is impossible, but not with God; for with God all things are possible.

K 10, 25
— 26
— 27

The kingdom of heaven is like unto a man that is a householder, which went out early in the morning to hire labourers into his vineyard. And when he had agreed with the labourers for a penny a day, he sent them into his vineyard. And he went out about the third hour, and saw others standing idle in the marketplace, and said unto them; Go ye also into the vineyard, and whatsoever is right I will give you. And they went their way. Again he went out about the sixth and the ninth hour, and did likewise. And about the eleventh hour he went out, and found others standing idle, and said unto them, Why stand ye here all the day idle? They said unto him, Because no man hath hired us. He said unto them, Go ye also into the vineyard; and whatsoever is right, that shall ye receive.

M 20, 1
— 2
— 3
— 4
— 5
— 6
— 7

So when even was come, the lord of the vine-

— 8

* *i.e.* a narrow arched gateway, still called in Syria, 'Es summ el Kayút,' the hole or eye of the needle.

Mar. 3. June 2.	**The Four Gospels arranged** Sep. 1. Dec. 1.

M 20, 8 — yard said unto his steward, Call the labourers, and give them their hire, beginning from the
— 9 — last unto the first. And when they came that were hired about the eleventh hour, they re-
— 10 — ceived every man a penny. But when the first came, they supposed that they should receive more; and they likewise received every man a
— 11 — penny. And when they had received it, they murmured against the goodman of the house,
— 12 — saying, These last have wrought but one hour, and thou hast made them equal unto us, which have borne the burden and heat of the day.
— 13 — But he answered one of them, and said, Friend, I do thee no wrong; didst not thou agree with
— 14 — me for a penny? Take that thine is, and go thy way; I will give unto this last, even as
— 15 — unto thee. Is it not lawful for me to do what I will with mine own? Is thine eye evil because
— 16 — I am good? So the last shall be first, and the first last; for many are called, but few chosen.
L 17, 7 — Which of you, having a servant ploughing or feeding cattle, will say unto him by and by, when he is come from the field, Go and sit
— 8 — down to meat? and will not rather say unto him, Make ready wherewith I may sup, and gird thyself, and serve me, till I have eaten and drunken; and afterward thou shalt eat and
— 9 — drink? Doth he thank that servant because

| Mar. 4. June 3. | in one Continuous Narrative. | Sep. 2. Dec. 2. |

he did the things that were commanded him? I trow not. So likewise ye, when ye shall have done all those things which are commanded you, say, We are unprofitable servants: we have done that which it was our duty to do.

L 17, 9
— 10

LXIII.
Mar. 4. June 3. Sep. 2. Dec. 2.
Ambition reproved. Blind Bartimeus receives his sight. Zaccheus receives Christ.

THEN came to Jesus the mother of Zebedee's children with her sons, James and John, worshipping him, and desiring a certain thing of him; saying, Master, we would that thou shouldest do for us whatsoever we shall desire. And he said unto them, What would ye that I should do for you? They said unto him, Grant unto us that we may sit, one on thy right hand, and the other on thy left hand in thy kingdom in glory. But Jesus answered and said, Ye know not what ye ask. Are ye able to drink of the cup that I shall drink of, and to be baptized with the baptism that I am baptized with? They said unto him, We are able. And he said unto them, Ye shall drink indeed of my cup, and be baptized with the baptism that I am baptized with: but to sit on

M 20, 20
K 10, 35
M 20, 20
K 10, 35

— 36
— 37

M 20, 21
— 22

— 23

Mar. 4.	Sep. 2.
June 3.	Dec. 2.

The Four Gospels arranged

M 20, 23 — my right hand, and on my left, is not mine to give, but for whom it is prepared of my Father.

— 24 — And when the ten heard it, they were moved with indignation against the two brethren. But

— 25 — Jesus called them unto him, and said, Ye know that the princes of the Gentiles exercise dominion over them, and they that are great

— 26 — exercise authority upon them. But it shall not be so among you; but whosoever will be great

— 27 — among you, let him be your minister; and whosoever will be chief among you, let him be

— 28 — your servant; even as the Son of man came not to be ministered unto, but to minister, and to give his life a ransom for many.

K 10, 46
L 19, 1
K 10, 46
M 20, 30

And they came nigh to Jericho, and Jesus entered and passed through; and as he went out of Jericho with his disciples and a great number of people, behold, two blind men sat by the highway side begging: one of them

K 10, 47
L 18, 36

was blind Bartimeus, the son of Timeus; and when he heard the multitude pass by, he asked

— 37 — what it meant. And they told him, that Jesus of Nazareth passed by.

— 38 — And he cried, saying, Jesus, thou Son of

— 39 — David, have mercy on me. And they which went before rebuked him, that he should hold his peace; but he cried so much the more, Thou Son of David, have mercy on me.

| Mar. 4. June 3. | in one Continuous Narrative. | Sep. 2. Dec. 2. |

And Jesus stood still, and commanded him to be called. And they called the blind man, saying unto him, Be of good comfort, rise; he calleth thee. And he, casting away his garment, rose, and came to Jesus. And Jesus answered and said unto him, What willest thou that I should do unto thee? The blind man said unto him, Lord, that I might receive my sight. So Jesus had compassion on him, and touched his eyes; and said unto him, Receive thy sight; thy faith hath saved thee, and hath made thee whole. Go thy way. And immediately he received his sight, and followed him, glorifying God; and all the people, when they saw it, gave praise unto God.   K 10, 49 — 50 — 51 M 20, 34 L 18, 42 K 10, 52 L 18, 43

And, behold, there was a man named Zaccheus, which was the chief among the publicans, and he was rich. And he sought to see Jesus who he was; and could not for the press, because he was little of stature. And he ran before, and climbed up into a sycamore tree to see him; for he was to pass that way. And when Jesus came to the place, he looked up, and saw him, and said unto him, Zaccheus, make haste, and come down; for to-day I must abide at thy house. And he made haste, and came down, and received him joyfully. And when they saw it, they all murmured, saying,   L 19, 2 — 3 — 4 — 5 — 6 — 7

L 19, 7	that he was gone to be guest with a man that is a sinner.
— 8	And Zaccheus stood, and said unto the Lord, Behold, Lord, the half of my goods I give to the poor; and if I have taken any thing from any man by false accusation, I restore to him four-
— 9	fold. And Jesus said unto him, This day is salvation come to this house, forasmuch as he also is a son of Abraham.

LXIV.

MAR. 5.   JUNE 4.   SEP. 3.   DEC. 3.

The parable of the talents.

L 17, 20	AND when Jesus was demanded by the Pharisees, when the kingdom of God would come, he answered them and said, The kingdom of God cometh not with observation;
— 21	neither shall they say, Lo here! or, Lo there! for, behold, the kingdom of God is within you.
L 19, 11	And as they heard these things, he added and spake a parable, because he was nigh to Jerusalem, and because they thought that the king-
— 12	dom of God would immediately appear. He said therefore, A certain nobleman went into a far country to receive for himself a kingdom,
— 13	and to return. And he called his ten servants,
M 25, 14 — 15	and delivered unto them his goods. And unto

| Mar. 5. June 4. | in one Continuous Narrative. | Sep. 3. Dec. 3. |

one he gave five talents, to another two, and to another one; to every man according to his several ability; and said unto them, Occupy till I come; and straightway took his journey. But his citizens hated him, and sent a message after him, saying, We will not have this man to reign over us. Then he that had received the five talents went and traded with the same, and made them other five talents. And likewise he that had received two, he also gained other two. But he that had received one went and digged in the earth, and hid his lord's money. And it came to pass, that after a long time, when he was returned, having received the kingdom, then he commanded those servants to be called unto him, to whom he had given the money, that he might know how much every man had gained by trading. Then the first, he that had received five talents, came and brought other five talents, saying, Lord, thou deliveredst unto me five talents; behold, I have gained beside them five talents more. His lord said unto him, Well done, thou good and faithful servant; thou hast been faithful over a few things, I will make thee ruler over many things; enter thou into the joy of thy lord: have thou authority over ten cities. And the second, he that had received two talents, came and said, Lord,

M 25, 15
L 19, 13
M 25, 15
L 19, 14
M 25, 16
— 17
— 18
L 19, 15
M 25, 19
L 19, 15
— 16
M 25, 20
— 21
L 19, 17
— 18
M 25, 22

| | Mar. 5.
June 4. | The Four Gospels arranged | Sep. 3.
Dec. 3. |

M 25, 22	thou deliveredst unto me two talents; behold, I have gained two other talents beside them.
— 23	His lord said unto him, Well done, good and faithful servant; thou hast been faithful over a few things, I will make thee ruler over many
L 19, 19	things; enter thou into the joy of thy lord. And he said likewise to him, Be thou also over five
— 20 M 25, 24	cities. And another, he which had received the one talent, came and said, Lord, I knew thee
L 19, 21	and feared thee because thou art an austere man; thou takest up that thou layedst not down, and reapest that thou didst not sow;
M 25, 25	and I was afraid, and went and hid thy talent
L 19, 20 M 25, 25	in a napkin, in the earth; lo, there thou hast that is thine. And he said unto him, Out of
L 19, 22	thine own mouth will I judge thee, thou wicked
M 25, 26	and slothful servant. Thou knewest that I was
L 19, 22	an austere man, taking up that I laid not down,
— 23	and reaping that I did not sow? Wherefore then gavest not thou my money into the bank, that at my coming I might have required mine
— 24	own with interest? And he said unto them
M 25, 28	that stood by, Take from him the talent and
L 19, 25	give it unto him which hath ten talents. (And they said unto him, Lord, he hath ten talents.)
M 25, 29	For unto every one that hath shall be given, and he shall have abundance; but from him that hath not shall be taken away even that

| Mar. 6. June 5. | in one Continuous Narrative. | Sep. 4. Dec. 4. |

which he seemeth to have. And cast ye the unprofitable servant into outer darkness: there shall be weeping and gnashing of teeth. But those mine enemies, which would not that I should reign over them, bring hither, and slay them before me. And when Jesus had thus spoken, he went before, ascending up to Jerusalem.

L 8, 18
M 25, 30
L 19, 27
— 28

LXV.
Mar. 6. June 5. Sep. 4. Dec. 4.
Mary anoints Christ with ointment of spikenard.

AND the Jews' passover was nigh at hand; and many went out of the country up to Jerusalem before the passover, to purify themselves. Then sought they for Jesus, and spake among themselves, as they stood in the temple, What think ye, that he will not come to the feast? Now both the chief priests and the Pharisees had given a commandment, that, if any man knew where he were, he should show it, that they might take him.

Then Jesus, six days before the passover, came to Bethany, where Lazarus was who had been dead, whom he raised from the dead. Much people of the Jews therefore knew that he was there; and they came, not for Jesus' sake only, but that they might

J 11, 55
— 56
— 57
J 12, 1
— 9

| Mar. 6. | The Four Gospels arranged | Sep. 4. |
| June 5. | | Dec. 4. |

J 12, 9
— 10
— 11

— 2
M 26, 6
J 12, 2

— 3
M 26, 7
J 12, 3
K 14, 3
M 26, 7
J 12, 3

K 14, 4

J 12, 4

— 5

— 6

K 14, 5
M 26, 10
K 14, 6
— 8

see Lazarus also, whom he had raised from the dead. But the chief priests consulted that they might put Lazarus also to death; because that by reason of him many of the Jews went away, and believed on Jesus. There they made him a supper, in the house of Simon the leper, and Martha served; but Lazarus was one of them that sat at the table with him. Then took Mary an alabaster box of very precious ointment of spikenard, very costly, and she brake the box, and poured the ointment on his head, as he sat at meat, and anointed the feet of Jesus, and wiped his feet with her hair; and the house was filled with the odour of the ointment.

And there were some that had indignation within themselves, and said, Why was this waste of the ointment made? Then said one of his disciples, Judas Iscariot, Simon's son, which should betray him, Why was not this ointment sold for three hundred pence, and given to the poor? This he said, not that he cared for the poor; but because he was a thief, and had the bag, and bare what was put therein. And they murmured against her. When Jesus understood it, he said unto them, Let her alone; why trouble ye her? she hath wrought a good work on me. She hath done what she could; she is come aforehand to anoint my body to the burying. For ye have the poor with you always, and whensoever ye will ye may do them good; but me ye have not always. Verily, I say unto you, wheresoever this gospel shall be preached throughout the whole world, this also that she hath done shall be spoken of for a memorial of her.

LXVI.

MAR. 7. JUNE 6. SEP. 5. DEC. 5.

Christ's public entry into Jerusalem. Christ a second time expels from the Temple the changers of money.

AND on the next day when they drew nigh unto Jerusalem, and were come to Bethphage, and Bethany, at the mount called the mount of Olives, Jesus sent two of his disciples, saying unto them, Go ye into the village over against you; in the which at your entering ye shall find an ass tied, and a colt with her, whereon never man sat; loose them, and bring them unto me. And if any man say aught unto you, ye shall say, The Lord hath need of them; and straightway he will send them.

And the disciples did as Jesus commanded them: they went their way, and found the colt

| Mar. 7. | | Sep. 5. |
| June 6. | The Four Gospels arranged | Dec. 5. |

K 11, 4 — tied by the door without in a place where two
— 5 — ways met; and they loosed him. And certain of them that stood there said unto them, What do ye, loosing the colt?

— 6 — And they said unto them even as Jesus had
M 21, 7 — commanded: and they let them go. And they
L 19, 35 — brought the ass, and the colt, and cast their
M 21, 7 — garments upon the colt, and they sat Jesus thereon.

— 4 — All this was done, that it might be fulfilled which was spoken by the prophet,* saying,
—, 5
J 12, 15 — Tell ye the daughter of Sion, Fear not, Behold, thy King cometh unto thee, meek, and sitting
— 16 — upon an ass's colt. These things understood not his disciples at the first; but when Jesus was glorified, then remembered they that these things were written of him, and that they had done these things unto him.

L 19, 36
M 21, 8
J 12, 12 — And, as he went, a very great multitude that were come to the feast, when they heard that
M 21, 8 — Jesus was coming to Jerusalem, spread their garments in the way; others cut down branches from the trees, and strewed them in the way.

L 19, 37 — And when he was come nigh, even now at
M 21, 9 — the descent of the mount of Olives, the multitudes that went before, and that followed,
L 19, 37 — began to rejoice and praise God with a loud

* Zech. ix, 9.

| Mar. 7. June 6. | in one Continuous Narrative. | Sep. 5. Dec. 5. |

voice for all the mighty works that they had seen. The people therefore that were with him when he called Lazarus out of his grave, and raised him from the dead, bare record. For this cause the people also met him, for that they heard that he had done this miracle. And they took branches of palm trees, and went forth to meet him, and cried, Hosanna! Blessed is the King of Israel that cometh in the name of the Lord.* Hosanna to the son of David! Peace in heaven, and glory in the highest!

The Pharisees therefore said among themselves, Perceive ye how ye prevail nothing? behold, the world is gone after him. And some of the Pharisees from among the multitude said unto him, Master, rebuke thy disciples. And he answered and said unto them, I tell you that, if these should hold their peace, the stones would immediately cry out.

And when he was come near, he beheld the city, and wept over it, saying, If thou hadst known, even thou, at least in this thy day, the things which belong unto thy peace! but now they are hid from thine eyes. For the days shall come upon thee, that thine enemies shall cast a trench about thee, and compass thee

L 19, 37
J 12, 17
— 18
— 13
M 21, 9
L 19, 38
J 12, 19
L 19, 39
— 40
— 41
— 42
— 43

* Psa. cxviii, 26.

Mar. 7. June 6.	**The Four Gospels arranged** — Sep. 5. Dec. 5.

L 19, 44 — round, and keep thee in on every side; and shall lay thee even with the ground, and thy children within thee; and they shall not leave in thee one stone upon another; because thou knewest not the time of thy visitation.*

M 21, 10 — And when he was come into Jerusalem, all
— 11 — the city was moved, saying, Who is this? And the multitude said, This is Jesus the prophet of Nazareth of Galilee.

— 12 — And Jesus went into the temple of God, and cast out all them that sold and bought in the temple, and overthrew the tables of the moneychangers, and the seats of them that sold
K 11, 16 — doves,† and would not suffer that any man should carry any vessel through the temple.
— 17 — And he taught, saying unto them, Is it not written,‡ My house shall be called of all nations the house of prayer? but ye have
— 18 — made it a den of thieves. And the scribes
L 19, 47 — and the chief priests heard it, and they with the chief of the people sought how they might
— 48 — destroy him; for they feared him, and could not find what they might do; for all the people were very attentive to hear him, and
K 11, 18 — were astonished at his doctrine.
M 21, 14 — And the blind and the lame came to him in
— 15 — the temple; and he healed them. And when

* Dan. ix, 24.   † Deut. xiv, 24-26.   ‡ Isa. lvi, 7.

	in one Continuous Narrative.	
Mar. 8. June 7.		Sep. 6. Dec. 6.

the chief priests and scribes saw the wonderful things that he did, and the children crying in the temple and saying, Hosanna to the son of David! they were sore displeased, and said unto him, Hearest thou what these say? And Jesus said unto them, Yea; have ye never read,* Out of the mouth of babes and sucklings thou hast perfected praise? And when he had looked round about upon all things, and now the eventide was come, he left them, and went out of the city into Bethany with the twelve; and he lodged there.

M 21, 15

— 16

K 11, 11
M 21, 17
K 11, 11
M 21, 17

LXVII.
MAR. 8. JUNE 7. SEP. 6. DEC. 6.
The fig tree withered. The parable of the two sons sent to work in the vineyard.

NOW in the morning as Jesus returned into the city, from Bethany, he hungered. And seeing a fig tree afar off having leaves, he came, if haply he might find any thing thereon: and when he came to it, he found nothing thereon but leaves only; for the time of figs was not yet. And Jesus answered and said unto it, Let no fruit grow on thee henceforward for ever. And his disciples heard it. And presently the fig tree withered away.

M 21, 18
K 11, 12
— 13

M 21, 19
K 11, 13
— 14
M 21, 19
K 11, 14
M 21, 19

* Psa. viii, 2.

| | Mar. 8.
June 7. | The Four Gospels arranged | Sep. 6.
Dec. 6. |

L 21, 38 K 11, 19 L 21, 37	And all the people came early in the morning to him in the temple, to hear him. And when even was come, he went out of the city. In the day time he was teaching in the temple; and at night he went out, and abode in the mount that is called the mount of Olives.
K 11, 20 M 21, 20 K 11, 21 — 22 — 23 M 21, 21 K 11, 23 M 21, 21 K 11, 23 — 24 M 21, 22	And in the morning, as they passed by, they saw the fig tree, dried up from the roots. And when the disciples saw it they marvelled. And Peter calling to remembrance said unto him, Master, behold, the fig tree which thou cursedst is withered away. And Jesus answering said unto them, Have faith in God; for, verily, I say unto you, if ye have faith, and doubt not, ye shall not only do this which is done to the fig tree, but whosoever shall say unto this mountain, Be thou removed, and be thou cast into the sea; and shall not doubt in his heart, but shall believe that those things which he saith shall come to pass; it shall be done, he shall have whatsoever he saith. Therefore I say unto you, What things soever ye desire, when ye pray, believe that ye receive them, and ye shall have them. All things whatsoever ye shall ask in prayer, believing, ye shall receive.
L 20, 1	And it came to pass, that on one of those days, as he taught the people in the temple, and preached the gospel, the chief priests and

| Mar. 8. June 7. | in one Continuous Narrative. | Sep. 6. Dec. 6. |

the scribes came upon him with the elders, and spake unto him, saying, Tell us, by what authority doest thou these things? or who is he that gave thee this authority? And Jesus answered and said unto them, I will also ask you one question, and answer me, and I will tell you by what authority I do these things. The baptism of John, whence was it? from heaven, or of men? answer me.

And they reasoned with themselves, saying, If we shall say, From heaven; he will say unto us, Why did ye not then believe him? But if we shall say, Of men; we fear the people will stone us; for all hold John as a prophet indeed. And they answered Jesus, and said, We cannot tell. And he said unto them, Neither tell I you by what authority I do these things. But what think ye? A certain man had two sons; and he came to the first, and said, Son, go work to-day in my vineyard. He answered and said, I will not; but afterward he repented, and went. And he came to the second, and said likewise. And he answered and said, I go, sir; and went not. Whether of them twain did the will of his father? They said unto him, The first. Jesus said unto them, Verily, I say unto you, the publicans and the harlots go into the kingdom of God before you. For John came unto

L 20, 2

K 11, 29

M 21, 25
K 11, 30

M 21, 25

— 26
L 20, 6
K 11, 32
M 21, 27

— 28

— 29

— 30

— 31

— 32

M 21, 32		you in the way of righteousness, and ye believed him not; but the publicans and the harlots believed him; and ye, when ye had seen it, repented not afterward, that ye might believe him.

LXVIII.
Mar. 9. June 8. Sep. 7. Dec. 7.
The parable of the vineyard let out to husbandmen. The tribute money.

M 21, 33	HEAR another parable, said Jesus: There was a certain householder, which planted a vineyard, and hedged it round about, and digged a winepress in it, and built a tower, and let it out to husbandmen, and went into a far
L 20, 9 M 21, 34	country for a long time. And when the time of the fruit drew near, he sent his servants to
L 20, 10	the husbandmen, that they might receive the fruit of the vineyard; but the husbandmen
M 21, 35	took his servants, and beat one, and killed
K 12, 4	another, and stoned another, and wounded him in the head, and sent him away shame-
— 5	fully handled. And again he sent another; and him they killed, and many others; beat-
L 20, 13	ing some, and killing some. Then said the lord of the vineyard, What shall I do? I will send my beloved son: it may be they will
— 14	reverence him when they see him. But when the husbandmen saw him, they reasoned among

| Mar. 9. June 8. | in one Continuous Narrative. | Sep. 7. Dec. 7. |

themselves, saying, This is the heir: come, let us kill him, and seize on his inheritance, and it shall be ours. And they caught him and cast him out of the vineyard and slew him. When the lord therefore of the vineyard cometh, what will he do unto those husbandmen? They said unto him, He will miserably destroy those wicked men, and will let out his vineyard unto other husbandmen, which shall render him the fruits in their seasons. Therefore say I unto you, The kingdom of God shall be taken from you, and given to a nation bringing forth the fruits thereof. And when they heard it, they said, God forbid.

And he beheld them, and said, What is this then that is written, in the scriptures,* The stone which the builders rejected, the same is become the head of the corner; this is the Lord's doing, and it is marvellous in our eyes? And whosoever shall fall on this stone shall be broken; but on whomsoever it shall fall, it will grind him to powder.†

And when the chief priests and the scribes and Pharisees had heard his parables, they perceived that he spake of them. But when they sought to lay hands on him, they feared the multitude, because they took him for a prophet. And they left him, and went their way.

L 20, 14
M 21, 38
K 11, 7
M 21, 39
— 40
— 41
— 43
L 20, 16
— 17
M 21, 42
— 44
— 45
L 20, 19
M 21, 45
— 46
K 12, 12

* Psa. cxviii, 22.   † Dan. ii, 34, 35.

Mar. 9.	Sep. 7.
June 8.	Dec. 7.

The Four Gospels arranged

M 22, 15	Then went the Pharisees, and took counsel how they might entangle him in his talk.
L 20, 20 M 22, 16 L 20, 20	And they watched him, and sent out unto him their disciples with the Herodians, spies, which should feign themselves just men, that they might take hold of his words, that so they might deliver him unto the power and authority of the governor.
K 12, 14	And when they were come, they said unto him, Master, we know that thou art true, and carest for no man; for thou regardest not the person of men, but
M 22, 17	teachest the way of God in truth; tell us therefore, What thinkest thou? is it lawful
K 12, 15	to give tribute unto Cæsar, or not? Shall we give, or shall we not give? But he, knowing
M 22, 18	their hypocrisy, said unto them, Why tempt
— 19	ye me, ye hypocrites? Show me the tribute money. And they brought unto him a penny.
— 20	And he said unto them, Whose is this image
— 21	and superscription? They said unto him, Cæsar's. Then said he unto them, Render therefore unto Cæsar the things that are Cæsar's; and unto God the things that are
L 20, 26	God's. And they could not take hold of his words before the people; and they marvelled
M 22, 22	at his answer, and held their peace; and left him, and went their way.

LXIX.

Mar. 10. June 9. Sep. 8. Dec. 8.

The woman that had had seven husbands. The great commandment. The Pharisees are unable to answer Christ.

THE same day came to Jesus certain of the Saducees, which deny that there is any resurrection; and they asked him, saying, Master, Moses wrote unto us,* If any man's brother die, having a wife, and he die without children, his brother shall take his wife, and raise up seed unto his brother. Now there were seven brethren; and the first took a wife, and dying left no seed; and the second took her, and died, neither left he any seed; and the third likewise; and the seven had her, and left no seed; last of all the woman died also. Therefore in the resurrection whose wife of them is she? for seven had her to wife.

And Jesus answering said unto them, The children of this world marry, and are given in marriage; but they which shall be accounted worthy to obtain that world, and the resurrection from the dead, neither marry, nor are given in marriage; neither can they die any more; but are as the angels of God in

* Deut. xxv, 5.

M 22, 23	
L 20, 27	
— 28	
K 12, 20	
— 21	
— 22	
L 20, 33	
— 34	
— 35	
— 36	
M 22, 30	

Mar. 10. June 9.	The Four Gospels arranged	Sep. 8. Dec. 8.

L 20, 36
K 12, 26
M 22, 31

K 12, 26

— 27
L 20, 38
K 12, 27
M 22, 29

— 33
L 20, 39

M 22, 34

K 12, 28
M 22, 35
K 12, 28
M 22, 35
K 12, 28
M 22, 36
K 12, 29

— 30

heaven; and are the children of God, being the children of the resurrection. And as touching the dead, that they rise; have ye not read that which was spoken unto you by God, in the book of Moses,* how in the bush God spake unto him, saying, I am the God of Abraham, and the God of Isaac, and the God of Jacob? He is not the God of the dead, but the God of the living; for all live unto him: ye therefore do greatly err, not knowing the scriptures, nor the power of God.

And when the multitude heard this, they were astonished at his doctrine. Then certain of the scribes answering said, Master, thou hast well said.

But when the Pharisees had heard that he had put the Sadducees to silence, they were gathered together. Then one of the scribes, which was a lawyer, having heard them reasoning together, and perceiving that he had answered them well, asked him a question, tempting him, and saying, Master, which is the first commandment of all in the law?

And Jesus answered him, The first of all the commandments is, Hear, O Israel; The Lord our God is one Lord:† and thou shalt love the Lord thy God with all thy heart, and with all

* Ex. iii, 6. † Deut. vi, 4, 5.

| Mar. 10. | | Sep. 8. |
| June 9. | in one Continuous Narrative. | Dec. 8. |

thy soul, and with all thy mind, and with all thy strength; this is the first and great commandment. And the second is like unto it, Thou shalt love thy neighbour as thyself.* On these two commandments hang all the law and the prophets. There is none other commandment greater than these. And the scribe said unto him, Well, Master, thou hast said the truth; for there is one God; and there is none but he; and to love him with all the heart, and with all the understanding, and with all the soul, and with all the strength, and to love his neighbour as himself, is more than all whole burnt offerings and sacrifices. And when Jesus saw that he answered discreetly, he said unto him, Thou art not far from the kingdom of God.

While the Pharisees were gathered together, Jesus asked them, as he taught in the temple, saying, What think ye of Christ? whose son is he? They said unto him, The son of David. He said unto them, How then doth David himself, by the Holy Ghost, call him Lord, saying, in the book of Psalms,† The Lord said unto my Lord, Sit thou on my right hand, till I make thine enemies thy footstool? David therefore himself calleth him Lord; and whence

* Lev. xix, 18.   † Psa. cx, 1.

| K 12, 87
| M 22, 46

is he then his son? And the common people heard him gladly. And no man was able to answer him a word, neither durst any man from that day forth ask him any more questions.

LXX.

Mar. 11. June 10. Sep. 9. Dec. 9.

The scribes and Pharisees condemned for their hypocrisy. The poor widow's two mites.

| M 23, 1
| L 20, 45
| M 23, 2
| — 3

| L 20, 46
| M 23, 3
| — 4

| — 5

| L 20, 46
| M 23, 6
| — 7
| — 8
| — 10

THEN spake Jesus to the multitude, and to his disciples, saying, in the audience of all the people, The scribes and the Pharisees sit in Moses' seat; all therefore whatsoever they bid you observe, that observe and do: but beware of the scribes; do not ye after their works; for they say, and do not. For they bind heavy burdens and grievous to be borne, and lay them on men's shoulders; but they themselves will not move them with one of their fingers. But all their works they do to be seen of men: they make broad their phylacteries, and enlarge the borders of their garments, and desire to walk in long robes, and love the uppermost places at feasts, and the chief seats in the synagogues, and greetings in the markets, and to be called of men, Rabbi, Rabbi. But be not ye called Rabbi; neither be

| Mar. 11. | | Sep. 9. |
| June 10. | in one Continuous Narrative. | Dec. 9. |

ye called masters; for one is your Master, even Christ; and all ye are brethren. And call no man your father upon the earth; for one is your Father, which is in heaven.*

Woe unto you, scribes and Pharisees, hypocrites! for ye devour widows' houses, and for a pretence make long prayer; therefore ye shall receive the greater damnation.

Woe unto you, scribes and Pharisees, hypocrites! for ye compass sea and land to make one proselyte, and when he is made, ye make him twofold more the child of hell than yourselves.

Woe unto you, ye blind guides, which say, Whosoever shall swear by the temple, it is nothing; but whosoever shall swear by the gold of the temple, he is a debtor! Ye fools and blind; for whether is greater, the gold, or the temple that sanctifieth the gold? And, Whosoever shall swear by the altar, it is nothing; but whosoever sweareth by the gift that is upon it, he is guilty. Ye fools and blind; for whether is greater, the gift, or the altar that sanctifieth the gift?† Whoso therefore shall swear by the altar, sweareth by it, and by all things thereon. And whoso shall swear by the temple, sweareth by it, and by him that dwelleth therein.

23, 8
— 9

— 14

— 15

— 16

— 17

— 18

— 19

— 20

— 21

* Mal. ii, 10. Isa. lxiii, 16.   † Ex. xxix, 37.

Mar. 11. June 10.	**The Four Gospels arranged**	Sep. 9. Dec. 9.

M 23, 29	Woe unto you, scribes and Pharisees, hypocrites! because ye build the tombs of the prophets, and garnish the sepulchres of the
— 30	righteous, and say, If we had been in the days of our fathers, we would not have been partakers with them in the blood of the pro-
— 31	phets. Wherefore ye are witnesses unto yourselves, that ye are the children of them which
L 11, 48	killed the prophets, for ye build their sepul-
M 23, 32	chres. Fill ye up then the measure of your
— 33	fathers. Ye serpents, ye generation of vipers, how can ye escape the damnation of hell?
L 11, 49	Therefore also said the wisdom of God, Be-
M 23, 34	hold, I send unto you prophets, and wise men, and scribes; and some of them ye shall kill and crucify; and some of them shall ye scourge in your synagogues, and persecute from city to
— 35	city; that upon you may come all the righteous
L 11, 50	blood shed upon the earth, from the foundation
M 23, 35	of the world, from the blood of righteous Abel* unto the blood of Zacharias son of Barachias, whom ye slew between the temple and the
— 36	altar.† Verily, I say unto you, all these things shall come upon this generation.
— 37	O Jerusalem, Jerusalem, thou that killest the prophets, and stonest them which are sent unto thee, how often would I have gathered thy

* Gen. iv, 8-10. † 2 Chron. xxiv, 20, 21.

Mar. 12.　　in one Continuous Narrative.　　Sep. 10.
June 11.　　　　　　　　　　　　　　　　Dec. 10.

children together, even as a hen gathereth her | M 23, 37
chickens under her wings, and ye would not !
Behold, your house is left unto you desolate ; | L 13, 35
and verily, I say unto you, ye shall not see
me, until the time come when ye shall say,
Blessed is he that cometh in the name of the
Lord.*

And Jesus sat over against the treasury, and | K 12, 41
he looked up, and beheld how the people cast | L 21, 1
money into the treasury ; and many that were | K 12, 41
rich cast in much. And there came a certain | — 42
poor widow, and she threw in two mites, which
make a farthing. And he called unto him his | — 43
disciples, and said unto them, Verily, I say
unto you, this poor widow hath cast more in,
than all they which have cast into the treasury ;
for all they did cast in of their abundance unto | — 44
the offerings of God ; but she of her want did | L 21, 4
cast in all that she had, even all her living. | K 12, 44

LXXI.

Mar. 12.　June 11.　Sep. 10.　Dec. 10.

Certain Greeks desire to see Christ.

AND there were certain Greeks among them | J 12, 20
that came up to worship at the feast ; the | — 21
same came therefore to Philip, which was of

* Psa. cxviii, 26.

Mar. 12.
June 11.

The Four Gospels arranged

Sep. 10.
Dec. 10.

J 12, 21	Bethsaida of Galilee, and desired him, saying,
— 22	Sir, we would see Jesus. Philip came and told Andrew; and again Andrew and Philip told
— 23	Jesus. And Jesus answered them, saying, The hour is come, that the Son of man should be
— 24	glorified. Verily, verily, I say unto you, except a corn of wheat fall into the ground and die, it abideth alone; but if it die, it bringeth forth much fruit.
— 27	Now is my soul troubled; and what shall I say, Father, save me from this hour? but, for
— 28	this cause came I unto this hour. Father, glorify thy name. Then came there a voice from heaven, saying, I have both glorified it,
— 29	and will glorify it again. The people therefore, that stood by, and heard it, said that it thundered; others said, An angel spake to
— 30	him. Jesus answered and said, This voice came not because of me, but for your sakes.
— 31	Now, is the judgment of this world; now shall
— 32	the prince of this world be cast out. And I, if I be lifted up from the earth, will draw all men
— 33	unto me. This he said, signifying what death he should die.
— 34	The people answered him, We have heard out of the law that Christ abide thfor ever;* and how sayest thou, The Son of man must be

* Ps. cx, 4.

lifted up? who is this Son of man? Then Jesus said unto them, Yet a little while is the light with you. Walk while ye have the light, lest darkness come upon you; for he that walketh in darkness knoweth not whither he goeth. While ye have light, believe in the light, that ye may be the children of light.

These things spake Jesus, and departed, and did hide himself from them. But though he had done so many miracles before them, yet they believed not on him; that the saying of Isaiah the prophet might be fulfilled, which he spake,* Lord, who hath believed our report? and to whom hath the arm of the Lord been revealed? Therefore they could not believe, because that Isaiah said again,† He hath blinded their eyes, and hardened their heart; that they should not see with their eyes, nor understand with their heart, and be converted, and I should heal them. These things said Isaiah, when he saw his glory, and spake of him.

Nevertheless among the chief rulers also many believed on him; but because of the Pharisees they did not confess him, lest they should be put out of the synagogue; for they loved the praise of men more than the praise of God.

Jesus cried and said, He that believeth on

* Isa. liii, 1.   † Isa. vi, 10.

	Mar. 13.	The Four Gospels arranged	Sep. 11.
	June 12.		Dec. 11.

J 12, 44	me, believeth not on me, but on him that sent
— 45	me. And he that seeth me seeth him that
— 46	sent me. I am come a light into the world, that whosoever believeth on me should not
— 47	abide in darkness. And if any man hear my words, and believe not, I judge him not; for I came not to judge the world, but to save the
— 48	world. He that rejecteth me, and receiveth not my words, hath one that judgeth him; the word that I have spoken, the same shall judge
— 49	him in the last day; for I have not spoken of myself; but the Father which sent me, he gave me a commandment, what I should say, and
— 50	what I should speak; and I know that his commandment is life everlasting. Whatsoever I speak therefore, even as the Father said unto me, so I speak.

LXXII.

MAR. 13.   JUNE 12.   SEP. 11.   DEC. 11.

The destruction of the temple foretold. The spirit of the world and the spirit of Christ are antagonistic.

M 24, 1	AND Jesus went out, and departed from the temple; and his disciples came to him to
L 21, 5	show him the buildings of the temple, how it was
M 24, 2	adorned with goodly stones and gifts. And Jesus said unto them, See ye not all these things?
L 21, 6	Verily, I say unto you, the days will come, in

Mar. 13. **in one Continuous Narrative.** Sep. 11.
June 12. Dec. 11.

the which there shall not be left one stone upon | L 21, 6
another, that shall not be thrown down.

And as he sat upon the mount of Olives | K 13, 3
over against the temple, the disciples, Peter | M 24, 3
and James and John and Andrew, asked him | K 13, 3
privately, saying, Master, tell us, when shall | L 21, 7
these things be? and what shall be the sign of | M 24, 3
thy coming, and of the end of the world? And | — 4
Jesus answered and said unto them, Take heed
that no man deceive you. For many will come | — 5
in my name, saying, I am Christ; and will
deceive many; and the time draweth near; go | L 21, 8
ye not therefore after them. And ye shall hear | M 24, 6
of wars and rumours of wars: see that ye be
not troubled: for all these things must first | L 21, 9
come to pass, but the end is not yet. For | M 24, 6
nation shall rise against nation, and kingdom | — 7
against kingdom; and there shall be famines,
and pestilences, and earthquakes, in divers
places; and fearful sights and great signs | L 21, 11
shall there be from heaven. All these are | M 24, 8
the beginning of sorrows. But beware of | M 10, 17
men; for before all these, they shall lay | L 21, 12
their hands on you, and persecute you, and
they will deliver you up to the councils, and | M 10, 17
into prisons, and they will scourge you in their | L 21, 12
synagogues; and ye shall be brought before | M 10, 17
governors and kings for my sake; and it shall | — 18
 | L 21, 13

| Mar. 13. | | Sep. 11. |
| June 12. | **The Four Gospels arranged** | Dec. 11. |

M 10, 18
L 12, 11

K 13, 11
L 12, 11
L 21, 15

— 14

L 12, 12
M 10, 20

L 12, 51

M 10, 34
L 12, 49

M 10, 35

— 36

L 12, 52

M 24, 10

M 10, 21

turn to you for a testimony against them and the Gentiles. And when they bring you unto the synagogues, and unto magistrates, and powers, take ye no thought beforehand how or what thing ye shall answer, or what ye shall say; for I will give you a mouth and wisdom, which all your adversaries shall not be able to gainsay nor resist. Settle it therefore in your hearts, not to meditate before what ye shall answer; for the Holy Ghost shall teach you in the same hour what ye ought to say. For it is not ye that speak, but the Spirit of your Father which speaketh in you.

Suppose ye that I am come to give peace on earth? I tell you, Nay; but rather division. I came not to send peace, but a sword. I am come to send fire on the earth; and what will I, if it be already kindled? For I am come to set a man at variance against his father, and the daughter against her mother, and the daughter in law against her mother in law. And a man's foes shall be they of his own household. For, henceforth there shall be five in one house divided, three against two, and two against three. Then shall many be offended, and will betray one another, and will hate one another. And the brother will deliver up the brother to death, and the father the child; and

Mar. 14. June 13.	in one Continuous Narrative.	Sep. 12. Dec. 12.

the children will rise up against their parents, and cause them to be put to death; ye shall be betrayed both by parents, and brethren, and kinsfolks, and friends; and will be hated of all men for my name's sake; but in your patience possess ye your souls. Fear not, little flock; for it is your Father's good pleasure to give you the kingdom; he that endureth to the end shall be saved. And I say unto you, my friends, Be not afraid of them that kill the body, but are not able to kill the soul; but I will forewarn you whom ye shall fear: fear him, who after he hath killed is able to destroy both soul and body in hell; yea, I say unto you, Fear him.	M 10, 21 L 21, 16 M 10, 22 L 21, 19 L 12, 32 M 10, 22 L 12, 4 M 10, 28 L 12, 5 M 10, 28 L 12, 5

LXXIII.

Mar. 14.　June 13.　Sep. 12.　Dec. 12.

The destruction of Jerusalem and the coming of false Christs foretold. Christ's second coming.

THIS gospel of the kingdom, said Jesus, must first be preached in all the world for a witness unto all nations; and then shall the end come. When ye therefore shall see Jerusalem compassed with armies, and the abomination of desolation, spoken of by Daniel the prophet,* standing in the holy place, where it ought not, (let him that	M 24, 14 K 13, 10 M 24, 14 — 15 L 21, 20 K 13, 14 M 24, 15 K 13, 14

* Dan. xii, 11.

| Mar. 14. June 13. | The Four Gospels arranged | Sep. 12. Dec. 12. |

L 21, 20 — readeth understand,) then know that the de-
— 21 — solation thereof is nigh. Then let them which are in Judæa flee to the mountains; and let them which are in the midst of it depart out; and let not them that are in the countries
K 13, 15 — enter thereinto; and let him that is on the housetop not go down into the house, neither enter therein, to take any thing out of his
— 16 — house; and let him that is in the field not
L 17, 32 — turn back again to take up his garment. Remember Lot's wife.* For these are the days
L 21, 22 — of vengeance, that all things which are written
M 24, 19 — may be fulfilled. And woe unto them that are with child, and to them that give suck in those
— 20 — days! But pray ye that your flight be not in
— 21 — the winter, neither on the sabbath day; for
L 21, 23 — then shall be great tribulation in the land, and
M 24, 21 — wrath upon this people, such as was not since the beginning of the world to this time, no,
L 21, 24 — nor ever shall be. And they shall fall by the edge of the sword, and shall be led away captive into all nations; and Jerusalem shall be trodden down of the Gentiles, until the times
M 24, 22 — of the Gentiles be fulfilled. And except those days should be shortened, there would no flesh
K 13, 20 — be saved; but for the elect's sake whom he
M 24, 22 — hath chosen, those days shall be shortened.

* Gen. xix, 26.

| Mar. 14.
June 13. | in one Continuous Narrative. | Sep. 12.
Dec. 12. |

And he said unto the disciples, The days will come, when ye will desire to see one of the days of the Son of man, and ye shall not see it. And then if any man shall say to you, Lo, here is Christ; or, Lo, he is there; believe him not; for there will arise false Christs, and false prophets, and will show great signs and wonders; to seduce, if it were possible, even the very elect, and will deceive many. And because iniquity will abound, the love of many will wax cold. But take ye heed; behold, I have foretold you all things. Wherefore if they shall say unto you, Behold, he is in the desert; go not forth; Behold, he is in the secret chambers; believe it not, go not after them, nor follow them. For as the lightning, that lighteneth out of the one part under heaven, shineth unto the other part under heaven; so shall also the Son of man be in his day. And they answered and said unto him, Where, Lord? And he said unto them, Wheresoever the body is, thither will the eagles be gathered together.*	L 17, 22 K 13, 21 M 24, 24 K 13, 22 M 24, 24 — 11 — 12 K 13, 23 M 24, 26 L 17, 23 — 24 — 37
Immediately after the tribulation of those days there shall be signs in the sun, and in the moon, and in the stars; the sun shall be darkened, and the moon shall not give her light, and the stars shall fall from heaven, and	M 24, 29 L 21, 25 M 24, 29

* Job xxxix, 30.

	The Four Gospels arranged	
Mar. 15. June 14.		Sep. 13. Dec. 13.

M 24, 29
L 21, 25
the powers of the heavens shall be shaken; and upon the earth there shall be distress of nations, with perplexity; the sea and the waves

— 26
roaring; men's hearts failing them for fear, and for looking after those things which are

M 24, 30
coming on the earth. And then shall appear the sign of the Son of man in heaven; and then shall all the tribes of the earth mourn, and they shall see the Son of man coming in the clouds of heaven with power and great

— 31
glory.* And he shall send his angels with a great sound of a trumpet, and they shall

K 13, 27
gather together his elect from the four winds, from the uttermost part of the earth to the

L 21, 28
uttermost part of heaven. And when these things begin to come to pass, then look up, and lift up your heads; for your redemption draweth nigh.

LXXIV.

MAR. 15. JUNE 14. SEP. 13. DEC. 13.

The world asleep at Christ's second coming. Watchfulness enjoined.

L 21, 29
K 13, 28
AND Jesus spake to them a parable: Behold the fig tree, and all the trees; when her branch is yet tender, and putteth forth

L 21, 30
leaves, ye see and know of your own selves

* Dan. vii, 13.

| Mar. 15. June 14. | in one Continuous Narrative. | Sep. 13. Dec. 13. |

that summer is now nigh at hand. So like- | L 21, 31
wise ye, when ye see these things come to pass,
know ye that the kingdom of God is nigh at
hand, even at the doors. Verily, I say unto | K 13, 29
you, this generation shall not pass away, till | L 21, 32
all be fulfilled. Heaven and earth shall pass | — 33
away; but my words shall not pass away.

But of that day and that hour knoweth no | K 13, 32
man, no, not the angels which are in heaven,
neither the Son, but my Father only. But as | M 24, 36
the days of Noah were, so shall also the | — 37
coming of the Son of man be. For as in
the days that were before the flood they were | — 38
eating and drinking, marrying and giving in
marriage, until the day that Noah entered into
the ark, and knew not until the flood came, | — 39
and destroyed them all; likewise also as it was | L 17, 27
in the days of Lot; they did eat, they drank, | — 28
they bought, they sold, they planted, they
builded; but the same day that Lot went out | — 29
of Sodom it rained fire and brimstone from
heaven, and destroyed them all; even thus | — 30
shall it be in the day when the Son of man is
revealed. I tell you, that in that night there | — 34
shall be two men in one bed; the one shall be
taken, and the other shall be left. Two women | — 35
shall be grinding together at the mill; the one | M 24, 41
shall be taken, and the other left. Two men | L 17, 35

| Mar. 15. | The Four Gospels arranged | Sep. 13. |
| June 14. | | Dec. 18. |

L 17, 36
K 13, 33
M 24, 43

shall be in the field, the one shall be taken, and the other left. Take ye heed, watch, and pray; for ye know not when the time is. But know this, that if the goodman of the house had known in what watch the thief would come, he would have watched, and would not have suffered his house to be broken up.

— 44

Therefore be ye also ready: for in such an hour as ye think not the Son of man cometh.

L 21, 34

Take heed to yourselves, lest at any time your hearts be overcharged with surfeiting, and drunkenness, and cares of this life, and

— 35

so that day come upon you unawares. For as a snare shall it come on all them that dwell on

— 36

the face of the whole earth. Watch ye therefore, and pray always, that ye may be accounted worthy to escape all these things that

K 13, 34

shall come to pass, and to stand before the Son of man. For the Son of man is as a man taking a far journey, who left his house, and gave authority to his servants, and to every man his work, and commanded the porter to

— 35

watch. Watch ye therefore; for ye know not when the master of the house cometh, at even, or at midnight, or at the cock-crowing, or in

— 36

the morning; lest, coming suddenly, he find

L 12, 41

you sleeping. Then Peter said unto him, Lord, speakest thou this parable unto us, or

| Mar. 15. | | Sep. 13. |
| June 14. | in one Continuous Narrative. | Dec. 13. |

even to all? And the Lord said, Who then is	L 12, 42
that faithful and wise steward, whom his lord	L 12, 42
shall make ruler over his household, to give	
them their portion of meat in due season?	
What I say unto you I say unto all, Watch.	K 13, 37
Blessed is that servant, whom his lord when	L 12, 43
he cometh shall find so doing. Of a truth I	— 44
say unto you, that he will make him ruler over	
all that he hath. But if that servant say in his	— 45
heart, My lord delayeth his coming; and shall	
begin to beat the men-servants and maidens,	
and to eat and drink, and to be drunken; the	— 46
lord of that servant will come in a day when he	
looketh not for him, and at an hour when he	
is not aware, and will cut him in sunder, and	
will appoint him his portion with the unbe-	
lievers, and with the hypocrites; there shall be	M 24, 51
weeping and gnashing of teeth. And that ser-	L 12, 47
vant, which knew his lord's will, and prepared	
not himself, neither did according to his will,	
shall be beaten with many stripes. But he that	— 48
knew not, and did commit things worthy of	
stripes, shall be beaten with few stripes. For	
unto whomsoever much is given, of him shall	
much be required; and to whom men have	
committed much, of him they will ask the	
more.	

LXXV.

MAR. 16. JUNE 15. SEP. 14. DEC. 14.

The parable of the ten virgins. Kindness to others accepted by Christ as done to himself.

M 25, 1 THEN, said Jesus, shall the kingdom of heaven be likened unto ten virgins, which took their lamps, and went forth to
— 2 meet the bridegroom. And five of them
— 3 were wise, and five were foolish. They that were foolish took their lamps, and took no
— 4 oil with them; but the wise took oil in their
— 5 vessels with their lamps. While the bridegroom tarried, they all slumbered and slept.
— 6 And at midnight there was a cry made, Behold, the bridegroom cometh! go ye out to
— 7 meet him. Then all those virgins arose, and
— 8 trimmed their lamps. And the foolish said unto the wise, Give us of your oil; for our
— 9 lamps are gone out. But the wise answered, saying, Not so; lest there be not enough for us and you; but go ye rather to them that sell,
— 10 and buy for yourselves. And while they went to buy, the bridegroom came; and they that were ready went in with him to the marriage; and

| Mar. 16. June 15. | in one Continuous Narrative. | Sep. 14. Dec. 14. |

the door was shut. Afterward came also the other virgins, saying, Lord, Lord, open to us. But he answered and said, Verily, I say unto you, I know you not. Watch therefore, for ye know neither the day nor the hour wherein the Son of man cometh. Let your loins be girded about, and your lights burning; and ye yourselves like unto men that wait for their lord, when he shall return from the wedding; that when he cometh and knocketh, they may open unto him immediately. Blessed are those servants, whom the lord when he cometh shall find watching; Verily, I say unto you, he will gird himself, and make them to sit down to meat, and will come forth and serve them. And if he shall come in the second watch, or come in the third watch, and find them so, blessed are those servants.

When the Son of man shall come in his glory, and all the holy angels with him, then shall he sit upon the throne of his glory; and before him shall be gathered all nations; and he shall separate them one from another, as a shepherd divideth his sheep from the goats; and he shall set the sheep on his right hand, but the goats on the left. Then shall the King say unto them on his right hand, Come, ye blessed of my Father, inherit the kingdom prepared for you

M 25, 11
— 12
— 13
L 12, 35
— 36
— 37
— 38
M 25, 31
— 32
— 33
— 34

| Mar. 16. | The Four Gospels arranged | Sep. 14. |
| June 15. | | Dec. 14. |

M 25, 35   from the foundation of the world; for I was a hungered, and ye gave me meat; I was thirsty, and ye gave me drink; I was a stranger, and
— 36   ye took me in; naked, and ye clothed me; I was sick, and ye visited me; I was in prison,
— 37   and ye came unto me. Then shall the righteous answer him, saying, Lord, when saw we thee a hungered, and fed thee; or thirsty, and gave
— 38   thee drink? When saw we thee a stranger, and took thee in? or naked, and clothed thee?
— 39   Or when saw we thee sick, or in prison, and
— 40   came unto thee? And the King shall answer and say unto them, Verily, I say unto you, inasmuch as ye have done it unto one of the least of these my brethren, ye have done it unto me.
— 41   Then shall he say also unto them on the left hand, Depart from me, ye cursed, into everlasting fire, prepared for the devil and his
— 42   angels; for I was a hungered, and ye gave me no meat; I was thirsty, and ye gave me no
— 43   drink; I was a stranger, and ye took me not in; naked, and ye clothed me not; sick, and
— 44   in prison, and ye visited me not. Then shall they also answer him, saying, Lord, when saw we thee a hungered, or athirst, or a stranger, or naked, or sick, or in prison, and did not
— 45   minister unto thee? Then shall he answer them, saying, Verily, I say unto you, inas-

much as ye did it not to one of the least of these, ye did it not to me. And these shall go away into everlasting punishment: but the righteous into life eternal.

M 25, 45
— 46

LXXVI.

Mar. 17. June 16. Sep. 15. Dec. 15.

Judas Iscariot covenants to betray Christ. The last supper.

AND it came to pass, when Jesus had finished all these sayings, that he said unto his disciples, Ye know that after two days is the feast of the passover, and of unleavened bread;* and the Son of man is betrayed to be crucified.

M 26, 1
— 2
K 14, 1
M 26, 2

Then assembled together the chief priests, and the scribes, and the elders of the people, unto the palace of the high priest, who was called Caiaphas, and consulted that they might take Jesus by subtilty, and kill him. But they said, Not on the feast day, lest there be an uproar among the people; for they feared the people.

— 3
— 4
— 5
L 22, 2

Then entered Satan into Judas surnamed Iscariot, being of the number of the twelve.

— 3

* Ex. xii, 3-27.

Mar. 17. June 16.	Sep. 15. Dec. 15.

The Four Gospels arranged

L 22, 4	And he went his way, and communed with the chief priest and captains, how he might be-
M 26, 15	tray him unto them, and said unto them, What will ye give me, and I will deliver him unto
L 22, 5	you? And they were glad, and covenanted to
M 26, 15 — 16 L 22, 6	give him thirty pieces of silver. And he promised, and from that time sought opportunity to betray him unto them in the absence of the multitude.
K 14, 12 M 26, 17 K 14, 13 L 22, 8	And the first day of the feast of unleavened bread, when they killed the passover, he sent forth two of his disciples, Peter and John, saying, Go and prepare us the passover that we may
— 9	eat. And they said unto him, Where wilt thou
K 14, 13	that we go and prepare? And he said unto them, Go ye into the city, and there shall meet you a man bearing a pitcher of water; follow
— 14	him. And wheresoever he shall go in, say ye
L 22, 11	to the goodman of the house, The Master saith
M 26, 18	unto thee, My time is at hand; I will keep the passover at thy house. Where is the guest-
K 14, 14	chamber, where I shall eat the passover with
— 15	my disciples? And he will show you a large upper room furnished and prepared; there
— 16	make ready for us. And his disciples went forth, and came into the city, and found as he had said unto them; and they made ready the passover.

| Mar. 17. | in one Continuous Narrative. | Sep. 15. |
| June 16. | | Dec. 15. |

And in the evening when the hour was come, he sat down, and the twelve apostles with him. Now before the feast of the passover, when Jesus knew that his hour was come that he should depart out of this world unto the Father, having loved his own which were in the world, he loved them unto the end; and he said unto them, With desire I have desired to eat this passover with you before I suffer; for I say unto you, I will not any more eat thereof, until it be fulfilled in the kingdom of God. And he took the cup, and gave thanks, and said, Take this, and divide it among yourselves; for I say unto you, I will not drink henceforth of this fruit of the vine until that day when I drink it new with you in my Father's kingdom. And he took bread, and gave thanks, and brake it, and gave unto them, saying, Take, eat, this is my body which is given for you; this do in remembrance of me. Likewise also the cup after supper, saying, This cup is the new testament in my blood, which is shed for you, for the remission of sins. Drink ye all of it. And they all drank of it. And he said, This do ye, as oft as ye drink it, in remembrance of me.

K 14, 17
L 22, 14
J 13, 1

L 22, 15

— 16

— 17

— 18
M 26, 29

L 22, 19
M 26, 26

L 22, 20

M 26, 28
— 27
K 14, 23
1Cor. 11,
[25

LXXVII.

Mar. 18. June 17. Sep. 16. Dec. 16.

Christ washes his disciples' feet, and foretells his betrayal by Judas Iscariot.

J 13, 2	SUPPER being ended, Jesus, knowing that
— 3	the Father had given all things into his hands, and that he was come from God
— 4	and went to God, rose from supper, and laid aside his garments; and took a towel, and
— 5	girded himself. After that he poured water into a basin, and began to wash the disciples' feet, and to wipe them with the towel where-
— 6	with he was girded. Then came he to Simon Peter; and Peter said unto him, Lord, dost
— 7	thou wash my feet? Jesus answered and said unto him, What I do thou knowest not now;
— 8	but thou shalt know hereafter. Peter said unto him, Thou shalt never wash my feet. Jesus answered him, If I wash thee not, thou
— 9	hast no part with me. Peter said unto him, Lord, not my feet only, but also my hands
— 10	and my head. Jesus said to him, He that is washed needeth not save to wash his feet, but is clean every whit; and ye are clean, but not
— 11	all. For he knew who would betray him;

| Mar. 18. | | Sep. 16. |
| June 17. | in one Continuous Narrative. | Dec. 16. |

therefore said he, Ye are not all clean. So after he had washed their feet, and had taken his garments, and was sat down again, he said unto them, Know ye what I have done to you? Ye call me Master and Lord; and ye say well; for so I am. If I then, your Lord and Master, have washed your feet; ye also ought to wash one another's feet. For I have given you an example, that ye should do as I have done to you. If ye know these things, happy are ye if ye do them. I speak not of you all; I know whom I have chosen; but that the scripture may be fulfilled,* He that eateth bread with me hath lifted up his heel against me. Now I tell you before it come, that, when it is come to pass, ye may believe that I am he.

When Jesus had thus said, he was troubled in spirit, and as they sat and did eat, he testified, and said, Verily, verily, I say unto you, one of you which eateth with me will betray me: his hand is on the table. And they were exceedingly sorrowful, and began every one of them to say unto him, Lord, is it I? And he answered and said unto them, It is one of the twelve, that dippeth with me in the dish. The Son of man indeed goeth,

* Psa. xli, 9.

J 13, 12
— 13
— 14
— 15
— 17
— 18
— 19

— 21
K 14, 18
J 13, 21
K 14, 18
L 22, 21
M 26, 22

K 14, 20
— 21

K 14 21	as it is written of him?* but woe to that man by whom the Son of man is betrayed! good were it for that man if he had never been born.
J 13, 22	Then the disciples looked one on another,
— 23	doubting of whom he spake. Now there was leaning on Jesus' bosom one of his disciples,
— 24	whom Jesus loved. Simon Peter therefore beckoned to him, that he should ask who it
— 25	was of whom he spake. He then lying on Jesus' breast said unto him, Lord, who is it?
— 26	Jesus answered, He it is, to whom I shall give a sop, when I have dipped it. And when he had dipped the sop, he gave it to Judas
M 26, 25	Iscariot, the son of Simon. Then Judas, which betrayed him, answered and said, Master, is it
J 13, 27	I? He said unto him, Thou hast said. And after the sop Satan entered into him. Then said Jesus unto him, That thou doest, do
— 28	quickly. Now no man at the table knew for
— 29	what intent he spake this unto him. For some of them thought, because Judas had the bag, that Jesus had said unto him, Buy those things that we have need of against the feast; or, that he should give something to the poor.
— 30	He then having received the sop went imme-
— 31	diately out; and it was night. Therefore, when he was gone out, Jesus said, Now is the

* Isa. liii, 3-9.

| Mar. 19. June 18. | in one Continuous Narrative. | Sep. 17. Dec. 17. |

Son of man glorified, and God is glorified in him. If God is glorified in him, God shall also glorify him in himself, and shall straightway glorify him. | J 13, 31
— 32

LXXVIII.
MAR. 19. JUNE 18. SEP. 17. DEC. 17.

Christ's last discourse: the vine and its branches, brotherly love, the world's hatred.

I AM the true vine, said Jesus, and my Father is the husbandman. Every branch in me that beareth not fruit he taketh away; and every branch that beareth fruit, he purgeth it, that it may bring forth more fruit. Now ye are clean through the word which I have spoken unto you. Abide in me, and I in you. As the branch cannot bear fruit of itself, except it abide in the vine; no more can ye, except ye abide in me. I am the vine, ye are the branches: he that abideth in me, and I in him, the same bringeth forth much fruit; for without me ye can do nothing. If a man abide not in me, he is cast forth as a branch, and is withered; and men gather them, and cast them into the fire, and they are burned. If ye abide in me, and my words abide in you, ye shall ask what ye will, and it shall be done unto you. Herein is my Father glorified,

J 15, 1
— 2
— 3
— 4
— 5
— 6
— 7
— 8

J 15, 8	that ye bear much fruit; so shall ye be my disciples.
— 9	As the Father hath loved me, so have I loved you: continue ye in my love. If ye keep my commandments, ye shall abide in my love; even as I have kept my Father's commandments, and abide in his love. These things have I spoken unto you, that my joy might remain in you, and that your joy might be full. A new commandment I give unto you; and this is my commandment, That ye love one another, as I have loved you. By this shall all men know that ye are my disciples. Greater love hath no man than this, that a man lay down his life for his friends. Ye are my friends, if ye do whatsoever I command you. Henceforth I call you not servants; for the servant knoweth not what his lord doeth; but I have called you friends; for all things that I have heard of my Father I have made known unto you. Ye have not chosen me, but I have chosen you, and ordained you, that ye should go and bring forth fruit, and that your fruit should remain; that whatsoever ye shall ask of the Father in my name, he may give it you. These things I command you, that ye love one another.
— 10	
— 11	
J 13, 34	
J 15, 12	
J 13, 35	
J 15, 13	
— 14	
— 15	
— 16	
— 17	
— 18	If the world hate you, ye know that it hated

| r. 19. June 18. | in one Continuous Narrative. | Sep. 17. Dec. 17. |

me before it hated you. If ye were of the world, the world would love its own; but because ye are not of the world, but I have chosen you out of the world, therefore the world hateth you. Remember the word that I said unto you, The servant is not greater than his lord. If they have persecuted me, they will also persecute you; if they have kept my saying, they will keep yours also. But all these things will they do unto you for my name's sake, because they know not him that sent me. If I had not come and spoken unto them, they had not had sin; but now they have no cloak for their sin. He that hateth me hateth my Father also. If I had not done among them the works which none other man did, they had not had sin; but now have they both seen and hated both me and my Father. But this cometh to pass, that the word might be fulfilled that is written in their law,* They hated me without a cause. But when the Comforter is come, whom I will send unto you from the Father, even the Spirit of truth, which proceedeth from the Father, he shall testify of me; and ye also shall bear witness, because ye have been with me from the beginning.

J 15, 19
— 20
— 21
— 22
— 23
— 24
— 25
— 26
— 27

* Psa. xxxv, 19.

LXXIX.

Mar. 20. June 19. Sep. 18. Dec. 18.

The Comforter promised; prayer to be made to the Father in the name of Christ.

J 16, 1 — THESE things have I spoken unto you, said Jesus, that ye should not be offended.
— 2 They shall put you out of the synagogues; yea, the time cometh, that whosoever killeth you
— 3 will think that he doeth God service. And these things will they do unto you, because
— 4 they have not known the Father, nor me. But these things have I told you, that when the time shall come, ye may remember that I told you of them. And these things I said not unto you at the beginning, because I was with you.
— 5 But now I go my way to him that sent me; and none of you asketh me, Whither goest
— 6 thou? But because I have said these things
— 7 unto you, sorrow hath filled your heart. Nevertheless I tell you the truth; it is expedient for you that I go away; for if I go not away, the Comforter will not come unto you; but if I depart, I will send him unto you. And when he
— 8 is come, he will reprove the world of sin, and
— 9 of righteousness, and of judgment: of sin, be-
— 10 cause they believe not on me; of righteousness, because I go to my Father, and ye see me no

| Mar. 20. June 19. | in one Continuous Narrative. | Sep. 18. Dec. 18. |

more; of judgment, because the prince of this world is judged. I have yet many things to say unto you, but ye cannot bear them now. Howbeit when he, the Spirit of truth, is come, he will guide you into all truth; for he shall not speak of himself; but whatsoever he shall hear, that shall he speak; and he will show you things to come. He shall glorify me; for he shall receive of mine, and shall show it unto you. All things that the Father hath are mine; therefore said I, that he shall take of mine; and shall show it unto you. A little while, and ye shall not see me; and again, a little while, and ye shall see me, because I go to the Father.

Then said some of his disciples among themselves, What is this that he saith unto us, A little while, and ye shall not see me; and again, a little while, and ye shall see me; and, Because I go to the Father? They said therefore, What is this that he saith, A little while? we cannot tell what he saith.

Now Jesus knew that they were desirous to ask him, and said unto them, Do ye inquire among yourselves of that I said, A little while, and ye shall not see me; and again, a little while, and ye shall see me? Verily, verily, I say unto you, ye shall weep and lament, but the world shall rejoice; and ye shall be sorrowful,

J 16, 11
— 12
— 13
— 14
— 15
— 16
— 17
— 18
— 19
— 20

Mar. 20. June 19.	Sep. 18. Dec. 18.

The Four Gospels arranged

J 16, 21   but your sorrow shall be turned into joy. A woman when she is in travail hath sorrow, because her hour is come;* but as soon as she is delivered of the child, she remembereth no more the anguish, for joy that a man is born into the world. And ye now therefore have sorrow; but

— 22   I will see you again, and your heart shall rejoice, and your joy no man taketh from you.

— 23   And in that day ye shall ask me nothing. Verily, verily, I say unto you, whatsoever ye shall ask the Father in my name, he will give

— 24   it you. Hitherto ye have asked nothing in my name; ask, and ye shall receive, that your joy

— 25   may be full. These things have I spoken unto you in proverbs; but the time cometh, when I shall no more speak unto you in proverbs, but

— 26   I shall show you plainly of the Father. In that day ye shall ask in my name; and I say not unto you, that I will pray the Father for you;

— 27   for the Father himself loveth you, because ye have loved me, and have believed that I came

— 28   out from God. I came forth from the Father, and am come into the world; again, I leave the world, and go to the Father.

— 29   His disciples said unto him, Lo, now speakest
— 30   thou plainly, and speakest no proverb. Now are we sure that thou knowest all things, and

* Gen. iii, 16.

needest not that any man should ask thee; by J 16, 30
this we believe that thou camest forth from God.
Jesus answered them, Do ye now believe? Be-   — 31
hold, the hour cometh, yea, is now come, that   — 32
ye shall be scattered, every man to his own,
and shall leave me alone ; and yet I am not
alone, because the Father is with me. These   — 33
things I have spoken unto you, that in me ye
might have peace. In the world ye shall have
tribulation ; but be of good cheer; I have over-
come the world.

LXXX.

MAR. 21. JUNE 20. SEP. 19. DEC. 19.

Christ's prayer for His disciples. His oneness with the Father.

THESE words spake Jesus, and lifted up   J 17, 1
his eyes to heaven, and said, Father, the
hour is come; glorify thy Son, that thy Son
also may glorify thee ; as thou hast given him   — 2
power over all flesh, that he should give eternal
life to as many as thou hast given him. And   — 3
this is life eternal, that they might know thee
the only true God, and Jesus Christ, whom thou
hast sent. I have glorified thee on the earth;   — 4
I have finished the work which thou gavest me
to do. And now, O Father, glorify thou me   — 5
with thine own self with the glory which I had

| | Mar. 21. June 20. | The Four Gospels arranged | Sep. 19. Dec. 19. |

J 17, 6 with thee before the world was. I have manifested thy name unto the men which thou gavest me out of the world; thine they were, and thou gavest them me; and they have kept thy word.
— 7 Now they have known that all things whatso-
— 8 ever thou hast given me are of thee. For I have given unto them the words which thou gavest me; and they have received them, and have known surely that I came out from thee, and they have believed that thou didst
— 9 send me. I pray for them; I pray not for the world, but for them which thou hast given
— 10 me; for they are thine. And all mine are thine, and thine are mine; and I am glorified
— 11 in them. And now I am no more in the world, but these are in the world, and I come to thee. Holy Father, keep through thine own name those whom thou hast given me, that they may
— 12 be one, as we are. While I was with them in the world, I kept them in thy name; those that thou gavest me I have kept, and none of them is lost, but the son of perdition; that the
— 13 scripture might be fulfilled.* And now come I to thee; and these things I speak in the world, that they might have my joy fulfilled
— 14 in themselves. I have given them thy word;
— 16 and the world hath hated them, because they

* Psa. xli, 9.

| Mar. 21. June 20. | in one Continuous Narrative. | Sep. 19. Dec. 19. |

are not of the world, even as I am not of the world. I pray not that thou shouldest take them out of the world, but that thou shouldest keep them from the evil. Sanctify them through thy truth ; thy word is truth. As thou hast sent me into the world, even so have I also sent them into the world. And for their sakes I sanctify myself, that they also might be sanctified through the truth. Neither pray I for these alone, but for them also which shall believe on me through their word ; that they all may be one ; as thou, Father, art in me, and I in thee, that they also may be one in us ; that the world may believe that thou hast sent me. And the glory which thou gavest me I have given them ; that they may be one, even as we are one : I in them, and thou in me, that they may be made perfect in one ; and that the world may know that thou hast sent me, and hast loved them, as thou hast loved me. Father, I will that they also, whom thou hast given me, be with me where I am ; that they may behold my glory, which thou hast given me ; for thou lovedst me before the foundation of the world. O righteous Father, the world hath not known thee ; but I have known thee, and these have known that thou hast sent me. And I have declared unto them thy name, and will declare	J 17, 14 — 15 — 17 — 18 — 19 — 20 — 21 — 22 — 23 — 24 — 25 — 26

J 17, 26	it; that the love wherewith thou hast loved me may be in them, and I in them.
J 14, 1	Let not your heart be troubled; ye believe
— 2	in God, believe also in me. In my Father's house are many mansions; if it were not so, I would have told you. I go to prepare a place
— 3	for you. And if I go and prepare a place for you, I will come again, and receive you unto myself; that where I am, there ye may be also.
— 4	And whither I go ye know, and the way ye know.
— 5	Thomas said unto him, Lord, we know not whither thou goest; and how can we know
— 6	the way? Jesus said unto him, I am the way, the truth, and the life; no man cometh unto
— 7	the Father but by me. If ye had known me, ye should have known my Father also; and from henceforth ye know him, and have seen him.
— 8	Philip said unto him, Lord, show us the
— 9	Father, and it sufficeth us. Jesus said unto him, Have I been so long time with you, and yet hast thou not known me, Philip? he that hath seen me hath seen the Father; how sayest
— 10	thou then, Show us the Father? Believest thou not that I am in the Father, and the Father in me? the words that I speak unto you I speak not of myself; but the Father that

Mar. 22. June 21. **in one Continuous Narrative.** Sep. 20. Dec. 20.

dwelleth in me, he doeth the works. Believe me that I am in the Father, and the Father in me; or else believe me for the very works' sake. Verily, verily, I say unto you, he that believeth on me, the works that I do shall he do also; and greater works than these shall he do; because I go unto my Father. And whatsoever ye shall ask in my name, that will I do, that the Father may be glorified in the Son. If ye shall ask anything in my name, I will do it.

J 14, 11
— 12
— 13
— 14

LXXXI.

MAR. 22. JUNE 21. SEP. 20. DEC. 20.

The test of love. The Comforter promised. Peter's denial foretold.

IF ye love me, said Jesus, keep my commandments. And I will pray the Father, and he shall give you another Comforter, that he may abide with you for ever; even the Spirit of truth; whom the world cannot receive, because it seeth him not, neither knoweth him; but ye know him; for he dwelleth with you, and shall be in you. I will not leave you comfortless; I will come to you. Yet a little while, and the world seeth me no more; but ye see me; because I live, ye shall live also. In that day ye shall know that I am in my

J 14, 15
— 16
— 17
— 18
— 19
— 20

Mar. 22. June 21.	𝕮𝖍𝖊 𝕱𝖔𝖚𝖗 𝕲𝖔𝖘𝖕𝖊𝖑𝖘 𝖆𝖗𝖗𝖆𝖓𝖌𝖊𝖉	Sep. 20. Dec. 20.

J 14, 21 — Father, and ye in me, and I in you. He that hath my commandments, and keepeth them, he it is that loveth me; and he that loveth me shall be loved of my Father, and I will love

— 22 — him, and will manifest myself to him. Judas said unto him, not Iscariot, Lord, how is it that thou wilt manifest thyself unto us, and

— 23 — not unto the world? Jesus answered and said unto him, If a man love me, he will keep my words; and my Father will love him, and we will come unto him, and make our abode with

— 24 — him. He that loveth me not keepeth not my sayings; and the word which ye hear is not

— 25 — mine, but the Father's which sent me. These things have I spoken unto you, being yet

— 26 — present with you; but the Comforter, which is the Holy Ghost, whom the Father will send in my name, he shall teach you all things, and bring all things to your remembrance, whatsoever I have said unto you.

— 27 — Peace I leave with you, my peace I give unto you; not as the world giveth, give I unto you. Let not your heart be troubled, neither

— 28 — let it be afraid. Ye have heard how I said unto you, I go away, and come again unto you. If ye loved me, ye would rejoice, because I said, I go unto the Father; for my

— 29 — Father is greater than I. And now I have

| Mar. 22. June 21. | in one Continuous Narrative. | Sep. 20. Dec. 20. |

told you before it come to pass, that, when it is come to pass, ye might believe. Hereafter I will not talk much with you; for the prince of this world cometh, and hath nothing in me. But that the world may know that I love the Father; as the Father gave me commandment, even so I do. Arise, let us go hence. J 14, 29 — 30 — 31

And Jesus said, Little children, yet a little while I am with you. Ye shall seek me: and as I said unto the Jews, Whither I go, ye cannot come; so now I say to you. Simon Peter said unto him, Lord, whither goest thou? Jesus answered him, Whither I go, thou canst not follow me now; but thou shalt follow me afterwards. Peter said unto him, Lord, why cannot I follow thee now? I will lay down my life for thy sake. Jesus answered him, Wilt thou lay down thy life for my sake? Verily, verily, I say unto thee, this night, before the cock crow, thou wilt deny me thrice. But he spake the more vehemently, Though I should die with thee, I will not deny thee, in any wise. Likewise also said they all. J 13, 33 — 36 — 37 — 38 M 26, 34 K 14, 31 M 26, 35 K 14, 31

Then said Jesus unto them, All ye will be offended because of me this night; for it is written,* I will smite the shepherd, and the sheep of the flock shall be scattered abroad. M 26, 31

* Zech. xiii, 7.

| Mar. 22. June 21. | The Four Gospels arranged | Sep. 20. Dec. 20. |

M 26, 32
— 33

L 22, 31

— 32

— 33

— 34

K 14, 30

L 22, 34

— 35

— 36

— 37

— 38

But after I am risen again, I will go before you into Galilee. Peter answered and said unto him, Though all men shall be offended because of thee, yet will I never be offended. And the Lord said, Simon, Simon, behold, Satan hath desired to have you, that he may sift you as wheat; but I have prayed for thee, that thy faith fail not: and when thou art converted, strengthen thy brethren. And he said unto him, Lord, I am ready to go with thee, both into prison, and to death. And he said, I tell thee, Peter, that this day, even in this night, before the cock crow twice, thou wilt thrice deny that thou knowest me.

And he said unto them, When I sent you without purse, and scrip, and shoes, lacked ye anything? And they said, Nothing. Then said he unto them, But now, he that hath a purse, let him take it, and likewise his scrip; and he that hath no sword, let him sell his garment, and buy one. For I say unto you, that this that is written* must yet be accomplished in me, And he was reckoned among the transgressors; for the things concerning me have an end. And they said, Lord, behold, here are two swords. And he said unto them, It is enough.

* Isa. liii, 12.

| Mar. 23. June 22. | in one Continuous Narrative. | Sep. 21. Dec. 21. |

When Jesus had spoken these words, and when they had sung a hymn, they went out, as he was wont, to the mount of Olives.

J 18, 1
M 26, 30
L 22, 39

LXXXII.

Mar. 23. June 22. Sep. 21. Dec. 21.

Christ's agony and betrayal in Gethsemane.

THEN came Jesus with them over the brook Cedron, unto a place called Gethsemane, where was a garden, into the which he entered, and his disciples. And when he was at the place, he said unto them, Sit ye here, and pray that ye enter not into temptation, while I go and pray yonder.

And he took with him Peter and the two sons of Zebedee, James and John, and began to be sore amazed, and to be sorrowful, and very heavy. Then said he unto them, My soul is exceedingly sorrowful, even unto death: I have a baptism to be baptized with: and how am I straitened till it be accomplished! Tarry ye here, and watch with me.

And he went a little farther, and he was withdrawn from them about a stone's cast, and kneeled down, and fell on his face, and prayed, saying, O my Father, if it be possible, let this cup pass from me; nevertheless not as I will,

M 26, 36
J 18, 1
M 26, 36
J 18, 1
L 22, 40

M 26, 36
L 22, 40
M 26, 36
— 37
K 14, 33
M 26, 37
— 38
L 12, 50
M 26, 38

— 39

251

| | Mar. 23.
June 22. | **The Four Gospels arranged** | Sep. 21.
Dec. 21. |

L 22, 45

K 14, 37
M 26, 40
L 22, 46
M 26, 41

but as thou willest. And when he rose up from prayer, and was come to his disciples, he found them sleeping for sorrow, and said unto Peter, Simon, sleepest thou? What! could ye not watch with me one hour? And he said unto them, Why sleep ye? rise, watch and pray, that ye enter not into temptation: the spirit indeed is willing, but the flesh is weak.

— 42

He went away again the second time, and prayed, saying, O my Father, if this cup may not pass away from me, except I drink it, thy will be done.

K 14, 40

M 26, 44

L 22, 44

And when he returned, he found them asleep again, for their eyes were heavy, neither wist they what to answer him. And he left them, and went away again, and prayed the third time, saying the same words. And being in an agony he prayed more earnestly; and his sweat was as it were great drops of blood falling down to the ground. And there appeared an angel unto him from heaven, strengthening him.

— 43

M 26, 45
K 14, 41
M 26, 45
K 14, 41

M 26, 46

Then came he to his disciples the third time, and said unto them, Sleep on now, and take your rest; it is enough, the hour is come; behold, the Son of man is betrayed into the hands of sinners. Rise, let us be going; behold, he is at hand that doth betray me.

| Mar. 23. June 22. | in one Continuous Narrative. | Sep. 21. Dec. 21. |

And while ye yet spake, lo, Judas, one of the twelve, which knew the place, for Jesus ofttimes resorted thither with his disciples, came, and with him a great multitude with swords and staves, and lanterns and torches; having received a band of men and officers from the chief priests and Pharisees, and the scribes and elders of the people.	M 26, 47 J 18, 2 K 14, 43 J 18, 3 K 14, 43 M 26, 47
Now he that betrayed him went before them, and he had given them a token, saying, Whomsoever I shall kiss, that same is he; take him, hold him fast, and lead him away safely. And forthwith he came to Jesus, and said, Hail, master! and kissed him. And Jesus said unto him, Friend, wherefore art thou come? Judas, betrayest thou the Son of man with a kiss! Jesus therefore, knowing all things that should come upon him, went forth, and said unto them, Whom seek ye? They answered him, Jesus of Nazareth. Jesus said unto them, I am he. And Judas also, which betrayed him, stood with them. As soon then as he had said unto them, I am he, they went backward, and fell to the ground. Then asked he them again, Whom seek ye? And they said, Jesus of Nazareth. Jesus answered, I have told you that I am he; if therefore ye seek me, let these go their way; that the saying might be fulfilled, which he	— 48 L 22, 47 K 14, 44 M 26, 48 K 14, 44 M 26, 49 — 50 L 22, 48 J 18, 4 — 5 — 6 — 7 — 8 — 9

| Mar. 23. | The Four Gospels arranged | Sep. 21. |
| June 22. | | Dec. 21. |

J 18, 9   spake, *Of them which thou gavest me have I lost none.

L 22, 49   When they which were about him saw what would follow, they said unto him, Lord, shall
M 26, 51   we smite with the sword? And, behold, one
J 18, 10   of them which were with Jesus, Simon Peter,
M 26, 51   stretched out his hand, and drew his sword,
J 18, 10   and smote the high priest's servant, and cut off his right ear. The servant's name was Malchus.
L 22, 51   And Jesus answered and said, Suffer ye thus far.
J 18, 11   And he touched his ear, and healed him. Then said Jesus unto Peter, Put up thy sword into
M 26, 52   the sheath; for all they that take the sword
— 53   shall perish with the sword.† Thinkest thou that I cannot now pray to my Father, and he shall presently give me more than twelve legions
— 54   of angels? But how then shall the scriptures
J 18, 11   be fulfilled,‡ that thus it must be? The cup which my Father hath given me, shall I not
L 22, 52   drink it? Then Jesus said unto the chief priests, and captains of the temple, and the
M 26, 55 / L 22, 52   elders, and to the multitudes, which were
M 26, 55   come to him, Are ye come out as against a thief with swords and staves to take me? I sat daily with you teaching in the temple,
L 22, 53   and ye stretched forth no hands against

* John, xvii, 12.   Section lxxx.
† Gen. ix, 6.   Ezek. xxxv, 5, 6.   ‡ Isa. liii, 5-12.

| Mar. 24. June 23. | in one Continuous Narrative. | Sep. 22. Dec. 22. |

me; but this is your hour, and the power of darkness.   L 22, 53

But all this was done, that the scriptures of the prophets might be fulfilled.* Then all the disciples forsook him, and fled. And the band and the captain and officers of the Jews took Jesus, and bound him, and led him away. And there followed him a certain young man, having a linen cloth cast about his naked body; and the young men laid hold on him; and he left the linen cloth, and fled from them naked.

M 26, 56
J 18, 12
K 14, 51
— 52

LXXXIII.

MAR. 24. JUNE 23. SEP. 22. DEC. 22.

Peter's denial of Christ. Christ before Caiaphas.

AND they led Jesus away to Annas first; for he was father-in-law to Caiaphas, who was the high priest that same year. Now Caiaphas was he, who gave counsel to the Jews, that it was expedient that one man should die for the people.

J 18, 13
— 14

And Simon Peter followed Jesus afar off, and so did another disciple; that disciple was known unto the high priest, and went in with Jesus into

— 15
M 26, 58
J 18, 15

* Gen. iii, 15. Psa. xxii, 1. Isa. liii, 5-12. Dan. ix, 24-26. Zech. xiii, 1.

	Mar. 24.	The Four Gospels arranged	Sep. 22.
	June 23.		Dec. 22.

J 18, 16 — the palace of the high priest. But Peter stood at the door without. Then went out that other disciple, which was known unto the high priest, and spake unto her that kept the door, and
J 18, 18
L 22, 55 brought in Peter. And the servants and officers
J 18, 18 stood there, and when they had kindled a fire
L 22, 55 in the midst of the hall, for it was cold, and
M 26, 58 were set down together, Peter sat down among
K 14, 54 them, with the servants, to see the end, and
— 66 warmed himself at the fire.

J 18, 17 And as Peter was beneath in the palace, there came the damsel that kept the door,
K 14, 66 one of the maids of the high priest; and
— 67 when she saw Peter warming himself, as he
L 22, 56 sat by the fire, she earnestly looked upon him, and said unto Peter, Art not thou also
J 18, 17 one of this man's disciples? Thou also wast
K 14, 67
M 26, 69 with Jesus of Nazareth of Galilee. But he
— 70 denied him before them all, saying, Woman,
L 22, 57 I know him not, neither understand I what
K 14, 68 thou sayest. And he went out into the porch; and the cock crew.

L 22, 58 And after a little while, when he was gone
M 26, 71 out into the porch, another maid saw him, and said unto them that were there, This fellow also
— 72 was with Jesus of Nazareth. And again he denied, with an oath, I do not know the man.
L 22, 59
J 18, 26 And about the space of one hour after, one of

| Mar. 24. June 23. | in one Continuous Narrative. | ep. 22. Dec. 22. |

the servants of the high priest, being his kinsman whose ear Peter cut off, said, Did not I see thee in the garden with him? Another confidently affirmed, saying, Of a truth this fellow also was with him, for he is a Galilean; his speech agreeth thereto.

Then began he to curse and to swear, saying, I know not this man of whom ye speak. And immediately, while he yet spake, the cock crew the second time; and the Lord turned, and looked upon Peter; and Peter called to mind the word that Jesus had said unto him, Before the cock crow twice, thou wilt deny me thrice. And when he thought thereon he went out, and wept bitterly.

And the men that held Jesus mocked him, and smote him. And when they had blindfolded him, they struck him on the face, and asked him, saying, Prophesy unto us, thou Christ; who is he that smote thee? And many other things blasphemously spake they against him.

And as soon as it was day, the elders of the people and the chief priests and the scribes came together, and led him into their council, for 'Annas had sent Jesus bound unto Caiaphas the high priest, who then asked Jesus of his disciples, and of his doctrine. Jesus answered him, I spake openly to the world; I ever

J 18, 26

L 22, 59

K 14, 70
— 71
L 22, 60

K 14, 72
L 22, 61
K 14, 72

M 26, 75

L 22, 63
— 64
M 26, 68
L 22, 65

— 66

J 18, 24
M 26, 57
J 18, 19
— 20

| Mar. 24. | | Sep. 22. |
| June 23. | **The Four Gospels arranged** | Dec. 22. |

J 18, 20   taught in the synagogue, and in the temple, whither the Jews always resort; and in secret
— 21   have I said nothing. Why askest thou me? ask them which heard me, what I have said unto them; behold, they know what I said.
— 22   And when he had thus spoken, one of the officers which stood by struck Jesus with the palm of his hand, saying, Answerest thou the
— 23   high priest so? Jesus answered him, If I have spoken evil, bear witness of the evil; but if well, why smitest thou me?

M 26, 59   Now the chief priests, and elders, and all the council, sought false witness against Jesus,
K 14, 55   to put him to death; and found none. For
— 56   many bare false witness against him, but their
— 57   witness agreed not together. And there arose certain, and bare false witness against him,
— 58   saying, We heard him say, I will destroy this temple that is made with hands, and within three days I will build another made without
M 26, 60   hands. At the last came two false witnesses,
— 61   and said, This fellow said, I am able to destroy the temple of God, and to build it in three
K 14, 59   days. But neither so did their witness agree together.
— 60   And the high priest stood up in the midst, and asked Jesus, saying, Answerest thou nothing? what is it which these witness against

| Mar. 24. June 23. | in one Continuous Narrative. | Sep. 22. Dec. 22. |

thee? But Jesus held his peace. And the elders of the people and the chief priests and the scribes asked him, saying, Art thou the Christ? tell us. And he said unto them, If I tell you, ye will not believe; and if I also ask you, ye will not answer me, nor let me go. Nevertheless, I say unto you, hereafter shall ye see the Son of man sitting on the right hand of the power of God, and coming in the clouds of heaven.

Then said they all, Art thou then the Son of God? And the high priest said unto him, I adjure thee by the living God, that thou tell us whether thou art the Christ, the Son of God. Jesus said unto him, Thou hast said. Again the high priest asked him, and said unto him, Art thou the Christ, the Son of the Blessed? And Jesus said, I am.

Then the high priest rent his clothes, saying, He hath spoken blasphemy; what further need have we of witnesses? behold, now ye have heard his blasphemy of his own mouth. What think ye? They answered and said, He is guilty to death. Then did they spit in his face.

M 26, 63
L 22, 66
— 67
— 68
M 26, 64
L 22, 69
M 26, 64
L 22, 70
M 26, 63
— 64
K 14, 61
— 62
M 26, 65
L 22, 71
M 26, 66
— 67

LXXXIV.

MAR. 25. JUNE 24. SEP. 23. DEC. 23.

Christ before Pontius Pilate and Herod.

M 27, 1
K 15, 1

M 27, 2
L 23, 1
J 18, 28
M 27, 2
J 18, 28

— 29

— 30

— 31

— 32

L 23, 2

WHEN the morning was come, all the chief priests and elders of the people and the scribes took counsel against Jesus to put him to death; and when they had bound him, the whole multitude of them arose, and led him from Caiaphas unto the hall of judgment, and delivered him to Pontius Pilate the governor. And it was early; and they themselves went not into the judgment hall, lest they should be defiled; but that they might eat the passover. Pilate then went out unto them, and said, What accusation bring ye against this man? They answered and said unto him, If he were not a malefactor, we would not have delivered him up unto thee. Then said Pilate unto them, Take ye him, and judge him according to your law. The Jews therefore said unto him, It is not lawful for us to put any man to death; that the saying of Jesus might be fulfilled, which he spake, signifying what death he should die. And they began to accuse him, saying, We found this fellow perverting the nation, and forbidding

| Mar. 25. June 24. | in one Continuous Narrative. | Sep. 23. Dec. 23. |

to give tribute to Cæsar, saying that he himself is Christ a King. Then Pilate entered into the judgment hall again, and called Jesus, and said unto him, Art thou the King of the Jews? Jesus answered him, Sayest thou this thing of thyself, or did others tell it thee of me? Pilate answered, Am I a Jew? Thine own nation and the chief priests have delivered thee unto me; what hast thou done? Jesus answered, My kingdom is not of this world; if my kingdom were of this world, then would my servants fight, that I should not be delivered to the Jews; but now is my kingdom not hence. Pilate therefore said unto him, Art thou a king then? Jesus answered, That thou sayest, I am, a king. To this end was I born, and for this cause came I into the world, that I should bear witness unto the truth. Every one that is of the truth heareth my voice. Pilate said unto him, What is truth? And when he had said this, he went out again unto the Jews, and said unto them, I find in him no fault at all.	L 23, 2 J 18, 33 — 34 — 35 — 36 — 37 — 38
And the chief priests and elders accused him of many things; but he answered nothing. And Pilate asked him again, saying, Answerest thou nothing? behold how many things they witness against thee. But Jesus yet answered nothing;	K 15, 3 M 27, 12 K 15, 3 — 4 — 5

| Mar. 25. June 24. | The Four Gospels arranged | Sep. 23. Dec. 23. |

M 27, 14
L 23, 4
— 5

so that Pilate marvelled greatly. Then said Pilate to the chief priests and to the people, I find no fault in this man. And they were the more fierce, saying, He stirreth up the people, teaching throughout all Jewry, beginning

— 6

from Galilee to this place. When Pilate heard of Galilee, he asked whether the man were a

— 7

Galilean. And as soon as he knew that he belonged unto Herod's jurisdiction, he sent him to Herod, who himself also was at Jerusalem at that time.

— 8

And when Herod saw Jesus, he was exceedingly glad; for he was desirous to see him of a long season, because he had heard many things of him; and he hoped to see some

— 9

miracle done by him. Then he questioned with him in many words; but he answered

— 10
— 11

him nothing. And the chief priests and scribes stood and vehemently accused him. And Herod with his men of war set him at naught, and mocked him, and arrayed him in a gorgeous

— 12

robe, and sent him again to Pilate. And the same day Pilate and Herod were made friends together; for before they were at enmity between themselves.

— 13

And Pilate, when he had called together the chief priests and the rulers and the people,

— 14

said unto them, Ye have brought this man

| Mar. 25. June 24. | in one Continuous Narrative. | Sep. 23. Dec. 23. |

unto me, as one that perverteth the people; and, behold, I, having examined him before you, have found no fault in this man touching those things whereof ye accuse him; no, nor yet Herod; for I sent you to him; and, lo, nothing worthy of death is done unto him. I will therefore chastise him, and release him. Now at that feast the governor was wont to release unto the people one prisoner, whomsoever they desired. Therefore when they were gathered together, and the multitude crying aloud began to desire him to do as he had ever done unto them, Pilate answered them, saying, Ye have a custom, that I should release unto you one at the passover; will ye therefore that I release unto you the King of the Jews? For he knew that the chief priests had delivered him for envy. But the chief priests and elders moved the people, that he rather should release unto them a notable prisoner, called Barabbas, and destroy Jesus. Now Barabbas was a robber, who for a certain sedition made in the city, and for murder, was cast into prison, and lay bound with them that had made insurrection with him. The governor answered and said unto them, Whether of the twain will ye that I release unto you? And they cried out all at once,

L 23, 14
— 15
— 16
M 27, 15
K 15, 6
M 27, 17
K 15, 8
— 9
J 18, 39
K 15, 10
M 27, 20
K 15, 11
M 27, 16
— 20
J 18, 40
L 23, 19
K 15, 7
M 27, 21
L 23, 18

| Mar. 26. | The Four Gospels arranged | Sep. 24. |
| June 25. | | Dec. 24. |

L 23, 18
K 15, 12

M 27, 22
K 15, 12
— 13
— 14

saying, Away with this man, and release unto us Barabbas! And Pilate answered and said again unto them, What will ye then that I shall do unto Jesus who is called Christ? him whom ye call the King of the Jews? And they cried out again, Crucify him! Then Pilate said unto them, Why, what evil hath he done? And they cried out the more exceedingly, Crucify him!

LXXXV.

Mar. 26. June 25. Sep. 24. Dec. 24.

Pilate's wife's dream; the purple robe and the crown of thorns. Judas Iscariot's repentance and suicide.

M 27, 19

L 23, 20

— 21
— 22

— 23

WHEN Pilate was sat down on the judgment seat, his wife sent unto him, saying, Have thou nothing to do with that just man; for I have suffered many things this day in a dream because of him. Pilate therefore, willing to release Jesus, spake again to them. But they cried, saying, Crucify him! Crucify him! And he said unto them the third time, Why, what evil hath he done? I have found no cause of death in him; I will therefore chastise him, and let him go. And they were instant with loud voices, requiring

| Mar. 26. June 25. | in one Continuous Narrative. | Sep. 24. Dec. 24. |

that he might be crucified. And the voices of them and of the chief priests prevailed.	L 23, 23
Pilate therefore took Jesus and scourged him.	J 19, 1
Then the soldiers of the governor took	M 27, 27
Jesus away into the common hall, called Præ-	K 15, 16
torium; and gathered unto him the whole	M 27, 27
band of soldiers. And they stripped him, and	— 28
put on him a purple robe. And when they	J 19, 2
had platted a crown of thorns, they put it upon his head, and a reed in his right hand; and they bowed the knee before him, and mocked him, saying, Hail, King of the Jews!	M 27, 29
And they smote him with their hands, and	— 30
they spat upon him, and took the reed, and	J 19, 3
smote him on the head. Pilate therefore went	— 4
forth again, and said unto them, Behold, I bring him forth to you, that ye may know that I find no fault in him. Then came Jesus	— 5
forth, wearing the crown of thorns, and the purple robe. And Pilate said unto them, Behold the man! When the chief priests	— 6
therefore and officers saw him, they cried out, saying, Crucify him! Crucify him! Pilate said unto them, Take ye him, and crucify	
him; for I find no fault in him. The Jews	— 7
answered him, We have a law, and by our law he ought to die, because he made himself the Son of God. When Pilate therefore heard	— 8

| Mar. 26. June 25. | The Four Gospels arranged | Sep. 24. Dec. 24. |

J 19, 9 — that saying, he was the more afraid; and went again into the judgment hall, and said unto Jesus, Whence art thou? But Jesus gave
— 10 — him no answer. Then said Pilate unto him, Speakest thou not unto me? knowest thou not that I have power to crucify thee, and have
— 11 — power to release thee? Jesus answered, Thou couldest have no power at all against me, except it were given thee from above; therefore he that delivered me unto thee hath the
— 12 — greater sin. And thenceforth Pilate sought to release him; but the Jews cried out, saying, If thou let this man go, thou art not Cæsar's friend; whosoever maketh himself a king speaketh against Cæsar.
— 13 — When Pilate therefore heard that saying, he brought Jesus forth, and sat down in the judgment seat in a place that is called the Pavement, but in the Hebrew, Gabbatha, and he
— 14 —
— 15 — said unto the Jews, Behold your King! But they cried out, Away with him! Away with him! Crucify him! Pilate said unto them, Shall I crucify your King? The chief priests answered, We have no king but Cæsar.

M 27, 24 — When Pilate saw that he could prevail nothing, but rather that a tumult was made, he took water, and washed his hands before the multitude, saying, I am innocent of the

| Mar. 26. June 25. | in one Continuous Narrative. | Sep. 24. Dec. 24. |

blood of this just person; see ye to it. Then answered all the people, and said, His blood be on us, and on our children! M 27, 25

And so Pilate, willing to content the people, gave sentence that it should be as they required. And he released unto them him that for sedition and murder had been cast into prison, whom they had desired; but he delivered Jesus unto them to be crucified. And it was the preparation of the passover, and about the third hour.*

K 15, 15
L 23, 24
— 25

J 19, 16
— 14
K 15, 25

Then Judas, who had betrayed him, when he saw that he was condemned, repented himself, and brought again the thirty pieces of silver to the chief priests and elders, saying, I have sinned in that I have betrayed the innocent blood. And they said, What is that to us? see thou to that. And he cast down the pieces of silver in the temple, and departed, and went and hanged himself; and falling headlong, he burst asunder in the midst, and all his bowels gushed out.

M 27, 8

— 4

— 5

A 1, 18

And the chief priests took the silver pieces, and said, It is not lawful to put them into the treasury, because it is the price of blood. And they took counsel, and bought with them the potter's field, to bury strangers in. And it

M 27, 6
— 7
A 1, 19

* *i. e.* 9 A.M.

| Mar. 27. | The Four Gospels arranged | Sep. 25. |
| June 26. | | Dec. 25. |

A 1, 19
M 27, 8
A 1, 19
M 27, 8

was known unto all the dwellers at Jerusalem. Wherefore that field was called, in their proper tongue, Aceldama, that is to say, The field of blood, unto this day.

— 9

Then was fulfilled that which was spoken by the prophet,* saying, And they took the thirty pieces of silver, the price of him that was valued, whom they of the children of Israel did value,

— 10

and gave them for the potter's field, as the Lord appointed me.

LXXXVI.

MAR. 27. JUNE 26. SEP. 25. DEC. 25.

*Christ bears his cross. The crucifixion.
The dying thief saved.*

M 27, 31
K 15, 20
M 27, 31
J 19, 17
M 27, 32

AND after that they had mocked Jesus they took the purple robe off from him, and put his own raiment on him, and led him away to crucify him. And he bearing his cross went forth. And as they came out, they found a man of Cyrene, Simon by name, the father of

K 15, 21
L 23, 26

Alexander and Rufus, who passed by, coming out of the country, and on him they laid the cross, that he might bear it after Jesus.

— 27

And there followed him a great company of people, and of women, which also bewailed

* Zech. xi, 12, 13.

| Mar. 27.
June 26. | in one Continuous Narrative. | Sep. 25.
Dec. 25. |

and lamented him. But Jesus turning unto them said, Daughters of Jerusalem, weep not for me, but weep for yourselves, and for your children. For, behold, the days are coming, in the which they shall say, Blessed are the barren, and the wombs that never bare, and the paps which never gave suck. Then shall they begin to say to the mountains, Fall on us; and to the hills, Cover us. For if they do these things in a green tree, what shall be done in the dry?

And when they were come to the place, which is called Calvary, and in the Hebrew, Golgotha; which is, being interpreted, The place of a skull; they gave him vinegar to drink mingled with gall: and when he had tasted thereof, he would not drink. And it was the third hour,* and there they crucified him; and with him they crucified two thieves; the one on his right hand, and the other on his left, and Jesus in the midst. And the Scripture was fulfilled, which saith,† And he was numbered with the transgressors. Then said Jesus, Father, forgive them; for they know not what they do.

And Pilate wrote a title of his accusation, and put it on the cross, over his head: and

L 23, 28

— 29

— 30

— 31

— 33
J 19, 17
K 15, 22
M 27, 34

K 15, 25
L 23, 33
K 15, 27

J 19, 18
K 15, 28

L 23, 34

J 19, 19
K 15, 26
J 19, 19
M 27, 37

* *i.e.* 9 A.M.   † Isa. liii, 12.

| Mar. 27. | | Sep. 25. |
| June 26. | The Four Gospels arranged | Dec. 25. |

L 23, 38   the writing was, THIS IS JESUS OF NAZARETH THE KING OF THE
J 19, 19   JEWS. And it was written in Hebrew,
— 20   and Greek, and Latin. This title then read many of the Jews: for the place where Jesus
— 21   was crucified was nigh to the city. Then said the chief priests of the Jews to Pilate, Write not, The King of the Jews; but that
— 22   he said, I am King of the Jews. Pilate answered, What I have written I have written.

— 23   Then the soldiers, when they had crucified Jesus, took his garments, and made four parts, to every soldier a part; and also his coat: now the coat was without seam, woven from the
— 24   top throughout. They said therefore among themselves, Let us not rend it, but cast lots for it, whose it shall be; that the scripture might be fulfilled which saith,* They parted my raiment among them, and for my vesture they did cast lots. These things therefore the
M 27, 36   soldiers did. And sitting down they watched
L 23, 36   him there, and mocked him, saying, If thou
— 37   art the King of the Jews, save thyself.
M 27, 39   And they that passed by reviled him, wagging their heads, and saying, Ah, thou that destroyest the temple, and buildest it in three

* Psa. xxii, 19.

| Mar. 27. June 26. | in one Continuous Narrative. | Sep. 25. Dec. 25. |

days, save thyself. If thou art the Son of God, come down from the cross. And the people stood beholding; and the rulers also with them; likewise also the chief priests mocking said among themselves with the scribes and elders, He saved others; himself he cannot save. If he is the Christ, the chosen of God, the King of Israel, let him now come down from the cross, and we will believe him. He trusted in God; let him deliver him now, if he will have him; for he said, I am the Son of God. The thieves also, which were crucified with him, cast the same in his teeth.*

And one of the malefactors which were hanged railed on him, saying, If thou art Christ, save thyself and us. But the other answering rebuked him, saying, Dost not thou fear God, seeing thou art in the same condemnation? And we indeed justly; for we receive the due reward of our deeds; but this man hath done nothing amiss. And he said unto Jesus, Lord, remember me when thou comest into thy kingdom. And Jesus said unto him, Verily, I say unto thee, to-day shalt thou be with me in paradise.

M 27, 40
L 23, 35

K 15, 31

M 27, 41
L 23, 35
M 27, 42

— 43

— 44

L 23, 39

— 40

— 41

— 42

— 43

* Psa. xxii, 7, 8.

LXXXVII.

MAR. 28. JUNE 27. SEP. 26. DEC. 26.

Christ's death and burial.

J 19, 25 — NOW there stood by the cross of Jesus his mother, and his mother's sister, Mary, the wife of Cleophas, and Mary Magdalene.

K 15, 40 — There were also women looking on afar off; among whom were Mary, the mother of James

M 27, 56
L 23, 49 — the less and of Joses, and Salome, the mother of Zebedee's children, and all his acquaintance,

K 15, 41 — and the women, who also, when he was in Galilee, followed him, and ministered unto him, and many other women which came up with him unto Jerusalem.

J 19, 26 — When Jesus therefore saw his mother, and the disciple standing by, whom he loved, he said unto his mother, Woman, behold thy son!

— 27 — Then said he to the disciple, Behold thy mother! And from that hour that disciple took her unto his own home.

K 15, 33 — And when the sixth hour* was come there was darkness over the whole land until the

— 34 — ninth hour.† And at the ninth hour Jesus cried with a loud voice, saying, Eloi, Eloi, lama sabachthani? which is, being interpreted,

* *i.e.* noon. † *i.e.* 3 P.M.

| Mar. 28. June 27. | in one Continuous Narrative. | Sep. 26. Dec. 26. |

My God, my God, why hast thou forsaken me?* And some of them that stood by, when they heard it, said, Behold, he calleth Elijah. The rest said, Let be, let us see whether Elijah will come to save him.

After this, Jesus knowing that all things were now accomplished, that the scripture might be fulfilled,† said, I thirst. Now there was set a vessel full of vinegar; and straightway one of them ran, and took a sponge, and filled it with vinegar, and put it upon hyssop, and put it to his mouth. When Jesus therefore had received the vinegar, he said, It is finished. And when he had cried again with a loud voice, Father, into thy hands I commend my spirit,‡ he bowed his head, and gave up the ghost.

Now when the centurion, which stood over against him, saw that he so cried out, and gave up the ghost, he glorified God, saying, Certainly this was a righteous man. And all the people that came together to that sight, beholding the things which were done, feared greatly, and smote their breasts, and returned, saying, Truly this was the Son of God.

And the sun was darkened, and the veil of the temple was rent in twain from the top to the bottom.

* Psa. xxii, 1.   † Psa. lxix, 21.   ‡ Psa. xxxi, 5.

Side references:
K 15, 34
— 35
M 27, 49
J 19, 28
— 29
M 27, 48
J 19, 29
— 30
M 27, 50
L 23, 46
J 19, 30
M 27, 54
K 15, 39
L 23, 47
— 48
M 27, 54
L 23, 48
M 27, 54
L 23, 45
K 15, 38

| Mar. 23. | | Sep. 26. |
| June 27. | **The Four Gospels arranged** | Dec. 26. |

J 19, 31 — The Jews, because it was the preparation, that the bodies should not remain upon the cross on the sabbath day, (for that sabbath day was a high day,) besought Pilate that their legs might be broken, and that they might be taken

— 32 away. Then came the soldiers, and broke the legs of the first, and of the other which was cru-

— 33 cified with him. But when they came to Jesus, and saw that he was dead already, they broke

— 34 not his legs; but one of the soldiers with a spear pierced his side, and forthwith came there-

— 35 out blood and water. And he that saw it bore record, and his record is true; and he knoweth

— 36 that he saith true, that ye might believe. For these things were done that the scripture should be fulfilled,* A bone of him shall not be broken.

— 37 And again another scripture saith, †They shall look on him whom they pierced.

K 15, 42 — And now when the even was come, that is,
— 43
M 27, 57 the day before the sabbath, Joseph, a rich man
L 23, 51
K 15, 43 of Arimathea, a city of the Jews, an honour-
L 23, 50 able counsellor, a good man, and a just, (the
— 51 same had not consented to the counsel and
J 19, 38 deed of them), being a disciple of Jesus, but secretly for fear of the Jews, who also himself
K 15, 43 waited for the kingdom of God, went in boldly
J 19, 38 and besought Pilate that he might take away

* Ex. xii, 46.   † Zech. xii, 10.

| Mar. 28. June 27. | in one Continuous Narrative. | Sep. 2?. Dec. 26. |

the body of Jesus. And Pilate marvelled if he was already dead : and calling unto him the centurion, he asked him whether he had been any while dead. And when he knew it of the centurion, he commanded the body to be delivered to Joseph.	K 15, 44 — 45 M 27, 58 K 15, 45
And he bought fine linen, and took him down; and there came also Nicodemus, who at the first came to Jesus by night, and brought a mixture of myrrh and aloes, about a hundred pound weight. Then took they the body of Jesus, and wound it in clean linen clothes with the spices, as the manner of the Jews is to bury.	— 46 J 19, 39 M 27, 59 J 19, 40
Now in the place where he was crucified there was a garden ; and in the garden a new sepulchre, Joseph of Arimathea's own new tomb, which he had hewn out in the rock ; and wherein never man before was laid.* There laid they Jesus therefore, for the sepulchre was nigh at hand. And Mary Magdalene and Mary the mother of Jesus, and the women also which came with him from Galilee, followed after, and beheld the sepulchre, and how the body was laid. And Joseph rolled a great stone to the door of the sepulchre, and departed. And there were Mary Magdalene and the other Mary sitting over against the sepulchre.	— 41 M 27, 60 L 23, 53 J 19, 42 K 15, 47 L 23, 55 M 27, 60 — 61

* Isa. liii, 9.

| | Mar. 29. June 28. | The Four Gospels arranged | Sep. 27. Dec. 27. |

LXXXVIII.

MAR. 29.   JUNE 28.   SEP. 27.   DEC. 27.

A guard placed at the sepulchre. The resurrection of Christ. The women come to the sepulchre. Christ appears to Mary Magdalene.

M 27, 62

— 63

— 64

— 65

— 66

K 16, 2

J 20 1

M 28, 2

— 3

NOW the next day, that followed the day of the preparation, the chief priests and Pharisees came together unto Pilate, saying, Sir, we remember that that deceiver said,* while he was yet alive, After three days I will rise again. Command therefore that the sepulchre be made sure until the third day, lest his disciples come by night, and steal him away, and say unto the people, He is risen from the dead; so the last error shall be worse than the first. Pilate said unto them, Ye have a watch; go your way, make it as sure as ye can. So they went, and made the sepulchre sure, sealing the stone, and setting a watch.

Very early in the morning, when it was yet dark, behold, there was a great earthquake; for the angel of the Lord descended from heaven, and came and rolled back the stone from the door, and sat upon it. His countenance was like lightning, and his raiment white

* Luke ix 22. Section xliii.

| Mar. 29. June 28. | in one Continuous Narrative. | Sep. 27. Dec. 27. |

as snow; and for fear of him the keepers did shake, and became as dead men. And the rocks rent; and the graves were opened; and many bodies of the saints which slept arose, and came out of the graves after his resurrection, and went into the holy city, and appeared unto many.

And some of the watch came into the city, and showed unto the chief priests all the things that were done. And when they were assembled with the elders, and had taken counsel, they gave large money unto the soldiers, saying, Say ye, His disciples came by night, and stole him away while we slept. And if this come to the governor's ears, we will persuade him, and secure you. So they took the money, and did as they were taught; and this saying is commonly reported among the Jews until this day.

In the end of the sabbath, as it began to dawn toward the first day of the week, came Mary Magdalene and the other Mary, the mother of James, and Salome, to see the sepulchre, and brought sweet spices that they might anoint him. And they said among themselves, Who shall roll us away the stone from the door of the sepulchre? for it was very great. And when they looked, they saw that the stone was rolled away.

M 28, 4
M 27, 51
— 52
— 53

M 28, 11
— 12
— 13
— 14
— 15

— 1
K 16, 1
M 28, 1
K 16, 1
— 3
— 4

| Mar. 29. June 28. | The Four Gospels arranged | Sep. 27. Dec. 27. |

J 20, 2 — Then Mary Magdalene ran, and came to Simon Peter, and to the other disciple, whom Jesus loved, and said unto them, They have taken away the Lord out of the sepulchre, and we know not where they have laid him.

K 16, 2
M 28, 2
— 5
— 6

And the women came unto the sepulchre at the rising of the sun, and an angel sat upon the stone; and said unto the women, Fear not ye, for I know that ye seek Jesus who was crucified. He is not here; for he is risen, as he said.* Come, see the place where the Lord lay.

K 16, 5
— 6
— 7
M 28, 7
K 16, 7

And entering into the sepulchre, they saw a young man sitting on the right side, clothed in a long white garment, and they were affrighted. And he said unto them, Be not affrighted: ye seek Jesus of Nazareth, who was crucified. He is risen; he is not here. Behold the place where they laid him. But go your way quickly, and tell his disciples and Peter, that he goeth before you into Galilee; there shall ye see him, as he said unto you.†

M 28, 7
K 16, 8
M 28, 8
K 16, 8
M 28, 8
J 20, 2

Lo, I have told you. And they went out quickly, and fled from the sepulchre with fear and great joy; neither said they anything to any man, for they were afraid, and did run to bring his disciples word.

Mary Magdalene having told Peter and that

* Luke ix, 22. Sect. xliii.   † John xvi, 22. Sect. lxxix.

| Mar. 29. June 23. | in one Continuous Narrative. | Sep. 27. Dec. 27. |

other disciple, they went forth and came to the sepulchre. So they ran both together; and the other disciple did outrun Peter, and came first to the sepulchre. And he stooping down, and looking in, saw the linen clothes lying; yet went he not in. Then came Simon Peter following him, and went into the sepulchre, and saw the linen clothes lie, and the napkin, that was about his head, not lying with the linen clothes, but wrapped together in a place by itself. Then went in also that other disciple, which came first to the sepulchre, and he saw, and believed. For as yet they knew not the scripture,* that he must rise again from the dead. Then the two disciples went away again unto their own home, wondering at that which was come to pass.

But Mary stood without at the sepulchre weeping; and as she wept, she stooped down, and looked into the sepulchre, and saw two angels in white sitting, the one at the head, and the other at the feet, where the body of Jesus had lain. And they said unto her, Woman, why weepest thou? She said unto them, Because they have taken away my Lord, and I know not where they have laid him. And when she had thus said, she turned

J 20, 3
— 4
— 5
— 6
— 7
— 8
— 9
— 10
L 24, 12
J 20, 11
— 12
— 13
— 14

* Psa. xvi, 10.

Mar. 30. June 29.	The Four Gospels arranged	Sep. 28. Dec. 28.

J 20, 14
— 15
herself back, and saw Jesus standing, and knew not that it was Jesus. Jesus said unto her, Woman, why weepest thou? whom seekest thou? She, supposing him to be the gardener, said unto him, Sir, if thou hast borne him hence, tell me where thou hast laid him, and I will take him away. Jesus said unto her,
— 16
Mary! She turned herself, and said unto him,
— 17
Rabboni! which is to say, Master! Jesus said unto her, Touch me not; for I am not yet ascended to my Father: but go to my brethren and say unto them, I ascend unto my Father, and your Father; and to my God, and your God.

— 18
K 16, 10
J 20, 18
K 16, 11
Mary Magdalene came and told the disciples that had been with him, as they mourned and wept, that she had seen the Lord, and that he had spoken these things unto her. And they, when they had heard that he was alive, and had been seen of her, believed not.

LXXXIX.

MAR. 30. JUNE 29. SEP. 28. DEC. 28.

Christ appears to the women, and afterwards to the two disciples going to Emmaus.

M 28, 9
AND as the women went to tell Jesus' disciples, behold, Jesus met them, saying, All hail! And they came and held him by
— 10
the feet and worshipped him. Then said Jesus

| Mar. 80. June 29. | in one Continuous Narrative. | Sep. 28. Dec. 28. |

unto them, Be not afraid; go tell my brethren that they go into Galilee, and there shall they see me. And the women also which came with him from Galilee, having prepared spices and ointments, and rested the sabbath day according to the commandment,* came unto the sepulchre very early in the morning, upon the first day of the week, bringing the spices which they had prepared; and certain others with them. And they found the stone rolled away from the sepulchre; and they entered in; and found not the body of the Lord Jesus. And it came to pass as they were much perplexed thereabout, behold, two men stood by them in shining garments. And as they were afraid, and bowed down their faces to the earth, they said unto them, Why seek ye the living among the dead? He is not here; but is risen. Remember how he spake unto you, when he was yet in Galilee, saying, The Son of man must be delivered into the hands of sinful men, and be crucified; and the third day rise again.†

And they remembered his words, and returned from the sepulchre, and told all these things unto the eleven, and to all the rest. It was Mary Magdalene, out of whom he had cast seven devils, and Joanna, and Mary the

M 28, 10
L 23, 55
— 56
L 24, 1
— 2
— 3
— 4
— 5
— 6
— 7
— 8
— 9
— 10
K 16, 9
L 24, 10

* Ex. xx, 10. † Luke ix, 22. Section xliii.

Mar. 30.	Sep. 28.
June 29.	Dec. 28.

The Four Gospels arranged

L 24, 10	mother of James, and other women that were with them, which told these things unto the
— 11	apostles. And their words seemed to them as idle tales, and they believed them not.
— 13	And, behold, two of them went that same day to a village called Emmaus, which was
— 14	from Jerusalem about threescore furlongs.* And they talked together of all these things which
— 15	had happened. And it came to pass, that, while they communed together and reasoned, Jesus himself drew near, and went with them.
— 16	But their eyes were holden that they should
K 16, 12	not know him, for he appeared in another
L 24, 17	form. And he said unto them, What manner of communications are these that ye have one
— 18	to another, as ye walk, and are sad? And the one of them, whose name was Cleophas, answering said unto him, Art thou only a stranger in Jerusalem, and hast not known the things which are come to pass there in these
— 19	days? And he said unto them, What things? And they said unto him, Concerning Jesus of Nazareth, which was a prophet mighty in deed
— 20	and word before God and all the people; and how the chief priests and our rulers delivered him to be condemned to death, and have
— 21	crucified him. But we trusted that it had

* Seven miles and a half.

| Mar. 30. June 29. | in one Continuous Narrative. | Sep. 28. Dec. 28. |

been he which should have redeemed Israel; and beside all this, to day is the third day since these things were done. Yea, and certain women also of our company made us astonished, which were early at the sepulchre: and when they found not his body, they came, saying, that they had also seen a vision of angels, which said that he was alive. And certain of them which were with us went to the sepulchre, and found it even so as the women said; but him they saw not.

Then he said unto them, O fools, and slow of heart to believe all that the prophets have spoken; ought not Christ to have suffered these things, and to enter into his glory? And beginning at Moses and all the prophets, he expounded unto them in all the scriptures the things concerning himself. And they drew nigh unto the village, whither they went; and he made as if he would have gone further. But they constrained him, saying, Abide with us; for it is toward evening, and the day is far spent. And he went in to tarry with them. And it came to pass, as he sat at meat with them, that he took bread and blessed it, and brake, and gave to them. And their eyes were opened, and they knew him; and he vanished out of their sight.

L 24, 21
— 22
— 23
— 24
— 25
— 26
— 27
— 28
— 29
— 30
— 31

| Mar. 31. June 30. | The Four Gospels arranged | Sep. 29. Dec. 29. |

L 24, 32 — And they said one to another, Did not our heart burn within us, while he talked with us by the way, and while he opened to us the
— 33 — scriptures? And they rose up the same hour, and returned to Jerusalem, and found the eleven gathered together, and them that were
— 34 — with them, saying, The Lord is risen indeed,
— 35 — and hath appeared to Simon. And they told
K 16, 13 — unto the residue what things were done in the
L 24, 35 — way, and how he was known to them in break-
K 16, 13 — ing of bread; but neither believed they them.

XC.

MAR. 31.   JUNE 30.   SEP. 29.   DEC. 29.

Christ appears to the disciples as they sit at meat.

L 24, 36
K 16, 14
J 20, 19 — AND as the disciples thus spake, while they sat at meat, the same day at evening, being the first day of the week, when the doors were shut where they were assembled for fear
L 24, 36 — of the Jews, came Jesus himself and stood in the midst, and said unto them, Peace be unto
— 37 — you! But they were terrified and affrighted,
— 38 — and supposed that they saw a spirit. And he said unto them, Why are ye troubled? and
K 16, 14 — why do thoughts arise in your hearts? And he upbraided them with their unbelief and

| Mar. 31. June 30. | in one Continuous Narrative. | Sep. 29. Dec. 29. |

hardness of heart, because they believed not them which had seen him after he was risen. And he said, Behold my hands and my feet, that it is I myself; handle me, and see; for a spirit hath not flesh and bones, as ye see me have. And when he had thus spoken, he showed them his hands, and his side, and his feet. Then were the disciples glad, when they saw the Lord.

And while they yet believed not for joy, and wondered, he said unto them, Have ye here any meat? And they gave him a piece of a broiled fish, and of a honeycomb. And he took it, and did eat before them. And he said unto them, These are the words which I spake unto you, while I was yet with you, that all things must be fulfilled, which were written in the law of Moses, and in the prophets, and in the Psalms, concerning me. Then opened he their understanding, that they might understand the scriptures, and said unto them, Thus it is written, and thus it behoved Christ to suffer,* and to rise from the dead the third day; and that repentance and remission of sins should be preached in his name among all nations, beginning at Jerusalem. And ye are witnesses of these things. And behold, I send

* Isa. liii, 5.

K 16, 14
L 24, 39
— 40
J 20, 20
L 24, 40
J 20, 20
L 24, 41
— 42
— 43
— 44
— 45
— 46
— 47
— 48
— 49

Mar. 31. June 30.	𝕮𝖍𝖊 𝕱𝖔𝖚𝖗 𝕲𝖔𝖘𝖕𝖊𝖑𝖘 𝖆𝖗𝖗𝖆𝖓𝖌𝖊𝖉	Sep. 29. Dec. 29.

L 24, 49	the promise of my Father* upon you ; but tarry ye in the city of Jerusalem, until ye be endued with power from on high.
J 20, 21	Then said Jesus to them again, Peace be unto you ! As my Father hath sent me, even so send I you. Ye shall be witnesses unto me, in Jerusalem and in all Judæa and in Samaria, and unto the uttermost parts of the earth. Go ye into all the world, and preach the gospel to every creature. He that believeth and is baptized shall be saved ; but he that believeth not shall be damned. And these signs shall follow them that believe ; in my name shall they cast out devils ; they shall speak with new tongues ; they shall take up serpents, and tread on scorpions, and have power over all the power of the enemy ; and nothing shall by any means hurt them. If they drink any deadly thing, it shall not hurt them ; and they shall lay hands on the sick, and they shall recover.
A 1, 8	
K 16, 15	
— 16	
— 17	
— 18 L 10, 19	
K 16, 18	
J 20, 22	And when he had said this, he breathed on them, and said unto them, Receive ye the Holy Ghost ; whosesoever sins ye remit, they are remitted unto them ; and whosesoever sins ye retain, they are retained. Verily, I say unto you, whatsoever ye shall bind on earth shall be bound in heaven ; and whatsoever ye shall
— 23	
M 18, 18	

* Isa. xliv, 8   Joel ii, 28.

| Mar. 31. | | Sep. 29. |
| June 30. | in one Continuous Narrative. | Dec. 29. |

loose on earth, shall be loosed in heaven. Again I say unto you, that if two of you shall agree on earth as touching any thing that they shall ask, it shall be done for them of my Father which is in heaven; for where two or three are gathered together in my name, there am I in the midst of them.	M 18, 18 — 19 — 20
But Thomas, called Didymus, one of the twelve, was not with them when Jesus came. The other disciples therefore said unto him, We have seen the Lord! But he said unto them, Except I shall see in his hands the print of the nails, and put my finger into the print of the nails, and thrust my hand into his side, I will not believe.	J 20, 24 — 25
And after eight days, again his disciples were within, and Thomas with them; then came Jesus, the doors being shut, and stood in the midst, and said, Peace be unto you! Then said he to Thomas, Reach hither thy finger, and behold my hands; and reach hither thy hand, and thrust it into my side; and be not faithless, but believing. And Thomas answered and said unto him, My Lord and my God! Jesus said unto him, Thomas, because thou hast seen me, thou hast believed; blessed are they that have not seen, and yet have believed.	— 26 — 27 — 28 — 29

XCI.

Apl. 1. July 1. Sep. 30. Dec. 30.

Christ appears to the disciples at the sea of Tiberias. Christ's ascension to heaven.

J 21, 1 — AFTER these things Jesus showed himself again to the disciples, at the sea of Tiberias; and on this wise showed he himself.
— 2 — There were together Simon Peter, and Thomas called Didymus, and Nathanael of Cana in Galilee, and the sons of Zebedee, and two
— 3 — other of his disciples. Simon Peter said unto them, I go a fishing. They said unto him, We also go with thee. They went forth, and entered into a ship immediately; and that
— 4 — night they caught nothing. But when the morning was now come, Jesus stood on the shore; but the disciples knew not that it was
— 5 — Jesus. Then Jesus said unto them, Children, have ye any meat? They answered him, No.
— 6 — And he said unto them, Cast the net on the right side of the ship, and ye shall find. They cast therefore, and then they were not able to
— 7 — draw it for the multitude of fishes. Therefore that disciple whom Jesus loved said unto Peter, It is the Lord. Then when Simon Peter heard that it was the Lord, he girt his fisher's coat

| Apl. 1. July 1. | in one Continuous Narrative. | Sep. 30. Dec. 30. |

unto him (for he was naked), and did cast himself into the sea. And the other disciples came in a little ship; (for they were not far from land, but as it were two hundred cubits,) dragging the net with fishes. As soon then as they were come to land, they saw a fire of coals there, and fish laid thereon, and bread. Jesus said unto them, Bring of the fish which ye have now caught. Simon Peter went up, and drew the net to land full of great fishes, a hundred and fifty and three; and for all there were so many, yet was not the net broken. Jesus said unto them, Come and dine. And none of the disciples durst ask him, Who art thou? knowing that it was the Lord. Jesus then came and took bread, and gave them, and fish likewise. This is the third time that Jesus showed himself to his disciples, after that he was risen from the dead.

So when they had dined, Jesus said to Simon Peter, Simon, son of Jonas, lovest thou me more than these? He said unto him, Yea, Lord; thou knowest that I love thee. He said unto him, Feed my lambs. He said to him again, the second time, Simon, son of Jonas, lovest thou me? He said unto him, Yea, Lord; thou knowest that I love thee. He said unto him, Feed my sheep. He said unto him the third

J 21, 7
— 8
— 9
— 10
— 11
— 12
— 13
— 14
— 15
— 16
— 17

| Apl. 1. | | Sep. 30. |
| July 1. | **The Four Gospels arranged** | Dec. 30. |

J 21, 17 — time, Simon, son of Jonas, lovest thou me? Peter was grieved because he said unto him the third time, Lovest thou me? And he said unto him, Lord, thou knowest all things; thou knowest that I love thee. Jesus said unto him,

— 18 Feed my sheep. Verily, verily, I say unto thee, when thou wast young, thou girdedst thyself, and walkedst whither thou wouldest: but when thou shalt be old, thou shalt stretch forth thy hands, and another shall gird thee, and carry thee whither thou wouldest not.

— 19 This spake he, signifying by what death he should glorify God. And when he had spoken

— 20 this, he said unto him, Follow me. Then Peter, turning about, saw the disciple whom Jesus loved following; which also leaned on his breast at supper, and said, Lord, which is

— 21 he that betrayeth thee? Peter seeing him, said to Jesus, Lord, and what shall this man do?

— 22 Jesus said unto him, If I will that he tarry till I come, what is that to thee? follow thou me.

— 23 Then went this saying abroad among the brethren, that that disciple should not die; yet Jesus said not unto him, He shall not die; but, If I will that he tarry till I come, what is that to thee?

— 24 This is the disciple which testifieth of these things, and wrote these things; and we know that his testimony is true.

| Apl. 1. July 1. | in one Continuous Narrative. | Sep. 30. Dec. 30. |

Then the eleven disciples went away into Galilee, into a mountain where Jesus had appointed them. And when they saw him, they worshipped him, but some doubted. And Jesus came and spake unto them, saying, All power is given unto me in heaven and on earth. Go ye therefore, and teach all nations, baptizing them in the name of the Father, and of the Son, and of the Holy Ghost; teaching them to observe all things whatsoever I have commanded you; and, lo, I am with you alway, even unto the end of the world. | M 28, 16 — 17 — 18 — 19 — 20

After that, he was seen of above five hundred brethren at once, of whom the greater part remain unto this present, but some are fallen asleep. After that, he was seen of James, then of all the apostles. To whom also he showed himself alive after his passion, by many infallible proofs, being seen of them forty days, and speaking of the things pertaining to the kingdom of God, until the day in which he was taken up, after that he through the Holy Ghost had given commandments unto the apostles whom he had chosen. | 1 C. 15, 6 — 7 A 1, 3 — 2

And he led them out as far as to Bethany, and he lifted up his hands, and blessed them. And it came to pass, while he blessed them, that he was parted from them, and a cloud received | L 24, 50 — 51 A 1, 9

| Apl. 1. | | Sep. 30. |
| July 1. | The Four Gospels arranged | Dec. 30. |

L 24, 51
K 16, 19
L 24, 52
A 1, 10

— 11

— 12
L 24, 52
A 1, 12

L 24, 53
K 16, 20

J 20, 30

J 21, 25

J 20, 31

him out of their sight; and he was carried up into heaven, and sat on the right hand of God. And they worshipped him.

And while they looked steadfastly toward heaven as he went up, behold, two men stood by them in white apparel, which also said, Ye men of Galilee, why stand ye gazing up into heaven? this same Jesus, who is taken up from you into heaven, shall so come in like manner as ye have seen him go into heaven.

Then returned they with great joy unto Jerusalem from the mount called Olivet, which is from Jerusalem a sabbath-day's journey, and were continually in the temple, praising and blessing God. And they went forth, and preached every where, the Lord working with them, and confirming the word with signs following.

And many other signs truly did Jesus in the presence of his disciples, which are not written in this book; the which, if they should be written every one, I suppose that even the world itself could not contain the books that should be written. But these are written, that ye might believe that Jesus is the Christ, the Son of God; and that believing ye might have life through his name. Amen.

XCII.

For Apl. 2, July 2, and Oct. 1, see page 1.

December 31.

The genealogy of Christ through Joseph.

THE book of the generation of Jesus Christ, the son of David, the son of Abraham. Abraham begat Isaac; and Isaac begat Jacob; and Jacob begat Judah and his brethren; and Judah begat Pharez and Zarah of Tamar; and Pharez begat Hezron; and Hezron begat Ram; and Ram begat Amminadab; and Amminadab begat Nahshon; and Nahshon begat Salmon; and Salmon begat Boaz of Rahab; and Boaz begat Obed of Ruth; and Obed begat Jesse; and Jesse begat David the king.

And David the king begat Solomon of her that had been the wife of Uriah; and Solomon begat Rehoboam; and Rehoboam begat Abijah; and Abijah begat Asa; and Asa begat Jehoshaphat; and Jehoshaphat begat Jehoram; and Jehoram begat Uzziah; and Uzziah begat Jotham; and Jotham begat Ahaz; and Ahaz begat Hezekiah; and Hezekiah begat Manasseh; and Manasseh begat Amon; and Amon begat Josiah; and Josiah begat Jeconiah and his brethren, about the time they were carried away to Babylon.

M 1, 1
— 2
— 3
— 4
— 5
— 6
— 7
— 8
— 9
— 10
— 11

M 1,12	And after they were brought to Babylon, Jeconiah begat Salathiel; and Salathiel be-
— 13	gat Zerubbabel; and Zerubbabel begat Abiud; and Abiud begat Eliakim; and Eliakim begat
— 14	Azor; and Azor begat Zadoc; and Sadoc begat
— 15	Achim; and Achim begat Eliud; and Eliud be- gat Eleazar; and Eleazar begat Matthan; and
— 16	Matthan begat Jacob; and Jacob begat Joseph the husband of Mary, of whom was born Jesus, who is called Christ.
— 17	So all the generations from Abraham to David are fourteen generations; and from David until the carrying away into Babylon are fourteen generations; and from the carrying away into Babylon unto Christ are fourteen generations.

XCIII.

FEB. 29. LEAP YEAR.

The genealogy of Christ through Mary.

L 3,23 — 24	JESUS himself was supposed to be the son of Joseph, who was the son of Heli, who was the son of Matthat, who was the son of Levi, who was the son of Melchi, who was the
— 25	son of Janna, who was the son of Joseph, who was the son of Mattathias, who was the son of Amos, who was the son of Nahum, who was

| Feb. 29. | in one Continuous Narrative. | Feb. 29. |

the son of Eli, who was the son of Naggia, who was the son of Maath, who was the son of Mattathias, who was the son of Shimei, who was the son of Joseph, who was the son of Juda, who was the son of Joanna, who was the son of Rhesa, who was the son of Zerubbabel, who was the son of Salathiel, who was the son of Neri, who was the son of Melchi, who was the son of Addi, who was the son of Cosam, who was the son of Elmodam, who was the son of Er, who was the son of Joses, who was the son of Eliezer, who was the son of Jorim, who was the son of Matthat, who was the son of Levi, who was the son of Simeon, who was the son of Judah, who was the son of Joseph, who was the son of Jonan, who was the son of Eliakim, who was the son of Melea, who was the son of Mainon, who was the son of Mattathias, who was the son of Nathan, who was the son of David, who was the son of Jesse,* who was the son of Obed, who was the son of Boaz, who was the son of Salmon, who was the son of Nahshon, who was the son of Amminadab, who was the son of Ram, who was the son of Hezron, who was the son of Pharez, who was the son of Judah, who was the son of Jacob, who was the son of

L 3, 2;
— 27
— 28
— 29
— 30
— 31
— 32
— 33
— 34

* Isa. xi, 1.

L 3, 34	Isaac, who was the son of Abraham, who was the son of Terah, who was the son of Nahor,
— 35	who was the son of Serug, who was the son of Reu, who was the son of Peleg, who was the
— 36	son of Eber, who was the son of Shelah, who was the son of Cainan, who was the son of Arphaxad, who was the son of Shem, who was the son of Noah, who was the son of
— 37	Lamech, who was the son of Methusaleh, who was the son of Enoch, who was the son of Jared, who was the son of Mahalaleel, who was the son of Cainan, who was the son of
— 38	Enos, who was the son of Seth, who was the son of Adam, who was the son of God.*

* Gen. v. 1.

INDEX,

SHOWING WHERE THE SUBJECT OF EVERY VERSE IN EACH OF THE FOUR GOSPELS MAY BE FOUND IN THIS WORK.

The Roman figures in the columns headed Verses *indicate that the very words of that verse, in whole or in part, have been used; and the Italic figures, that the sense of that verse has been given in the words of one of the other Gospels.*

Matthew.

Chap.	Verses.	Sec.	Chap.	Verses.	Sec.	Chap.	Verses.	Sec.
I	1-17	92	IV	23-25	15	VI	28-34	31
	18-25	3	V	1-12	19	VII	*1*	22
II	1-23	5		13, 14	19		2	22
III	1-3	6		*15*	19		*3-5*	22
	4	2		16, 20	19		6	48
	5-7	6		21-24	20		*7-11*	53
	8-10	6		*25*	20		12	21
	11	7		26, 30	20		13, 14	57
	12	7		*31*	61		15, 16	22
	13-15	7		32	61		17, 18	22
	16, 17	7		33-37	20		*19*	6
IV	*1*	7		38-47	21		*20*	22
	2	7		48	21		21	22
	3, 4	7	VI	1-8	21		22	57
	5	7		9-14	53		*23*	57
	6	7		*15*	53		*24*	22
	7-9	7		16-18	22		25	22
	10	7		19-21	31		*26, 27*	22
	11	7		*22*	20		*28, 29*	14
	12	11		23	20	VIII	1	23
	13-16	14		*24*	60		2-4	15
	17	11		25, 26	31		*5*	23
	18-22	14		*27*	31		6	23

297

Matthew.

Chap.	Verses.	Sec.	Chap.	Verses.	Sec.	Chap.	Verses.	Sec.
VIII	7, 10	23	X	30, 31	31	XIII	9	32
	11	57		32, 33	44		10, 11	33
	12	57		34-36	72		12	64
	13	23		37, 38	43		13-23	33
	14, 15	14		39	43		24-30	32
	16, 17	15		40, 41	36		31, 32	33
	18-20	34		42	36		33	33
	21	34	XI	1	36		34-36	33
	22	34		2	24		36-53	34
	23, 24	35		3-11	24		54-57	18
	25	35		12	24		58	18
	26, 27	35		13	24	XIV	1	24
	28-32	35		14	24		2	24
	33	35		15-19	24		3, 4	11
	34	35		20-24	25		5	11
IX	1	35		25-27	52		6-11	24
	2-4	16		28-30	50		12	24
	5-7	16	XII	1	27		13	37
	8, 9	16		2-4	27		14, 15	37
	10-13	16		5-8	27		16	37
	13	27		9	27		17	37
	14-16	16		10	27		18, 19	37
	17	16		11, 12	27		20	37
	18-23	17		13, 14	27		21	37
	24, 25	17		15	27		22-25	38
	26	17		16	28		26	38
	27-38	18		17-28	28		27-33	38
X	1	36		29	28		34, 35	38
	2-4	18		30	60		36	38
	5-11	36		31, 32	28	XV	1-3	40
	12, 13	36		33	22		4	40
	14, 15	36		34	28		5	40
	16	48		35	22		6-9	40
	17, 18	72		36, 37	28		10, 11	40
	19	72		38-40	29		12-15	40
	20-22	72		41-44	29		16, 17	40
	23-26	48		45-50	29		18-20	40
	26, 27	30	XIII	1	32		21-31	41
	28	72		2, 3	32		32	42
	29	31		4-8	32		33	42

Matthew.

Chap.	Verses.	Sec.	Chap.	Verses.	Sec.	Chap.	Verses.	Sec.
XV	34-36	42	XIX	22-26	62	XXIII	22	20
	37-39	42		27	43		23, 24	30
XVI	1-4	42		28	44		25	30
	5	42		29	43		26-28	30
	6	42		30	62		29-37	70
	7	42	XX	1-16	62		38, 39	70
	8-12	42		17	46	XXIV	1-8	72
	13-23	43		18	46		9	72
	24-26	43		19	46		10	72
	27	44		20-28	63		11, 12	73
	28	44		29	63		13	72
XVII	1, 2	44		30	63		14, 15	73
	3, 4	44		31-33	63		16-18	73
	5-7	44		34	63		19-22	73
	8	44	XXI	1-12	66		23	73
	9-13	44		13	66		24	73
	14, 15	45		14-17	66		25	73
	16, 17	45		18-22	67		26	73
	18	45		23, 24	67		27, 28	73
	19	45		25-32	67		29-31	73
	20, 21	45		33-35	68		32-35	74
	22	46		36, 37	68		36-39	74
	23-27	46		38-46	68		40	74
XVIII	1	46	XXII	1-13	58		41	74
	2	46		14	62		42	74
	3, 4	46		15-22	68		43, 44	74
	5	46		23	69		45-50	74
	6, 7	47		24-28	69		51	74
	8, 9	20		29-31	69	XXV	1-13	75
	10	47		32	69		14-26	64
	11	59		33-36	69		27	64
	12-14	59		37	69		28-30	64
	15-17	47		38-43	69		31-46	75
	18-20	90		44, 45	69	XXVI	1-5	76
	21-35	47		46	69		6, 7	65
XIX	1, 2	48	XXIII	1-10	70		8, 9	65
	3-13	61		11	46		10	65
	14	61		12	46		11-13	65
	15	61		13	30		14	76
	16-21	62		14-21	70		15-18	76

Matthew.

Chap.	Verses.	Sec.	Chap.	Verses.	Sec.	Chap.	Verses.	Sec.
XXVI	19, 20	76	XXVII	1, 2	84	XXVII	33	86
	21	77		3-10	85		34	86
	22	77		11	84		35	86
	23, 24	77		12	84		36, 37	86
	25	77		13	84		38	86
	26-29	76		14	84		39-44	86
	30-35	81		15-17	84		45-47	87
	36-42	82		18	84		48-54	87
	43	82		19	85		55	87
	44-56	82		20-22	84		56-61	87
	57-61	83		23	84		62-66	88
	62	83		24, 25	85	XXVIII	1-8	88
	63-72	83		26	85		9, 10	89
	73, 74	83		27-30	85		11-15	88
	75	83		31, 32	86		16-20	91

Mark.

Chap.	Verses.	Sec.	Chap.	Verses.	Sec.	Chap.	Verses.	Sec.
I	1	Intro.	I	35-39	15	II	23, 24	27
	2	24		40	15		25-28	27
	3-5	6		41-43	15	III	1-3	27
	6	2		44	15		4-8	27
	7	7		45	15		8-12	28
	8	7	II	1-4	16		13-17	18
	9, 10	7		5	16		18, 19	18
	11, 12	7		6	16		19-23	28
	13	7		7	16		24-26	28
	14, 15	11		8, 9	16		27-30	28
	16	14		10-12	16	IV	31	29
	17-19	14		13	16		32-35	29
	20-22	14		14	18		1-5	32
	23-25	14		15	16		6	32
	26-31	14		16, 17	16		7, 8	32
	32, 33	15		18, 19	16		9	32
	34	15		20-22	16		10-14	33

Mark.

Chap.	Verses.	Sec.	Chap.	Verses.	Sec.	Chap.	Verses.	Sec.
IV	15-18	33	VI	45	38	IX	47	20
	19, 20	33		46	38		48	20
	21	29		47-56	38		49, 50	19
	22	30	VII	1-6	40	X	1	48
	23	32		7	40		2-4	61
	24	22		8, 9	40		5	61
	24	33		10	40		6-9	61
	25	64		11-19	40		10	61
	26-29	32		20	40		11	61
	30, 31	33		21-23	40		12-14	61
	32-34	33		24-37	41		15	61
	35	34	VIII	1-7	42		16	61
	36-41	35		8, 9	42		17-27	62
V	1-8	35		10-20	42		28	43
	9	35		21	42		29, 30	43
	10-13	35		22-26	42		31	62
	14, 15	35		27	43		32-34	46
	16-21	35		28-30	43		35-37	63
	22	17		31-37	43		38-45	63
	23	17		38	44		46, 47	63
	24	17	IX	1, 3	44		48	63
	25-27	17		4, 5	44		49-52	63
	28	17		6	44	XI	1	66
	29, 30	17		7	44		2	66
	31	17		8	44		3	66
	32	17		9	44		4-6	66
	33-35	17		10	44		7-10	66
	36, 37	17		11	44		11	66
	38, 39	17		12, 13	44		12-14	67
	40-43	17		14-18	45		15	66
VI	1-6	18		19	45		16-18	66
	7-9	36		20-28	45		19-24	76
	10, 11	36		29	45		25, 26	53
	12, 13	36		30, 31	46		27, 28	67
	14	24		32	46		29, 30	67
	15, 16	24		33, 37	46		31	67
	17-20	11		38-40	45		32	67
	21-29	24		41	36		33	67
	30-43	37		42	47	XII	1-3	68
	44	37		43-46	20		4, 5	68

Mark.

Chap.	Verses.	Sec.	Chap.	Verses.	Sec.	Chap.	Verses.	Sec.
XII	6	68	XIII	30, 31	74	XIV	53	83
	7	68		32-37	74		54-62	83
	8-11	68	XIV	1	76		63-65	83
	12	68		2	76		66-68	83
	13	68		3-9	65		69	83
	14, 15	68		10, 11	76		70-72	83
	16, 17	68		12-17	76	XV	1	84
	18, 19	69		18	77		2	84
	20-22	69		19	77		3-14	84
	23-25	69		20, 21	77		15, 16	85
	26-37	69		22	76		17-19	85
	38-40	70		23	76		20-22	86
	41-44	70		24, 25	76		23, 24	86
XIII	1, 2	72		26-29	81		25-28	86
	3	72		30, 31	81		29, 31	86
	4-9	72		32	82		32	86
	10	73		33	82		33-35	87
	11	72		34-36	82		36, 37	87
	12, 13	72		37	82		38-47	87
	14-16	73		38, 39	82	XVI	1-8	88
	17-19	73		40, 41	82		9	89
	20-23	73		42	82		10, 11	88
	24-26	73		43, 44	82		12, 13	89
	27	73		45-50	82		14-18	90
	28, 29	74		51, 52	82		19, 20	91

Luke.

Chap.	Verses.	Sec.	Chap.	Verses.	Sec.	Chap.	Verses.	Sec.
I	1-4	Intro.	III	7	6	IV	16-30	13
	5-38	1		8-14	6		31-36	14
	17	44		15-18	7		37	14
	39-80	2		19, 20	11		38, 39	14
II	1-7	3		21-23	7		40-43	15
	8-39	4		23-38	93		44	15
	40-52	6	IV	1-13	7	V	1-11	14
III	1-6	6		14, 15	11		12	15

Luke.

Chap.	Verses.	Sec.	Chap.	Verses.	Sec.	Chap.	Verses.	Sec.
V	13	15	VIII	32, 33	35	X	25-42	53
	14-16	15		34-37	35	XI	1, 2	53
	17-39	16		38, 39	35		3	53
VI	1-3	27		40	35		4-13	53
	4, 5	27		41-43	17		14, 15	28
	6-9	27		44	17		16	29
	10	27		45-56	17		17-20	28
	11	27	IX	1	36		21, 22	28
	12, 13	18		2, 6	36		23	60
	14	18		7-9	24		24, 25	29
	15-19	18		10-13	37		26	29
	20, 21	19		14, 15	37		27-32	29
	22-26	19		16	36		33	19
	27-29	21		17	37		34-36	20
	30	21		18, 19	43		37-42	30
	30	22		20-22	43		43	70
	31	21		23-25	43		44-46	30
	32-36	21		26-36	44		47	70
	37, 38	22		37-43	45		48-50	70
	39	40		43-45	46		51	70
	40	48		46	46		52-54	30
	41-49	22		47, 48	46	XII	1-3	30
VII	1-17	23		49, 50	45		4, 5	72
	18-35	24		51-56	48		6, 7	31
	36-50	25		57, 58	34		8, 9	44
VIII	1-3	28		59-62	34		10	20
	4-6	32	X	1, 2	48		11, 12	72
	7	32		2	18		13-21	31
	8	32		3	48		22-24	31
	9, 10	33		4-8	36		25, 26	31
	11, 15	33		9	36		27	31
	16	19		10, 11	36		28	31
	17	30		12	36		29-31	31
	18	33		13, 14	65		32	72
	18	64		15	25		33	31
	19	29		16	36		34	31
	20	29		17, 18	52		35-38	75
	21	29		19	90		39, 40	74
	22	34		20-22	52		41-48	74
	22-31	35		23, 24	33		49	72

Luke.

Chap.	Verses.	Sec.	Chap.	Verses.	Sec.	Chap.	Verses.	Sec.
XII	50	82	XVIII	1-14	61	XX	37	69
	51, 52	72		15	61		38, 39	69
	53	72		16, 17	61		40, 41	69
	54-57	42		18	62		42	69
	58	19		19-23	62		43, 44	69
	59	20		24	62		45, 46	70
XIII	1-9	32		25-27	62		47	70
	10-17	57		28-30	43	XXI	1	70
	18-21	33		31, 32	46		2, 3	70
	22-33	57		33, 34	46		4	70
	34	70		35	63		5-9	72
	35	70		36-39	63		10	72
XIV	1-24	53		40, 41	63		11-16	72
	25	43		42, 43	63		17	72
	26	43	XIX	1-9	63		18	31
	27	43		10	59		19	72
	28-33	34		11-25	64		20-26	73
	34	19		26	64		27	73
	35	19		27, 28	64		28	73
	35	34		29, 30	66		29-36	74
XV	1-32	59		31-34	66		37, 38	67
XVI	1-15	60		35-44	66	XXII	1	76
	16	24		45, 46	66		2-6	76
	17	19		47, 48	66		7	76
	18	61	XX	1, 2	67		8, 9	76
	19-31	60		3-5	67		10	76
XVII	1, 4	47		6	67		11	76
	5, 6	45		7, 8	67		12, 13	76
	7-10	62		9, 10	68		14-20	76
	11-19	49		11, 12	68		21	77
	20, 21	64		13, 14	68		22, 23	77
	22-24	73		15	68		24-30	46
	25	43		16, 17	68		31-39	81
	26	74		18	68		40	82
	27-30	74		19, 20	68		41, 42	32
	31	73		21-25	68		43-49	82
	32	73		26	68		50	82
	33	43		27, 28	69		51-53	82
	34-36	74		29-32	69		54	83
	37	73		33-36	69		55-61	83

Luke.

Chap.	Verses.	Sec.	Chap.	Verses.	Sec.	Chap.	Verses.	Sec.
XXII	62	83	XXIII	26-31	86	XXIII	54	87
	63-71	83		32	86		55	87
XXIII	1, 2	84		33-35	86		55, 56	89
	3	84		36-43	86	XXIV	1-11	80
	4-16	84		44	87		12	88
	17	84		45-51	87		13-35	89
	18, 19	84		52	87		36-49	90
	20-25	85		53	87		50-53	91

John.

Chap.	Verses.	Sec.	Chap.	Verses.	Sec.	Chap.	Verses.	Sec.
I	1-14	3	VII	2-10	48	XIII	20	36
	15	7		11-31	49		21-32	77
	16, 17	3		32-53	50		33	81
	18	10	VIII	1-20	51		34, 35	78
	19-28	7		21-30	50		36-38	81
	29-51	8		31-59	52	XIV	1-14	80
II	1-25	9	IX	1-41	54		15-31	81
III	1-21	10	X	1-42	55	XV	1-27	78
	22-36	11	XI	1-46	56	XVI	1-33	79
IV	1-4	11		47-54	57	XVII	1-26	80
	5-42	12		55-57	65	XVIII	1	81
	43-54	13	XII	1-6	65		1-12	82
V	1-38	26		7, 8	65		13-24	83
	39-47	27		9-11	65		25	83
VI	1-9	37		12, 13	66		26	83
	10	37		14	66		27	83
	11-14	37		15-19	66		23-40	84
	15-17	38		20-24	71	XIX	1-16	85
	18	38		25	43		17-24	86
	19	38		26	44		25-42	87
	20	38		27-50	71	XX	1-18	83
	21	38	XIII	1	76		19-29	90
	22-26	38		2-15	77		30, 31	91
	27-71	39		16	48	XXI	1-25	91
VII	1	40		17-19	77			

Acts.			1 Corinthians.		
Chap.	Verses.	Sec.	Chap.	Verses.	Sec.
I	2, 3	91	XI	25	76
	8	90	XV	6, 7	91
	9-12	91			
	18, 19	85			

Alphabetical List of all Places mentioned in the Gospels.

Places.	First mentioned.	Places.	First mentioned.
Abilene	Luke iii, 1	†Gethsemane	Matt. xxvi, 36
Ænon	John iii, 23	†Golgotha	Matt. xxvii, 33
Arimathea	Matt. xxvii, 57	Gomorrha	Matt. x, 15
*Babylon	Matt. i, 11	Idumea	Mark iii, 8
Bethabara	John i, 28	Iturea	Luke iii, 1
Bethany	Matt. xxi, 17	Jacob's Well	John iv, 6
†Bethesda	John v, 2	Jericho	Mark x, 46
Bethlehem	Matt. ii, 1	Jerusalem	Matt. ii, 1
Bethphage	Matt. xxi, 1	Jordan R.	Matt. iii, 5
Bethsaida	Matt. xi, 21	Judæa	Matt. ii, 22
†Calvary	Luke xxiii, 33	,, Wilderness of	
Cana	John ii, 1	Magdala	Matt. xv, 39
Canaan	Matt. xv, 22	Nain	Luke vii, 11
Capernaum	Matt. iv, 13	Nazareth	Matt. ii, 23
Cedron	John xviii, 1	*Nineveh	Matt. xii, 41
Cæsarea Philippi	Matt. xvi, 13	†Olives, Mt. of	Matt. xxi, 1
Chorazin	Matt. xi, 21	Rama	Matt. ii, 18
*Cyrene	Matt. xxvii, 32	Salim	John iii, 23
Dalmanutha	Mark viii, 10	Samaria	Luke xvii, 11
Decapolis	Matt. iv, 25	Sarepta	Luke iv, 26
*Egypt	Matt. ii, 13	Sidon	Matt. xi, 21
Emmaus	Luke xxiv, 13	†Siloam	Luke xiii, 4
Ephraim	John xi, 54	Sodom	Matt. x, 15
Gadara	Mark v, 1	Sychar	John, iv, 5
Galilee	Matt. ii, 22	Syria	Matt. iv, 24
,, Sea of	Matt. iv, 18	Tiberias	John vi, 23
Gennesaret	Matt. xiv, 34	,, Sea of	John vi, 1
,, Lake of	Luke v, 1	Trachonitis	Luke iii, 1
Gergesa	Matt. viii, 28	Tyre	Matt. xi, 21

All these places are marked upon the Map at the beginning of this book, except those to which an * is prefixed, which are outside its area, and those with a †, which are in, or close to, Jerusalem.